Cork Proctor: The King of Ad-Libs! The expression his talent. A genius of laughter;
　　—Stan Irwin, former Entertainment L

　　　　　　　　　　　　　　Johnny Carson's Manager

Cork Proctor is always aware of everything and everyone around him. Nothing gets by him and his comments about those people and events are spot on the money. He's truly one of a kind.

　　　　　　　　　　　　　　—Tom Dreesen, Comedian

My Mind is an Open Mouth ... Yep, the perfect title for Cork's book. And should you have occasion to look into his open mouth, more often than not you'll find his foot as well.

　　　　　—William E. Martin, CEO, Service1st Bank of Nevada

Cork's willingness to look at himself and others with such an authentic and merciless eye makes him unique. No comic has ever surprised me more and made me laugh harder. When he riffs about his life experiences and personal foibles utilizing his unique framework of quirky associations, humility, esoteric references, perfect recall, and lightning fast delivery, you know you're in the presence of that rare entity—the jazz comic.
—Dr. Ron Carducci, Former Musician and Clinical Psychologist, Denver Broncos

How do you comment on someone who has broken all the rules of comedy and still succeeded? My dear friend, Cork Proctor, is the one and only jazz comedian who ever existed. He insisted on being fresh and new for the theme of any presentation. His intellectually slanted performances consisted of a generation of daring and mind-boggling ad-libs. They never failed to not only provoke laughter, but also instill a curiosity in the search for the truth. I've been blessed in my professional past to be associated with some of the great purveyors of laughter—Jack Benny, Milton Berle, Redd Foxx, Shecky Greene, Groucho and Harpo Marx. They, of course, were incomparable, but they were also rehearsed, and that's where the comparison ends. Insane or impossible, Cork did it "new" every night.

　　　　　　　—Jackie (JC) Curtiss, Actor/Comedian

When asked to write a little something for Cork's book, I was delighted. Unfortunately, that cheap bastard wanted me to buy my own copy.

　　　　　　　　　　　—Ray Malus, Recording Artist

While serving as best man at my wedding, in order to entertain the attending friends and family, he attempted to set the altar drapes on fire at the Little Church of the West in Las Vegas just before my bride appeared. He almost brought down (or emptied) the house.

—**Mark Tully Massagli, President Emeritus, American Federation of Musicians**

It has been a pleasure and honor to work with many of the greatest comedians of our time including Milton Berle, George Burns, Charlie Callas, Red Buttons, Buddy Hackett, Red Skelton, Sid Caesar, Pat Henry, Jackie Gayle, and so many more. The man, my friend for over thirty-five years, who was equally brilliant, was Cork Proctor. His creativity and delivery are at a level rarely achieved. One of the best ever!

—**Vinnie Falcone, Conductor/Arranger for Frank Sinatra**

My two favorite pimps: Joe Conforte and "Corky" Proctor. Joe the Purveyor of Pussy and Cork, the Purveyor of Humor, Mirth, and the Naked Realities of Life. Both dear friends for half a century.

—**George Flint, Doctor of Divinity, Lobbyist for the "Oldest Profession," and Founder of the Chapel of the Bells, Reno and Las Vegas**

Cork Proctor! He's a cross between Don Rickles and Attila the Hun. He's truly non-stop humor. Line after irreverent line. I've known Cork for over thirty years and the kamikaze approach to humor hasn't changed … just the hair.

—**George Joseph, CEO, Worldwide Casino Consulting, Inc.**

Eighty-years-old. Very scary that someone could keep his mouth open that long!

—**B. Mahlon Brown, Past President, National Association of Former United States Attorneys**

Cork Proctor is not only spontaneous and very funny, but an all-around great guy and good friend. He's as interesting a man as you'll ever meet.

—**Johnny Tillotson, Singer**

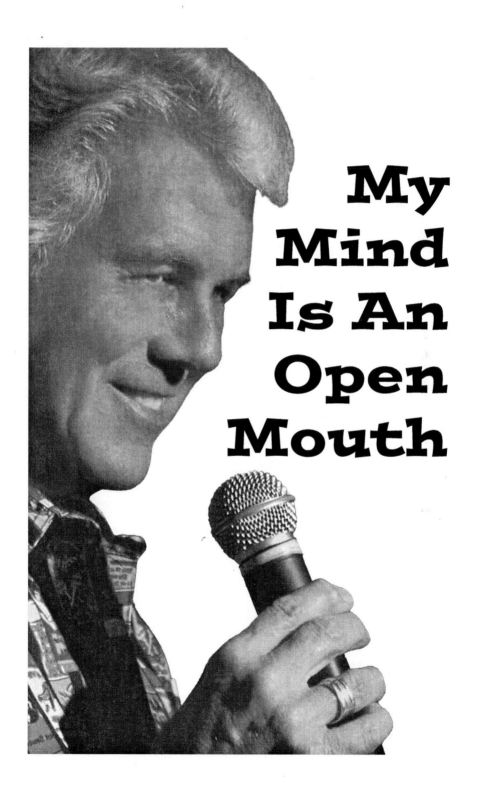

My Mind Is An Open Mouth

My Mind Is An Open Mouth

A Life Behind the Mic

Cork Proctor

with Carolyn Hamilton

LifeStories · Las Vegas, Nevada

Though every effort has been made to verify names, dates, and places
mentioned in this memoir, there may be still be some inaccuracies.
No disrespected or deception is intended.

This book would not have been possible without the tape-recorded and
transcribed interviews provided by University of Nevada Las Vegas
Special Collections Archivist Joyce Moore.

Credits
Cover Photograph: Ed Foster
Editor: Jami Carpenter
Book Designer: Sue Campbell
Production Assistance: Scott Harmon

First Printing
ISBN 978-1-935043-92-8 Trade Paper Edition
ISBN 978-1-935043-86-7 E-Book Edition
CorkProctorMemoir.com

LifeStories

AN IMPRINT OF STEPHENS PRESS
www.LifeStoriesBooks.com

Printed in United States of America

This book is appreciatively dedicated to the memories of Variety *entertainment columnist Bill Willard,* Las Vegas Review-Journal *entertainment columnist Forrest Duke, and* Las Vegas Sun *entertainment columnist Joe Delaney.*

Acknowledgments

This book has taken five years to come to some kind of organized completion. It would not be possible without the perseverance of Joyce Moore, Ken Hanlon, and Carolyn V. Hamilton.

I must extend a huge thank you to the University of Nevada Special Collections Archivist Joyce Moore, who patiently tape-recorded and transcribed my meandering tales that often bounced between place and time, sometimes in mid-sentence. To UNLV Arnold Shaw Popular Music Director Ken Hanlon, whose belief in the worthiness of this publication is warmly appreciated. And to my second wife, Carolyn V. Hamilton, who lived a lot of these adventures, listened over and over to these tales and so was able to remind me when I left something out of a story or contradicted myself in the telling. I'm sure she never anticipated that her editing of the transcriptions would turn into a time-consuming, ghostwriting experience.

I would like to acknowledge those professionals I consider to be my "mentors"—whether they knew it or not—influencing my musical learning, comedy delivery, and career direction: Dr. Walter Shudde, Jackie Gayle—who said "Lose the Drums"—Bernie Allen, J.C. Curtiss, Lennie Bruce, Herm

Saunders, Dick Clark, Joy Hamann, Leo Lewis, Louie Jordan, Joe Williams, Mike O'Callaghan, Myron Cohen, Norm Crosby, Ruthe Deskin, Shelly Manne, Stan Irwin, Tip O'Neill, Bob Flannigan, Tony Austin, Pete Matteo, Dee Dee Peters, Dick Capri, Shecky Greene, and Pete Barbutti.

It is with deep gratitude that I thank Dick Francisco, Greg Thompson, Michael Gaughan, Bill Harrah, Harold Smith, Flo Shrank, Roy Powers, and the Reviglio brothers (Tom and Jack) for consistently appreciating and rewarding my unpredictable spoutings with bill-paying employment.

At Stephens Press, a big hug to Carolyn Hayes Uber and a special thank you to Sue Campbell for the cover design and Jami Carpenter, copy editor. Ed Foster, who provided the cover photo, has photographed me at many events such as the Joe Williams concert and the Meatball Awards, always making me look good.

A special thanks to those of you who have been loyal fans, showing up at my performances time after time for a giggle and a laugh. You know who you are.

And lastly, I would like to give special mention to Louise Erickson Proctor. She was a compassionate, gracious partner, with a sense of humor and infinite patience, and without whom I wouldn't have my two beautiful daughters, Kathryn and Luann. Girls, thank you for not always liking, but loving and trusting your crazy dad.

FOREWORD

It is with a feeling of great pleasure and accomplishment that the UNLV Arnold Shaw Popular Music Research Center is involved in the publication of the autobiography of drummer and comedian Cork Proctor. Here is the story of a man who has been involved in the entertainment business of Las Vegas and Reno for nearly sixty years. He knows everyone and, of greater importance, everyone knows him. His nimble mind and quick wit have entertained countless tourists and locals over the last several decades—his reputation as a great "roastmaster" precedes him everywhere.

As with most great entertainers, Cork Proctor has given his time graciously to help raise funds for many Las Vegas charitable organizations. In the tradition of many comedians, his repartee continues off the stage, as well as on. Having lunch with him is a wonderful thing to experience because he entertains not only his friends, but also the food servers.

The Shaw Center is greatly in his debt for the many fine interviews of "Strip" personalities he has conducted over the years that are now part of the Center's archives for use by researchers, students and the public. Because of his intimate knowledge of the Las Vegas entertainment business and its many interesting personalities, Cork has produced some rare and interesting inter-views that delve into the heart of our city's entertainment culture. For that, the Shaw Center will be forever grateful.

Whether or not you are familiar with Cork's many talents, you certainly will find this biography a most entertaining and informative read. It is the work of the very creative and stream-of-conscious mind of a man whose greatest thrill is to entertain and make people laugh, something at which he excels. Enjoy!

—Ken Hanlon, Director, Arnold Shaw Popular Music Research Center, University of Nevada Las Vegas

My Mind is an Open Mouth: A Life Behind the Mic

The 1940s

Cat Fight

When my mother caught my father cheating with another woman, she got hysterical. I don't know if it was the first time she'd caught him, or the culmination of several events, but they had a huge cat fight, screaming at each other in front of their five-year-old son.

I'd never seen anything like that, and it scared me to death.

We lived in a house on 3rd and Adams in Phoenix, Arizona, where my father worked as an auditor for the Firestone Tire and Rubber Company. My mother, who had beautiful hands and bright red hair, had been a John Robert Powers model in Chicago in the 1920s. My father had been a student of certified public accounting at the University of Wisconsin. He never did get a degree, but he was probably one of the most intelligent guys I ever knew.

They met at a Kappa Sigma fraternity party, married in 1929, and went to the Broadmoor Hotel in Colorado Springs on their honeymoon in a new Ford that his father, a Ford and Lincoln dealer in the small town of Columbus, Wisconsin, had given them.

I was born on July 22nd, 1932, left-handed, dyslexic, and never circumcised—the cruelest cut of all.

Both my parents came from God-fearing Wisconsin Presbyterians. As a little kid, my grandparents took me to church where I was subjected for hours to those horrible preachers. I didn't know who—it wasn't Jesus Christ—they were talking about. It went on forever and if I wiggled, my grandfather, Alfred Henry Proctor, kicked me.

Alfred Henry, my father's father, was a stern, moral, Victorian-era kind of guy. His son, Alfred Samuel, was kind enough to name me Alfred Courtney, which I have since changed to Cork. As a little kid, I couldn't say, "Courtney." When people asked me my name, I would say, "Alfie Corky." It became Corky and later I dropped the 'y'.

My grandfather, Alfred Henry Proctor, was a Wisconsin farmer who later became a railroad engineer with the great Chicago railroads around Wisconsin. Ultimately he became president of a bank. He was a big guy, stout. At seventy-two, he had a fight with a guy who challenged him about some impropriety.

"Fred, I don't know what you're doing at the bank," the guy said, "but it looks like you're stealing."

My grandfather was a decent guy, quite well-respected in the community around Columbus. So right there, in the middle of a snowstorm, my offended grandfather knocked the guy down cold.

My mother's father had a cigar store in Madison and their family name was Courtney. He invented the strong box, which later became the safety deposit box.

From Wisconsin, my father and mother came out to Phoenix, Arizona, where he went to work for Firestone Tire and Rubber Company. My two strongest memories of being five-years-old and living in our house on 3rd and Adams are that "cat fight" over my father's philandering and the dog bite.

It was blistering hot in Phoenix with no air conditioning in those days. Across the street lived a Scotty dog. I was curious and attracted to the dog. "Hi doggie." The little prick came out and bit me on the ankle. I was a little kid with undeveloped bones. He bit all the way through, teeth marks on both sides. My mother came out of the house screaming. She rushed me to the emergency room where they gave me some shots because they were afraid

I might get rabies. They sewed me up and I still have the scar. Yet I never developed a fear of dogs. I love dogs.

Firestone transferred my father from Phoenix to Los Angeles, where we lived on a farm in Orange, California. The Firestone store was downtown at 11th and Figueroa. When the long commute grew tiresome, he made plans to move the family to Wyvernwood, an East Los Angeles development of homes at Olympic and Soto. Today the area is predominantly Hispanic and known as the Barrio.

He's Got Polio

My mother was five months pregnant, packing to move, when I got hit by a car. I was headed across the street to the neighbor's house. Riding my bicycle, I sped right out of a blind driveway into the street. I didn't look; when you're eight-years-old you don't look at anything. The kid in the Model A couldn't stop in time. I got slammed into the pavement, landing so hard I was out. The bicycle looked like a pretzel.

I was rushed to St. Joseph's Hospital, the same hospital where I'd been born, and diagnosed with a concussion and a broken leg. My left leg was put in traction, in the air with a pulley to align the bone. Very uncomfortable. They kept me in there a month. No television or radio, but my mother brought me a lot of books. The cast itched like a bitch. I wanted to get into that cast with a Chinese back scratcher. Mostly I stuck my finger inside it as far as I could and said, "Wow, that smells bad."

Today, my left leg is 3/8 inch shorter than my right. I may have also suffered some cranial damage because I suspect there are certain areas—synapses—that don't work very well.

When I got out of the hospital I was still in a cast. When the other kids saw me, they made fun of me. "Run away from him," they said. "He's got polio." That hurt. I didn't have polio—I had a broken leg.

My angry father tried to sue the guy who hit me for going too fast, but I was liable. They went to court, got me on the stand to testify, and my dad lost. That was painful for him because he had to pay all the court costs.

Right after the move to Wyvernwood, my mother again caught my father cheating. He spent a lot of time tea dancing at Los Angeles' stately Ambassador Hotel on Wilshire Boulevard. At five o'clock he and his friends would have martinis and meet wanton women with short skirts and high eyebrows. Hello.

Finally, she confronted him about his behavior—he had again come home drunk—and the screaming began. He was seated on a chest, sobbing, "I'll never do it again; I promise I'll never do it again."

A horrified, confused, eight-year-old, I watched it all from a corner in the living room.

By this time my mother, who was pregnant again, hated my father. I sensed that she didn't want to have the child she carried, and shortly after this fight, she indeed miscarried. She started to hemorrhage and two days later her mother came out from Wisconsin on the train. I'd never seen so much blood, and no one would tell me shit. Later I learned she had a fibroid tumor in her uterus, went into the hospital, and had a hysterectomy. I would remain an only child.

My father's position at Firestone changed to Field Auditor. He drove all around the famous Route 66, checking on Firestone dealers in little towns like Chandler, Bixby, Seligman, and Peach Springs. Sometimes I got to go with him on the road, which was great fun for a little kid.

Running Away

By 1941, my mother had had enough of my father's wayward behavior and decided to leave him. I heard the "D" word being discussed. She planned to take me and go back to Wisconsin to live with her mother, Ella White Courtney, a beautician on the Capital Square.

In the *L.A. Times* my mother saw an ad that read, "Lady driving to Wisconsin. Would like to have someone share the gas." (Twenty cents a gallon). The woman, Mrs. Brothers, had just gotten a divorce, was pleasant, and had a '40 Ford business coupe with jump seats in the back.

By the time we got to Albuquerque, I was filled with rage and wrath and pissed off about everything. I was pissed off at my mother for taking me to Wisconsin. I didn't want to go to Wisconsin—I hadn't forgotten those church sermons—so I ran away. My mother reached out to grab me, and tore off all of her beautiful fingernails. Crying, I kept on running. I didn't know why I was angry. What's the biggest fear you have as a child? Abandonment.

I didn't get far. My mother found me. It was tearful, and to this day I feel bad about it. She was beside herself. She didn't know how to handle me. She didn't know how to handle anything.

As soon as we arrived in Columbus, she got a job.

Those Boys at Wyler

Forty miles from where my grandparents lived in Columbus was Evansville, a little town with a military school called the Wyler Military Academy. My mother incarcerated me there with a bunch of you-name-its from homosexuals to car thieves. We were all kids from dysfunctional families. Between seventy and one hundred boys were there.

At the school I went off the swings trying to do a full swing and landed on my wrists, spraining them. In sports I broke an arm and was in a cast for six weeks, during which I got to stay with Grandma Ella in her small apartment on Hamilton Street. The war was still on and we didn't have a lot of food, but we had enough. I read a lot of books and did well in school.

In military school I developed an intense dislike for discipline and homosexuals. I don't mean homosexuals individually, but there were a lot of gay kids in that school, and I was real uncomfortable with all that mincing and prancing. I was twelve-years-old. What did I know?

One night I peed out of the second story window. A strict rule was that we were not to be moving around in the middle of the night going to the bathroom. Perhaps worried about the guys fraternizing? The next day at lunch, a gay teacher we figured was just weird, Mr. Bruce, publicly vilified me.

"And he urinated out of the second story dormitory last night." God, you would have thought I raped somebody's sister and cut off her head.

Emily and Carl Griffith—a couple in their sixties who ran the school— were decent people. Emily, a gorgeous woman with snow white hair, would sit in that tiled room, tapping her cane, watching us shower; she was "monitoring the class" to see that we didn't "do anything" we shouldn't do. I'd get a woody.

I never told my mother about it because she stood me up a few times at school and I figured she didn't care.

Captain Griffin was cool. When he got mad he'd yell at us. He was always adjusting his cock, like he couldn't decide on which side to dress it.

Mr. and Mrs. Griffin had a tough time because these kids were all miscreants. A judge would say, "Put this kid in military school before he burns down the neighborhood."

I wasn't a bad kid, just goofy. Most of us came from a shit childhood. We didn't know why we were there, and we didn't know why we dressed in these uniforms and wore these ties and practiced the manual of arms. It was basically a prep school for places like the Virginia Military Institute. A lot of kids went on to military careers and did thirty or forty years.

Sex on a Train

As a field auditor for Firestone, Las Vegas was one of the small towns my father visited. He would drive from Los Angeles to audit the Firestone store owned by James Cashman, in the same building as Cashman's Cadillac—the Buick, Pontiac, Oldsmobile, LaSalle, John Deere and Caterpillar Tractor dealership. Kids always liked to go in there because you could smell the tires and get to see exhibitions of race cars from Indianapolis. Today the Union Plaza Hotel sits on that spot. James Cashman and my dad became pretty tight. They were in the Elks together, enjoyed great times and drank together.

My father begged my mother to come back to him, and she did. She joined him where he was living at the Cherry Lynn Apartments in Boulder City. Those apartments are still there, two stories, painted white, on the east side of the street. I think my father chose Boulder City because he liked its proximity to Lake Mead and its charming little parks and beautiful little houses that had been built during the construction of Boulder/Hoover Dam.

Between the fifth and sixth grades at Wyler, I joined my parents in Boulder City for the summer. For the seventh grade, my parents took me out of military school and enrolled me in Basic Junior High school, so named after the local Basic Magnesium—BMI—plant.

My Mind is an Open Mouth: A Life Behind the Mic

When FDR died in 1944, I was twelve-years-old, and was having a difficult year at Basic, going from an all-boys cloistered environment into a setting
with kids who had little structure or discipline. At Basic there were kids who
were sixteen in the seventh grade.

During this time I traveled back and forth to Wisconsin by train. I liked
the train. The first time I saw sex was in the club car of the Santa Fe Chief,
going from the old downtown Las Vegas depot back to Chicago. I saw lots of
people making love. This was during the war, and women traveling by train
were often in the service. The service guys and women all had olive drab
underwear. Later, one of my stage jokes became, "To this day for me to get
aroused I have to see a bunch of half-naked people in the club car on a train
wearing olive drab underwear."

Guns to Go

My dad had an incredible collection of guns. He was a gun safety nut, but he
didn't always pay attention. In 1944 he took me dove hunting with him and
James Cashman at Moapa. All the men would drink, a customary part of
hunting. They shot a lot of doves, and periodically they also shot each other.

Back home at 99 Water Street in Henderson, drunk, Dad was running a
rag down the 32-inch barrel of his loaded Winchester 12-gauge shotgun. He
was holding it straight up when it went off, right through the plywood ceiling—there was no lathe or sheetrock—and out through the roof. A shotgun
pattern spreads; when it goes out of the barrel, it's an inch and a half, at four
feet it's four inches, and at twenty feet it spreads eighteen inches, depending
on the shot size.

My mother came into the room screaming, "Al, you and those god damned
guns!"

We all looked up to see daylight through the hole. The explosion in the
house scared us. Later when I was more mature I realized that when it went
off he could have been waving that gun around. It could have hit my mom, it
could have hit me, it could have hit him.

One afternoon a year later my dad took me down to the jail in Las Vegas
to meet Sheriff Glen Jones. The sheriff was also a drinking buddy from the

Elks. Everybody knew my dad. We walked right into Glen Jones' office. He made my dad a Cutty and water about a foot high and they both lit cigarettes. I sat and listened while they did the-how-are-you and what-are-you-doing and blah, blah, blah.

"You know, Al," Glen said, "We've been stopping a lot of guys on the street, and a lot of guys are coming out of WWII with guns, and we've confiscated a lot of stuff." He pointed across the room. "Go over to that drawer."

My dad rose from his chair and opened a drawer that looked like something in an industrial pantry. It had to have been three feet wide and three feet deep. When he pulled it open we could both see that it was packed full with pistols.

A common practice was for the police department to have the barrel cut off with a torch to make the gun inoperable. They'd give the guy who did this 400 guns at a time. He'd keep the ones he wanted and cut the barrels off the rest.

"Take whatever you want, Al," Glen said.

From the drawer, my dad filled a bag with six working pistols, including a Smith and Wesson, some German Lugars, and a Walther P.K.

Glen was a great guy. He and his wife had been to our house for dinner. I'd been over to his house on Bonanza, too, not far from the Binion ranch. As I recall, the Jones family had a swimming pool.

There was a substantial rumor that Glen had a piece of Roxie's at Four Mile Spring, the brothel out where the road dipped. Probably true. Why else wouldn't it have been closed down? Somebody had to be taking care of somebody. There were also successful brothels called The Cribs down on 3rd Street, not far from the post office. A lot of guys I knew went there, but I never did. I used to deliver newspapers there. I never heard that anybody used condoms in those days. I think the law looked the other way; everybody was getting greased.

Roxie's was nearly destroyed by fire in the 1950s. Somebody may have torched it or it may have burned by itself. Who knows? I don't think any of the sheriffs were so zealous that they would go out and burn down a chance to make some pin money. Another advantage to letting the brothels be was that

My Mind is an Open Mouth: A Life Behind the Mic

they could keep an eye on the girls and the pimps, and there was somebody watching out there—security, twenty-four hours a day.

Quejo's Cave

The Elks Club big production was the annual Las Vegas Helldorado Week, usually held in May, when weather temperatures had already climbed to hot as hell. For the whole week, everyone in town dressed in western costume. The big parade ended at the fairgrounds where people could visit Helldorado Village, pig out on corn dogs and cotton candy and take carnival rides and puke.

A highlight of the village was Quejo's Cave, which showed the dried body of this old Indian outlaw, Quejo. At the turn of the century, Quejo terrorized the Nelson and Searchlight areas of southern Nevada for twenty years by killing people at night and stealing their stuff. He had hidden out in the cave, where he finally died of starvation, I think, because he was in a fetal position.

His mummified body and all the contents of his cave were placed in a replica of the original cave, with a glass front. We could peer through the glass, see the body and the rifles and guns lining his cave. Quejo was always a huge attraction; everybody wanted to see him. As kids, we were all nonchalant because we'd seen him a million times. We'd knock on the glass and say, "Are you still asleep?"

As times changed, the exhibit disappeared. I've asked around, but nobody seems to know what happened to his remains after that.

Huntridge and Las Vegas High School

It's a shame my parents reunited because I would have been better off to stay with one of them. That old nonsense—that we stay together for the sake of the kids—ruins the kids. Kids feel every nerve center, every piece of agitation or angst. They can't relate because they have this terrible fear of what's going to happen to me if they split? I thought their splitting was my fault.

My father was having a real good time in Las Vegas, drinking and still fighting with my mother. So for the eighth grade, they sent me back to military school. When I came home from Wyler in the spring of 1945, it was not to the Cherry Lynn apartments, but to a little house they had bought in Las Vegas' first tract housing development, Huntridge.

In the fall of 1946 I began my freshman year at Las Vegas High School, which was placed on the National Register of historic places in 1991. Around the corner from our house at 1320 Norman Avenue, on Maryland Circle, lived future Nevada State Senator Richard Bryan, his brother Paul, and their parents, Lil and Oscar Bryan. Our neighbors across the back fence were the Rebers, whose son Rod would later found one of Las Vegas' most successful ad agencies, Kelly and Reber.

Huntridge homes were wonderful little stucco houses with one bathroom and two bedrooms, a living room, fireplace, kitchen, and shake roof. Lots were decent-sized, about 60 feet by 120 feet, and we lived there quite a while.

My mother worked at the White Cross Drug Stores. The downtown location was at Fremont and Third, and the Strip location at Las Vegas Boulevard South and Oakey is now closed and destined to reopen as a grocery store. She sold cosmetics and rotated between the two stores. People liked her. She was bright and did well, but it was a dumbass job. "Hi there; what cologne would you like?" and "The tampons are on aisle 4B." She probably made eighty cents an hour. Not very redeeming, but unfortunately she didn't have many skills. She had been to charm school and to college, but she didn't have a degree. As a refined woman, she found it comfortable at White Cross, and it was good for her at that time. She was probably well advanced for the town.

My old man continued to be an inveterate chippy having flagrant affairs and my Victorian-thinking mother put up with it. She didn't have, God bless her, the courage or conviction to leave. She came from a rigid, conservative family. "We don't talk about bowel movements. We call it 'BM.' When a woman is pregnant, she's 'PG.'"

I thought it was bullshit. Wisconsin bias and a lot of bigotry in both families. My mother and father blamed the Jews and the blacks for everything. I grew up in that environment, with those chain-smoking, biased, angry parents. They never traveled anywhere. I did more with my wife in a year than they did in an entire lifetime. But that was their choice. I don't mean to besmirch

Wisconsin. I'm sure everyone in Wisconsin isn't a bigot or a racist, but in my family, that's what came across.

I loved Las Vegas. There was Tule Springs and wonderful homes and ranches and forty-acre parcels on the south end of the Strip where I live now.

In Las Vegas I experienced a different attitude, a world quite different from that of my parents. At Las Vegas High, we had few blacks and Mexicans, and we never went out looking for black guys to beat up. I wasn't the kind of guy who would do that anyway.

That first year at Las Vegas High School was not fun. Feeling out of my element, I had a difficult time. I found most of my schoolmates snobbish. Don Pulliam and Blair Roach and Rod Reber and Richard Bryan had all grown up together. This was a cadre that I felt I couldn't break into.

I wasn't athletic, and I didn't want to play sports. I saw guys getting slammed and hurt. "I don't like pain," I announced. "I'm not doing that."

Mostly, I hung out with three or four guys from a different group. Bob MacKenzie, Doug Stewart, Kenny Freeman, George Cromer, Stanley Clifton—guys who just wanted to have fun. We had a club called the Riffs, after the musical term, and we belonged to a hotrod club called The Gamblers, the first real legitimate hotrod club in Las Vegas. We hung this magnesium club plate, the symbol of two dice—a five and a six—below the back bumper, where it swung on a chain.

My main interest was cars. There wasn't any sex in high school per se. Somebody was getting it, but it wasn't me because my mother told me, "You can get a venereal disease." She brought all of that Victorian mentality from Wisconsin into our family. I wasn't intimate until I was almost nineteen-years-old.

Years later when I had an affair with a cheerleader who was three years older than me, she said, "You know, you probably could have slept with half those girls because they thought you were so cute."

The Car Thief

After I arrived at Las Vegas High School I became my own miscreant. In 1946 all us guys in school were car crazy. Mad Man Muntz had a car lot on

East Fremont, and we'd go out there at night. They left all the keys in the cars, which were surrounded by a chain attached to poles spaced several feet apart. We'd lift the poles and lay them down, chain and all. We'd take a '38 Packard, four-door convertible and a .22 and drive over to the dump—where the Fox Charleston Plaza is now—and shoot rats for an hour. Then we'd take the car back. We'd back it in and leave it and put the chains and posts back.

One night Billy Burton and I walked three blocks to the Huntridge Theater to see Abbot and Costello, who were making a live appearance. An emcee in the theater would give us ten dollars if we would cut off our pant leg. As part of the shows, they gave away chickens and live animals, furniture and rabbits.

While we waited to get in, we got bored. We started messing with an old 1928 Chevrolet truck parked in the theater parking lot. We thought we'd take it and circle around the parking lot, do some donuts, have some fun. We were playing with the truck's little push-pull ignition switch and the next thing we knew, we were busted for auto theft.

The most embarrassing thing was that the cop who arrested us was Roy MacKenzie, the older brother of my schoolmate and best friend, Bob MacKenzie. Las Vegas cops had their own guns in those days. A lot of them had just come home from the military, the marines, or Japan. Roy walked up with his gun drawn and stuck it between my eyes.

His partner, Arthur 'Nic' Nickles, stuck his pearl-handled .38 in my navel and said, "If you move, I'll blow your ass off." The angle of deflection was down into my navel. It was a great turning point in my life—the end of my crime spree.

For a few nights they made Billy and me stay in the animal recovery barns on Bonanza Road. When I was let out, I was officially put on probation. Marie Morgan and Barney Berger, my probation officers, made me write down where I was and what I did and who I was with, but they were nice people, Barney and Marie.

My dad came and got me and we went home. It was quiet around the house for several days. Then he said, "You will never make a good criminal. You're not a good liar, and I suggest you give this some serious thought."

In my bedroom, I ruminated on it and decided that crime was not for me. I made up my mind to stay straight. Yet I couldn't resist when a girl named Margo Goumond, the daughter of multi-millionaire P.J. Goumond, loaned me her '40 Ford Convertible to drive, even though I was fourteen-years-old and didn't have a driver's license. I thought that had to be better than sex. No girl smelled as good as the leather in that convertible.

I think Billy Burton went on into crime and got killed. We never did get to see Abbot and Costello.

Not long after that five of us freshman, including George Cromer and Doug Stewart, decided to skip school. I had taken my parents' car keys out and had a duplicate key made. My mother was at work. My dad was at work at Archie Grant Ford at 5th & Stewart, across from City Hall, and he drove a company car, a pickup truck. The family car, a 1938 kelly green Oldsmobile four-door sedan, was sitting right there in the driveway.

So what if I stole my parents' car? I'd already been busted by the cops. I figured my parents couldn't be any worse than Metro.

We all climbed into the Olds and I drove us out to Lake Mead—a bunch of goofy fourteen-year-olds. Nobody had a driver's license. I drove carefully— no speeding. This side of the dam was a steep power line construction road. Not thinking about anything but having a joyous afternoon skipping school, I drove down that road to get to the edge the lake. At the bottom of the hill we got out and looked around. That's when I realized the angle of the hill.

Uh Ohhhhh. The car was stuck, and I couldn't get it to go back uphill.

At the edge of the lake were some folks in a jeep. They saw our predicament, came over and said, "Can we help?"

Because he was in the Sheriff's Posse, my father had a beautiful hand-braided horsehair lariat that he'd left in the car. We hooked it between the Olds and the Jeep, with the idea that the Jeep could haul the Olds uphill. That beautiful lariat tightened, pulled the Olds three feet and snapped into pieces.

No collective thinking there, only panic. Had I gotten all the guys to push the car while the jeep pulled it from the front, we could have made it up the hill.

I wanted to die from embarrassment. The guys thought it was funny as hell. It wasn't their father's car. We hitchhiked back to town. Terrified to go home, I went up the street to Earl Nelson's house, where I stayed for four or five hours. Looking for me, my father called around and tracked me down. About 10:00 p.m. he came to the Nelsons. I was hiding under the bed. He hauled me out, stood me up, and slapped me across the face.

"Give me the keys!"

I think he admired my spirit, though. Deep down inside he was thinking, *hey, this kid's alright. He's willing to take a chance.*

The next day, my father and I went back to get the car. It took a double-boom wrecker with 1,000 feet of steel cable to pull the Olds back to the highway. Luckily I hadn't hurt the motor or anything. I was self-conscious about driving the car, but you can imagine how stupid the whole thing was. Thank God, nobody got hurt.

So I was on probation for the rest of my life. You think I'd learn once. But hey, the difference was that when I stole the car at the Huntridge, the cop had a gun.

To School, or not to School

In 1947, the year they built the first Cashman Stadium in Las Vegas, I dropped out of school to work as a laborer. I drove a water truck, though I was only fifteen-years-old and didn't have a driver's license.

Jimmy Cashman, Jr. had come back from military service in Germany. Still in uniform, he came down to the site one day and said "hi" to everybody. It made me wonder, where was I going in my life? So I returned to school, where I hung out with my little Huntridge gang. We stuck together and we're still friends today. Mostly, we talked about hotrods and what we would do if we had that girl in our car.

Strippers and Silver Dollars

When I worked parking cars at the El Rancho Vegas, I went home every night with a sack full of silver dollars. Barely sixteen, I can't remember how I got the job, but my dad didn't get it for me. I went there to see a guy who knew a guy, all "broken nose" mob guys.

Nat King Cole, appearing in the showroom, was allowed to stay in the special cabanas in the back of the hotel. That was highly unusual because black entertainers were made to stay on the Westside, Las Vegas' black neighborhood, never in the hotels.

I think my parents were disturbed about me working there because I was "around showgirls." I did spend time watching Lilly Christine, "the cat girl," and Lili St. Cyr, one of the biggest strippers in America. I snuck into the showroom and stood in the back. They let me do it because I worked there.

I met guys like movie star Victor Mature, who tipped me a handful of silver dollars. After six weeks, the powers that be decided I was too young and fired me. Actually, it was a good job and they wanted to bring in someone else. I knew it was a week-to-week job to see how I worked out, but I didn't hit any cars or anything so I knew it wasn't about that.

The Lobster Ring

In 1951, my parents moved from Huntridge to a house on an acre of land on the western side of town, 4115 Del Monte, near Oakey and Charleston. This neighborhood was considered the outskirts of town, and the streets were oiled instead of paved. Saddle maker Jack Thomas lived next door. Emil Pahor and his brother also lived in that neighborhood. And a whole bunch of quail. My dad and I built a fence around the property, which still stands, and we had two Springer spaniels, Nip and Tuck.

The old Jack Porter ranch was up the street. I later went to high school with Jack Junior. Porter Senior had a side business with a guy named Doc Ladd and his son, Al, to import lobsters from Mexico. The single engine plane flew in at 11 o'clock at night to offload fresh lobsters from the beach below Ensenada, Mexico. Four cars on the street with their headlights on would show them where to land.

Al Ladd had a seafood company on Main Street, and he'd be out there with a truck to collect the lobsters. I rode my bike over to help him. The quality of the lobsters was wonderful. I don't think they cared whether or not what they were doing was legal; what they cared about was that they didn't have to pay any taxes. Eventually, they got busted. It was all bull. Somebody with his hand out probably didn't get greased. Who cared when everyone was getting all these great lobsters?

The newspaper headline read, "Cops Bust Big Fish Ring."

Corrupted by the Compton Tar Babies

A Compton, California football team, the Compton Tar Babies, came to Las Vegas to play Las Vegas High School. The Compton guys were big, older than regular guys, and they won the game. They were also all stoned on marijuana. Compton was a predominately black community, and most of those football players brought dope with them. After the game they passed the marijuana around. We all inhaled, got a buzz, and said, "Wow, isn't this great?" I'm sure the stuff was organically pure because this was before the wide use of pesticides.

At Vegas High, we knew there were two or three guys—one a Mexican—who were dealing, but we weren't much interested. There wasn't any focus on dope, no feeling that you had to get loaded. We were already passive kids. The good Mormons, of course, they didn't smoke anything. They went to church and to the Gold and Green Ball where they had good times dancing.

For a hoot, I got some seeds and decided to see if I could grow marijuana in our garage on Del Monte. I planted them in wooden Kraft cheese boxes and they did well. Hey, I was growing it for my own satisfaction, not marketing it.

One day I was tending my "garden" when my mom walked into the garage. She had a drink in one hand and a cigarette in the other. "You know that marijuana is addictive," she said.

"Mom, maybe you ought to go look in the mirror."

She was adamant. "Stop that shit or I'll tell your father."

I wasn't in the mood to deal with that, so I said, "Okay." It was fun because it was forbidden. I never was any dyed-in-the-wool pot smoker because it made me goofy. I was already goofy. I knew I didn't want to be any goofier. So, out went the Kraft cheese boxes.

The 1950s

Tahiti Felix

In the summer of 1950 I told my mother, "I'm gonna go to boot camp in San Diego for two weeks."

Ten of my buddies were going, and they'd asked me if I wanted to go. "Let's make a party out of it," they said.

So I joined the Naval Reserve and went to San Diego for the two-week training. There I became friends with Jimmy Nelson, the son of successful Columbia Pictures film director Sam Nelson. Their real family name was Von Falkinburg.

One day Jimmy and I and some of the other guys went down to the Pike in Long Beach, where there were arcade booths and rides. We met a tattoo artist named Tahiti Felix, and we all got tattoos. It was the thing to do if you were in the navy. On my bicep I got a wolf with three drops of blood dripping from his jaw.

When I went home to Vegas sporting my new tattoo, my mother's scream was higher than passing a toaster out of your rectum.

"What have you done?!"

My father didn't give a shit. He said, "Ah, if he wants it, he's got it."

The Elks Lodge

My mother had a few nice friends. Mary Todkill was a nurse married to Bert Todkill, who owned the Todkill-Lincoln Mercury dealership where the Stratosphere sits now. My mother was also tight with Lil Bryan, Oscar's wife, but even in Huntridge, my mother didn't socialize. She just worked. I don't think she had the confidence to knock on a door and say, "Hi, I'm Kay and I live two doors down. Do you want to come over for coffee?" Basically, her thrust was cooking for the old man. The only reason he lived as long as he did is because every night before he passed out from two or three martinis, she gave him a wonderful meal. She was a good cook, except she overcooked vegetables, so that they came out looking like stainless steel.

My father was drinking and chippying, a personification of the old joke, "He was good to his family—he never went home." Al Proctor was a popular member of the Lions and Kiwanis and the Sheriff's Posse and the Rotary Club. He must have gone to a meeting five nights a week. He seemed to do everything he could to avoid coming home.

After ten years, he had left Firestone and in 1951 managed the Ford Garage, the building next to City Hall at 5th and Stewart. When he did come home, he was two-thirds shit-faced. Everybody who knew him said he was a great guy. Most nights they were at the Elks Lodge, playing cards and drinking and drinking and drinking. That was the lifestyle. Lodge night was Thursday, so hey, Nellie, bar the door; "We're going to Lodge."

In the Elks my father went through all the chairs and became Exalted Ruler and later District Deputy, a pretty important job. Their pictures are still there, all of these past exhausted roosters, stern looks on their faces like they're angry at everything. It's the medley of the dead out there at the Elks Lodge.

Jim Cashman, a powerful man in Nevada, ran the Elks Lodge. Like Pat McCarran and later, Ralph Lamb, if Jim Cashman told you to leave town on the next flatbed train, you better be on the train. These guys weren't kidding. There were no pimps, no street drug dealers in Vegas. Only cheaters and drifters, which was why Benny Binion had his stock rule: "I'll pay you $27.00 a day (or whatever), and don't steal." The "or else" was understood.

My Mind is an Open Mouth: A Life Behind the Mic

The Elks Lodge was so bigoted and so racist; they told the guys on the Westside—the black community in Las Vegas, "You can get your own lodge." So there was the Benevolent Protective Order of Elks, and then on the Westside we had the Improved BPOE.

After I came home from the navy, Dad said, "You ought to join the lodge."

I said, "Screw you. I'll join your lodge when I can bring a Puerto Rican and a black guy in here for a drink."

"They have their own lodge," he said, his tone defensive.

"Dad, why don't you admit it? It's a racist, bigoted group. You're in it for the sake of being in it. You don't want anybody in it that doesn't measure up to your standards."

He became irate. "That's a hell of a thing to say."

"Look around. You see any blacks? You see any Puerto Ricans?"

Voices raised, we almost got into a physical confrontation. So I never joined anything. I decided those organizations are time-consuming and expensive, and I didn't ever want to join something where you wear a funny suit and have a trick handshake. It's not important to me. I just want to live my life and have a good time.

The guy in the cheap, wooden coffin

My old man was having a great time with his pals, full blown to the max, and I was drifting. In 1951, after four years of C's, F's and incompletes, I was still the little kid running away in Albuquerque. I didn't like what I was doing, and I didn't particularly like anybody outside of the guys I hung with. And you couldn't matriculate with C's, F's and incompletes.

That summer I stayed out of the house by getting a job as a grave digger at the cemetery on Foremaster Lane. In sun and hundred-plus degree heat, I dug graves by hand. I worked with an old black man, Ed Dingins, who wore WWI hobnailed boots with the toes cut out. He was a good worker and we shared a lot of laughs.

One day, in the potter's field at the extreme east end of the cemetery, we were lowering a guy in a cheap, wooden coffin into a gravesite. Suddenly there was a creaking sound.

Ed stopped. "Look man, the lid came off."

In a firm voice I said to the corpse, "Oh, no, you're not getting out of there now. Let me tell you something—we spent all day digging this hole!"

Ed laughed out loud. Then we realized the dead guy's relatives, in a nearby funeral car, had heard us.

That night when I got home, my father confronted me in anger.

"What are you doing down there?" He said George Maxwell, the manager of the funeral facility, had called him to tell him what I'd said, and that the dead guy's relatives were furious.

"I certainly wouldn't have done it if I thought the family was there," I said. "Who would think a guy in potter's field …? I guess the family had a funeral car they rented and came down to say goodbye to him." I explained that they hadn't exactly come to the gravesite. If they had been standing there, I never would have said anything.

By that time I knew I was nuts and that I could be funny. I think my father hated that I was funny, that I could upstage him. He worked at his kind of comedy, to tell jokes and stories well. I would just walk in and do something stupid, off the wall, and get big laughs.

"Tell George," I suggested, "next time he should get better screws for the box."

The Body in the Trunk

A series of odd jobs followed that. I worked for awhile on Main Street in the Archie Grant Ford Paint & Body Shop, where the Nevada Hotel is now. My dad got me the job. They paid me by the hour to mask and sandblast cars in preparation for painting, and I worked there on and off for a couple of years. I sanded a car that belonged to Jack Dennison, a former maitre'd who had opened a restaurant on the Vegas Strip called The Copper Cart. He then "forgot" to pay us, and Archie Grant, owner of the Ford dealership, sued him.

The worst experience was when the insurance company sent over a fine Cadillac convertible that had had a dead body in the trunk. In Vegas summer heat, that body had cooked. The body was gone when we got the car, but the odor would live forever. We tried everything, but we never could get that odor out.

High School Number Two: Manogue

I had spent four years at Las Vegas High as a sophomore, and out of complete frustration my parents arranged for me to transfer to Bishop Manogue High School up north in Reno. On McCarran Boulevard, right on the Trukee River, it used to be the old Flick Ranch. Even though we weren't Catholic, my parents convinced them I'd do well and they accepted me.

My mother, God love her, was a kind woman who sincerely believed that my dad was going to get his shit together and come back into the marriage. Talk about denial. She was so frustrated, and I felt so bad for her. On the drive to Reno, I asked, "Why don't you just leave?"

"Well, your father is getting his insurance," she said. I didn't understand her answer. I think she didn't know where to go because she didn't know how to do anything. She was a woman steeped in all that Wisconsin stuff. I asked her the same question on other occasions, but she always had an excuse.

Through the Catholic diocese, the Reno home of a widow who could use some income was recommended as a place where I could live. Mrs. Potter had a son, Bob, and daughter, Vivian, who also attended Bishop Manogue.

The two big hotels in Reno were the Mapes Hotel and the Riverside Hotel & Casino, owned by Mert Wertheimer. The Mapes was run by a nice old guy, Bill Peachard, who I think came from the purple gang in Detroit. He was a strange-looking cat, and we called him "beaky buzzard." Up the street was Fitzgerald's, owned by a bookkeeper for the purple gang. Once they came with shotguns and tried to kill him. But we liked it because though we were only seventeen, we could drink there.

Reno was a small, safe town. None of the kids ever stole a car, and there was zero violence. We just did crazy stuff. When there was a lot of snow on the road on the way to school out at the Flick ranch, we'd tie a forty-foot piece of rope to the back bumper of a car and ski behind it in our shoes, going thirty miles an hour.

Stealing the Turkey

The annual fundraiser dinner for the Knights of Columbus was held after the Catholic Youth Organization meeting at St. Anne's, a big, pretty church downtown. As CYO members, students were invited and some worked as organizers and servers.

I was seated at the table, eating, as they were about to raffle off a roasted 32-pound turkey.

"I don't think someone should win that turkey," I whispered to my friends. "I think we should take it home."

Four of us went into the kitchen. With kids serving, there was a lot of activity and no one paid any attention to us. There sat that big, beautiful turkey, destined for the raffle. Nearby was the skeleton of the turkey that had been stripped for the dinner. We took some mashed potatoes and stuffed them into the skeleton and covered it with a damp towel. Then we stole out the back door with the big, cooked turkey.

By the time they rolled out that turkey in front of 400 people for the raffle and uncovered it, we were long gone.

I took that baked turkey home to the Potter house and put it under the bed.

That same night one of the girls came home with me. She told her mother she was staying overnight with Vivian Potter, only Vivian and her mother weren't home. They had gone to visit friends at Lake Tahoe. She put on my pajamas and crawled into my bed and then said, "Now, I don't want to do anything."

I thought, *so what are you doing in my bed in my pajamas?*

"We're not going to do anything," I said, "We don't want to hurt that turkey under the bed."

She stayed the night and we didn't "do anything."

The next day we deboned the turkey, wrapped everything in a wet towel and put the pieces in the fridge. We made sandwiches four inches thick and gave them to friends who came by. I'd hand them a thigh and say, "Here, take this home."

The four of us were never actually caught, but Manogue's principal, Father Joseph Lindy, suspected me.

"Did you have anything to do with this?" he asked.

"Do you suspect me?"

His eyes narrowed. "I know you. We like you here, but we know you're a provocateur." Father Lindy had a well-developed vocabulary.

Stealing the turkey was kind of a cheap shot thing to do, and I'm reticent to admit it, but it's been fifty years, a lot of those people are dead, and I don't think the turkey cares. Boy, it was good.

Mighty Joe

Another prank involved the *Mighty Joe Young* billboard. Out by the railroad tracks, behind where the Sparks Nugget is now, was a drive-in theater. I went there with my friends Tom McGee and Jack Sorenson and as the theater was letting out, I noticed the ladder to the marquee.

I said, "Hey, you want to have some fun?"

The billboard read "Mighty Joe Young, starring Forest Tucker." I climbed the ladder and changed the letters to, "Mighty Joe Hung, starring Torest Fucker." We drove away in hysteria. Tears ran down my face because it looked so funny. Can you imagine people driving by?

The next day it was in the paper, "VANDALS ..."

But there were no vandals, never any gangs, never any guns, just silly pranks.

The mothers would say, "He seems to be a nice boy;" meanwhile, I was taking their kids on trips, doing crazy stuff.

The Big Reno Flood

One of my years at Manogue High School was the year of the Big Reno Flood. We all volunteered, sandbagging the whole downtown because when the Truckee River ran over, it took cars and everything with it. We drank a lot at the Koblantz bar. They gave us free drinks because we worked down there in the heat sandbagging. In the Penney's store hundreds of boxes of socks were floating around, argyles and such. They said, "Take anything you want." For days I had muddy socks at home, drying out on a line.

Two Boys and Trouble in a Cabin

I lived with the Potter family for a year. After school I worked at the Midtown Drugstore on west Second Street for 65 cents an hour.

At an inter-school party I met popular Jerry Poncia, who drove a yellow 1950 Mercury convertible. He was entrepreneurial—already running a string of slot machines, making $500 a week on them. He invited me to "come on out and live with me."

So for my last year at Manogue I lived with Jerry and his parents, Lola and Raymond Poncia. They operated the Sierra Turf Club, his father ran a race book, and they had a little ranch on Lakeside Drive.

A hundred feet from the main house on the edge of a pond was a cabin where Jerry and I stayed. For kicks, we shot at the beavers in the pond with an old pump 22. We'd get drunk, look out the window and yell, "There he is!" and grab the gun. We were pretty good shots, but we didn't want to kill them, just rustle them up a little.

Every weekend in that cabin became a party, beginning on Friday afternoons. I met a lot of Jerry's buddies. We didn't know how much we drank until spring came and the snow melted to reveal a pile of Sierra beer bottles about the height of a car.

Jerry had been accepted to the Northwestern University School of Architecture. His mother would say, "Corky, don't you go back there and mess with Jerry. He's trying to get an education."

Sometimes she would come out and knock on the door and say, "What are you boys doing in there?"

"Ooooh, we're just sleeping."

Then she would say to Jerry, "You have to stop that drinking. You and that Corky are out there drinking, and I know you're having sex with those girls." Like she could see the cabin moving around at night.

I bought a 1940 Ford Coupe, and every night I was illegally drag-racing. I was a pretty good driver—I'd challenge anybody. In Vegas, I lost my driver's license more than once for drag-racing. I'd get it back and they'd take it away again. Luckily I never hit anybody, because we'd race right down Reno's main street.

Jerry's mother would come out of the house and say, "What are all these cars doing in the driveway?"

Eventually, the inevitable happened in that cabin. I lost my virginity with Joan Clogston, the game warden's daughter, a fifteen-year-old sophomore. We were in school together. I had turned nineteen, a senior about to graduate. It was a miracle I didn't go to jail. It was a miracle she didn't get pregnant, because I never used protection. Talk about robbing the cradle and looking for eggs. But it was consensual.

Two-time High School Dropout

God love those nuns at Manogue High School. When I got some personalized attention from them—they made me feel like I belonged—my grades zoomed to B's and A's. I excelled in some things, which surprised me because I thought I was stupid. I didn't know that I had ADHD and OCD compounded by dyslexia. My left-handed penmanship is deplorable, and I've never been able to take notes. I wanted to be a good quality musician, but I couldn't learn to read music. I was all screwed up.

I think about what the education at the Catholic school did for me and I give those teachers high marks. It was a great period for me because it proved to me that I had more than a one-track mind.

Father Joseph Lindy, the principal, believed in me. One day I asked him, "What is it about God? What is God? Where is She? How does this work?"

He was pensive. "Well, look at the wall socket. The electricity is in there and we can't see it, but we know it's in there."

"Father Lindy, if I stick a hairpin in that wall socket, we'll know it's in there."

I was always given to oratory. I like to talk and at Manogue I began to refine my speaking skills.

The year I was destined to graduate, war in Korea broke out. I was a quarter short for graduation, and Father Welsh said, "I want you to do that speech over again."

I'd already done the speech and gotten a B+. I wasn't going to do it again.

"If you don't," he said, "you won't graduate."

He was breaking my balls. Father Welsh was one reason why I didn't become a Catholic. The other was Sister George, who planned to put my name in the yearbook as, "Court," and refused to correct it.

"Where does it say that you change my name to fit your yearbook?"

Boy, I was roaring. I was nineteen-years-old, likely to get drafted to go to Korea and get killed, and I didn't give a shit.

So, a quarter short, I didn't graduate. To this day Manogue Catholic High School occasionally sends me a mailer requesting a donation. Before I send it back, I write, "Send me my diploma, and I'll think about sending you some money."

Going to Korea to Die

I returned to Vegas, now a two-time high school dropout, to await my draft notice. I lived at home, had my own car—a green 1940 Ford four-door sedan—and spent most of my time hanging out with my old buddies. I had always worked hard and saved my money and bought cars, little Fords and coupes and roadsters.

My old man said, "You're not hanging around the house. Go get a job, or you're going to get in trouble." He may have been goofy, but my father had a work ethic.

I started out at the Park Market at 15th and Fremont. My good friend Bob Mackenzie and I started there together, and he subsequently had a long management career with Lucky Stores. Bored, I lasted about a month. From there I went to work at Safeway as an apprentice meat cutter. After I almost cut off two of my fingers, my dad said, "I don't think you're going to work out as a meat cutter."

So, back to construction and driving nails. I worked on the Joe W. Brown Race Track as an apprentice carpenter. I worked on a cement crew pouring concrete—hard work—out at Nellis. It was hot and there was no air conditioning in cars then, except for Cadillacs.

You name it, I did it.

The reports from Korea didn't look good. It was cold as a bitch there and the Koreans out-gunned us. They were kicking our asses. They were tougher than steel, defending their own turf. I'd already lost some good friends.

When my draft notice arrived, everybody came to see me off to Los Angeles for my physical. I had no plan to duck it. I'd accepted the idea that I was going to Korea and there I would die.

To my surprise, I didn't pass the physical. After tests and x-rays, the doctor said, "Your back is junk." He described a bad degenerated disc, fifth lower lumbar.

"Will you write that down?" I asked.

"Yes, you're not going. You can't be a foot soldier."

Even though I came home with an official paper in hand, my father started grinding on me because I wasn't going to Korea, if you can believe that.

"Aren't you going to go and save America?"

"Yeah, and what did you do in the war, Daddy?" I could see him walking around Hoover Dam with a flashlight and a cigarette saying, 'No Japs in here.'

"All my friends at the Elks Lodge wonder why you're still walking around town," he said.

"This isn't a popularity contest. I'm 4F." I waved the paper at him. "What does this say?"

He couldn't accept it. Between drinking and running around with women, he was in blitzville. He wasn't paying any attention to me.

But I thought, maybe I could beat this, and I consulted an orthopedic guy.

"Why don't you start doing weight training?" he suggested. "Start lifting and strengthening your back muscles if you want to go."

It wasn't that I wanted to go to Korea; I wanted to shove it up my dad's nose.

So I started working out. Soon, I could bench press 160 pounds. My goal was to be the strong guy who could bench his own body weight.

The Minesweeper

Already a member of the Naval Reserves, it occurred to me to try the navy. I went to the Naval Recruiting office in Las Vegas and, by God, they took me.

In March, 1953, at age nineteen, I went to boot camp in the United States Navy as a full specimen of what a good sailor was going to be.

At the end of boot camp when they began to give out the assignments, I kidded, "With my luck, I'll end up on a mine sweeper."

The *USS Illusive AM448* was a 620-ton aggressive class minesweeper made of laminated, glued-together pieces of plywood. It had four Packard ID1700 diesel engines, two shafts, and two controllable pitch propellers. The engines were made of beryllium. It was designed to degauss the fields in Korea's Yalu River. The Koreans had sub-surface mines you didn't even have to touch to set them off. If a metal mine sweeper went through there, boom, they went off. Lethal. Yes, I was going to Korea to die.

The 172-feet *Illusive* was part of a whole fleet, with a war time complement of thirty-six guys. It was being built at the Martinolich Ship Yard in San Diego. Tony Martinolich also built the joint off Desert Inn Road, The Colonial House. The Martinolich Ship Building Company sat on Harbor Drive next to a Breast of Chicken Tuna cannery, which is no longer there. At seven in the morning we would muster at the ship yard and then go back to our barracks. After 8 o'clock we'd have the whole day free, waiting for them to finish the ship.

I usually got into my car and went surfing. Man, I got a tan. I was chocolate and my hair, all bleached out, grew near down to my ass. In La Jolla we drank all night and I passed out. At dawn the next morning I was awakened by flies and a bad smell. I'd been sleeping with my head on a dead sea lion.

The captain was Lieutenant Commander John E. Ruzic, a gentleman with a southern accent. His first officer was a former architect named Swanson. These guys had been conscripted back into what was being called "the peace occupation of Korea" and "the Korean Conflict." Ruzic and Swanson had already done their time in WWII, had been sucked back into the Korean thing, and were as unhappy as they could be.

Captain Ruzic made me the captain's orderly. When they had inspection on the ship, I'd walk around behind him with a notepad. Captain Ruzic would eye one of the guys and say, "Proctor, this man needs a haircut."

My Mind is an Open Mouth: A Life Behind the Mic

I could feel the guy thinking, "aaaaah," mad because my own hair was so long.

Tony Martinolich

That was a great summer. On the weekends we took pocket rockets—amphetamines—to keep us awake to drive to Vegas. We'd leave at three o'clock in the afternoon from the naval base in San Diego, and be in Vegas by seven-thirty. That was a long haul on a two-lane road. It's a miracle that we didn't get killed. I was driving a '49 Ford two-door sedan, a great little car that would do 100 MPH, but it had no air conditioning, so we used the desert rat trick: soaking a tee shirt in water and putting it on wet. We could crank the windshield out and get a good wind against our bodies. It would work as an evaporative cooler for forty miles before we had to soak the tee shirt again.

I met Tony Martinolich and he took a liking to me. I think he was Slovakian. He started flying me to Las Vegas in his Cessna. He was building the Colonial House, and he knew I lived there. We'd go to Miramar Naval Station, which the guys called Top Gun Field because they were training there to be combat pilots, and we'd fly out of there. I'd never been in a small plane and it scared the shit out of me. But after a while, even though I'm a little anal and a control freak, I understood that I couldn't fly this plane from the jump seat, and Tony knew what he was doing. He'd throttle back, put the flaps down, and we'd come in to Las Vegas' McCarran Airport real slow. We'd taxi from the end of the airport where the big sculptures of three-bladed propellers mark the entrance all the way down to the old facility.

Tony Martinolich never let me fly his Cessna, but later I got to fly the mail plane between Vegas and Reno. An old Piper Apache twin engine, it carried 900 pounds of mail. All the exhaust stuff had been taken off. I've never heard noise like that. I was working for Bill Harrah at the time and his pilot, Tom Johnson, was great. I always tell people, if you are terrified of flying—and, God, I was wetting my pants until I was thirty-five-years-old—take some flying lessons. Get the feel of what the aircraft is doing.

Twenty-one in Tijuana

On my twenty-first birthday, July 22, 1953, my buddy, Bob Mackenzie, and some other guys took me to Tijuana. I drove us all in my '49 Ford two-door sedan.

In a bar called El Baron we found some working girls. We were already drunk, and we were supposed to each pick one. There was a pretty girl who looked like Marilyn Monroe except she had some gold teeth. She was eating, still on her lunch break. I would have to wait for her to finish before I could jump her bones for seven dollars.

When we went into the back room, in the corner next to the bed I saw a wooden Seven-Up crate full of crumpled used Kleenex. Somehow, that took all the romance out of it. I couldn't get aroused. No homo erectus. She wasn't helping me much, and it was embarrassing because I was totally impotent.

"You fok me, you fok me," she kept repeating.

"You know what," I said, "I can't do this."

It wasn't that it was below my dignity. God knows, when you're twenty-one your hormones are overactive. I just couldn't get into it. I went back to the bar and proceeded to get completely trashed. The mariachis played "Anchors Away," and by then my secret was out among all those damned sailors. That was my first and last experience in going to a brothel for sex.

Back on this side of the border, it was three in the morning when I dropped everybody off. My little Ford sedan had been lowered and had duel exhaust. As I left Bob's house I cranked a U-ie and nailed it, squealing the tires. Out of nowhere came the red lights, a young police officer out of San Diego. I immediately stopped and got out my driver's license and paperwork. He looked at my driver's license and probably realized he wasn't much older than I was.

"You got me," I said. "No mystery here." I was in the navy, it was my birthday, and I was feeling good.

"Have you been drinking?"

"Oh, yeah; we been to Tijuana."

"Are you drunk?"

"Not anymore," I said. "Not after you turned that red light on and got out with a gun in your hand."

He said, "Okay, just cool it."

So for my birthday, I got a pass.

The Launch

In the navy, when you are on a ship that is built from the get-go and part of the initial crew, you each get a plank owner's certificate with your name on it. I also have a picture of the ship. On November 14, 1953, the USS Illusive was commissioned. A bottle of something was busted across the bow, probably cheap beer.

Now we were ready to go, taking sea trials around San Diego. The degaussing test grounds were off the Channel Islands. A station monitored us to see if any of our metal products or anything on the ship were strong enough to detonate mines. As it turned out, they weren't. When we would go out to those islands, man, everybody would be throwing up, but it never did bother me. To this day, I've never been seasick.

The USS Illusive was an avante garde mine sweeper, a beautiful ship with real tile terrazzo floors. Built out of wood, it had brass tools, so there was nothing to set off those deadly Korean magnetic mines. Out the back of the ship trailed two sponsons that we called "pigs." They looked like pontoons, like what you'd see under the wings of sea planes. They were flotation devices that held the scissor device to cut the cable of a floating mine. With its shallow draft, the ship rode high in the water. The mines were maybe two feet below the water. The ship would scoot over them and the cutting cable between the two sponsons would cut the mine free or loosen it. Another electronic cable would detonate it. If for some reason that cable didn't detonate it, we could also blow it up by machine-gunning it from the rear of the ship. It was dangerous work. Few mine sweepers survived the Korean conflict.

When I reported as an able-bodied seaman, Captain Ruzic asked, "Can you type?"

"Sixty words a minute."

"Great. You can type the ship logs."

That's how I became a yeoman. My other job—special sea detail—was to report on all the functions at the back of the ship. If the ship got blown apart, it could actually be steered from the back, or aft end. It was spooky, but interesting. Even though I was a yeoman, I was stationed in the aft steering at the ass end of the boat. I didn't know what I was doing, but I had a gun. A lot of the time I was asleep—literally. Most of the time, I was back there smoking weed. The smell of the hemp from the ropes was so strong, you couldn't smell the dope. The rest of the time I was the real sailor, the yeoman who typed the ships log every day, recording what we ate, how much fuel we took on, etc.

One day something happened. We passed Catalina Island and headed out into the Channel Islands. Then one of the propellers on the Packard V-12 twin diesel engines went automatically into reverse. The Illusive had been designed with an automatic reverse pitch, so the ship could be thrown into reverse with no waiting. The effect was like slamming your car into reverse going thirty miles an hour.

That and the screaming and yelling woke me.

The propeller had backed over the electric detonation cable, which ran all the electric juice back into the ship. When the cable wound around the propeller, it bent the shaft. Captain Ruzic quickly shut down the power for the mine detonation system. Anyone in the ship touching metal could have been electrocuted instantly. We sat there waiting to figure out what to do. The action had thrown one of the motors out of sync. We had to be towed back into the shipyards, humiliated and embarrassed. A huge piece of black cable filled with copper wires was tied over the side of the ship.

A ceasefire had actually stopped the fighting in Korea on July 27, 1953, and shortly after the Illusive was commissioned, the war ended. My mother was ecstatic. When I called, she said, "Oh, the war's over. Are you coming home?"

"No." I had another seventeen months to go.

The Gun Thief

When you "stand a watch" on the ship it means you stand in one place at a lecture-like podium for four hours to screen people who might want to come on board. It could be the mid-watch or the middle of the night. I had a watch from two to six in the morning, and I didn't even drink coffee.

My Mind is an Open Mouth: A Life Behind the Mic

I took a sidearm—the gun went with the post. At the beginning of your watch you accepted it from the previous guy and signed for it in the log. Considered government property, it came with a belt and real ammunition. It was peacetime, but we were wearing a gun.

Being the inquisitive car thief that I was, during my boring watch I took that 45 caliber automatic out and field-stripped it. I spread out all the parts on the podium. I had the gun completely apart when an old man came up the gangway. I nearly had an accident in my shorts. With my arm I swept everything right into the water. I'll never forget that splash. Talk about a court martial—messing with the government's property…

What was I going to do? At the end of my watch I was supposed to hand off the gun, belt, and ammo to the next guy. I ran downstairs and got a guy who would stand in for me, wearing the gun belt, while I ran over to the minesweeper tied next to us where I knew a guy. I paid him to go into their ammunition locker and get me another 45, because he was stealing a federal firearm. It wasn't the same serial number, but nobody was going to check because you put ditto marks in the log for the "equipment." You signed out and the next guy signed in and you passed the gun and holster. That gun had been in the holster for three years, and nobody ever looked at the serial number; the log was a row of ditto marks. Nobody took the gun out and played with it. Only I would do that. The rest of the guys smoked and drank coffee.

I was only gone twenty minutes, which was acceptable because it was peacetime. You could get away with it, say you didn't feel well, and nobody gave a shit.

A Short Smokestack

In the Illusive we slept three high in bunks in a 20 x 20 foot area. You learn a great deal about getting along with your fellow man when a guy's ass is right over your nose.

We had a good cook named Martinez, but a lot of the guys were sick every morning. In the mess hall, some would feel ready to throw up. We all had terrible headaches and I came to the conclusion it wasn't from drinking the night before, though there was plenty of that. We were drinking, going to

Tijuana to the dog races, and acting crazy, having fun. We spent a lot of time listening to Humphrey Bogart and Lauren Bacall talk to each other on the ship-to-shore radio.

The more I thought about it, the more I was sure what it was—diesel fumes. Because of my hot-rod mechanical background I knew that you are not supposed to inhale exhaust, diesel or any other kind of fuel. It's not good for you to have that in your lungs. And you stink when you get up in the morning. At night while we slept, we were leaving the front hatch open to get fresh air. The diesel fumes in there would knock out a giraffe.

I went to the ship's doctor and told him that we were all getting headaches. He said something silly, so I waited a week and then went into the old man's office.

"Captain Ruzic," I said, "we have a serious problem."

"What is it, Proctor?"

"The intake/exhaust fans from the generator are so strong, they're sucking the diesel fumes back into the sleeping quarters at night. Everyone in the forward locker, all twenty-two of us, are waking up every morning with a gang-banger headache." I pointed out that some of the guys didn't even drink.

Captain Ruzic got right on it. Some guys, including an admiral, from 12th Naval District Board of Inspection and Survey came aboard. I met them all and Captain Ruzic had me explain my theory to them.

"Even though warm air rises," I told them, "the smokestack for that 300-kilowatt generator is too short."

The admiral gave me that look that said, *what does this kid know?*

I was always pretty mechanically minded, so I was confident. "I know a lot about race cars and engines and exhaust and such," I added, "and the stack needs to be higher. The diesel fumes coming out of the generator smokestack are rising and being sucked back into the air-conditioning system."

The looks on their faces were priceless. We went back to Long Beach and they stretched the smokestack another twelve to fifteen feet. They also tried to put a deflector on the generator. They retrofitted all those mine sweepers; I think there were thirty of them at one time in San Diego. It cost millions of dollars, and then they never got to Korea. Illusive later took part in joint

My Mind is an Open Mouth: A Life Behind the Mic

exercises with Japanese naval units and carried out maneuvers off Japan, the Philippines, and Okinawa. She finally decommissioned in 1990, and was sold by the navy for scrapping in February 1993 for $12,000.

After the diesel fume fiasco the duty was pretty good. We made runs out to the Channel Islands to the degaussing field. We went through, pulling all of our stuff to see how much magnetism we were giving off. I found it quite an interesting process.

I joined the navy and never left Southern California. I like to say we fought the invasion of Catalina Island and the landing at Ensenada, Mexico, our two biggest battles. Hey, I went. My intentions were good.

Save the Kidney

The following year, 1954, I developed hydronephrosis, a swelling of the kidney caused by an obstruction in the ureter. It could have been congenital or it could have been caused by a drunken fight I'd lost where I'd been kicked in the kidneys. The doctor said there was no way to tell which.

In those days they used to take out the kidney and the ureter. I was fortunate that the navy doctors diagnosed it early. The kidneys are not real big, about the size of your fist. A good kidney looks like a spider web. A bad kidney looks like a sack of rotten grapes and, boy, that scared me because only one kidney was perfect.

I went to Norco Naval Hospital in Corona, California for an exam. I said to the nurse, "When I take a deep breath it's agonizing." She said it was because the kidney was distended.

Dr. Walter Shudde, the head of urology, said, "We're going to get you in here. Go back to the ship, get your stuff, and come back here as fast as you can. The chances are real good that we'll save your kidney."

That was Friday. John MacRill, a guy from navy bootcamp who had become a good friend, and his parents drove me to Corona. Monday morning they cut me open and saved my kidney.

Dr. Shudde, a commander, must have been seventy when he operated on me. He'd been in the navy for forty-five years. He had arthritis so bad he could hardly hold the pen when he wrote the script. But his nurse said, "Let me tell you something. This guy is gold. He's forgotten more about kidney surgery and urology than most doctors will ever know."

Her words were comforting, but I was terrified. I woke up to tubes with a saline drip and sucking on a piece of washcloth around an ice cube.

"Can I have some water?"

"No, you may not."

"Can I have some morphine?"

"Yes, you may have some morphine."

Now I know how guys get hooked. I loved that morphine. They would shoot me up with it and I'd be like on opium … drifting … sailing … flying. After three days they took me off of it.

I called all the girls I knew and they all came and brought me cards. I enjoyed that part. One of the guys in my ward had just been circumsized, and he wasn't quite healed. But he was healed enough to take one of the nurses on a gurney into a private room. Afterward it looked like somebody slaughtered a lamb in there.

It took a month for me to recoup from the kidney surgery. By then I was on a first-name basis with Dr. Shudde, and he knew I hated the navy.

I said, "Walter, could you keep me here a while?"

"How long do you want to stay?"

"As long as I can. I don't want to go back to the minesweeper. It's sitting there in the water, and it'll never pass the inspection at Board of Survey because it's junk."

So he sent a note to Captain Ruzic saying, "We're keeping him for observation." What did they care? We weren't going anywhere on that ship anyway. The ship was dead, the war was over, big deal.

I stayed for four or five more months, working for Dr. Walter Shudde. I learned a lot about urology. I worked in the lab with urologist Doctor Conrad Stryker, whose father invented the Stryker Frame for people with a broken back. I took all the specimens and put them in formalin in the bottle with the gauze and typed out the label. Dr. Stryker was a cool guy, a German who was probably still a Nazi. We had a lot of conversations about World War II in which he made comments that led me to think that.

But they all liked me. I was nuts, but I got along.

I still have the kidney and it's working well. Dr. Shudde told me that beer is good. "It's a diuretic," he said, "but be careful of drinking too much vodka and hard liquor unless it's distilled well, because they're hard on the tissue and hard on your brain."

Well, obviously, I didn't heed all of his advice.

Discharge

When Captain Ruzic left a big, tall skinny dude named Henry replaced him as commander. Henry was a real navy guy, everything by the book. Stiff and goofy, he looked like Abraham Lincoln would have if he'd been in the navy.

Henry told me, "I don't think I'm going to recommend you for reenlistment, Proctor."

"Write that down immediately," I said.

In 1955, almost two years to the day, my commitment to the navy was up. I typed my own discharge papers—thank you very much—gave myself a substantial leave credit and a few vacation days and that was the end of my naval career.

When I got out I had a new Ford that I bought through my dad. It was in the parking lot on Highway 101, opposite the gate.

There was a rule that you had to be in uniform for the first twenty-four hours after your discharge, and I was still in the Reserve. You had to behave with navy decorum, and that meant you had to treat your sea bag with respect. To piss off the Marine guard at his entry post, I dropped my navy sea bag in front of him and dragged it all the way across Highway 101 to the parking lot.

That night I drove to L.A. to celebrate. Maynard Sloate, who I would later work with in Vegas, had a club called Strip City where I went to get a drink. I was driving my new Ford, I'd gotten out of the navy, I was glad to be an American, glad I didn't have to go to Korea on a mine sweeper, glad I was going home. Man, I had a great attitude. There was a comedian performing onstage. I didn't know who he was, and I started ad-libbing with him. Talk about asking to get your head cut off. He came over after the show and said, "Wow, man, I don't know who you are or what you do, but you are quick."

He was Lenny Bruce.

Do Something

I got home to Vegas Easter week of 1955, in the middle of a terrible storm. It rained and rained, filling the Charleston and Bonanza underpass. A sign of things to come? I moved in with my parents in the house on Del Monte. Bad mistake, bad mistake. I'd been in the service and was no longer the little naïve kid. Now I knew too much. Now I was a big kid, 6 feet 1½ inches, 200 pounds. I'd been lifting weights and my build was fairly substantial.

And I'd discovered girls.

One evening I brought one home to the house for the night. I shouldn't have done that. It didn't sit well with the folks.

Almost every day my dad asked, "What do you want to do?" He was always bugging me to do something.

"I don't know," I said. "I just got out of two years in the navy."

I tried selling cars, but it bored me. Then I went to work at the Sahara Hotel as a lifeguard. There I again met Victor Mature. Handsome and charming, he came in and invited everybody to sit and drink with him. Boy, could he drink—vodka out of an eight-ounce highball glass.

"Sit down, come on, we have room."

I told him I was twenty-three, just out of the navy. That I met him years before when he came to the El Rancho in his 1947 canary yellow Cadillac convertible. But he was almost completely shit-faced, and I could tell he didn't remember.

"Yeah," he said, "so what are we going to do? There must be some starlets we can bang or something. What do you do?"

"I'm the lifeguard here." I was actually swimming right there while he downed a six-pack of vodka.

That same year I started dating a cocktail waitress from the Golden Nugget named Marie, and I was in love. I had a '52 Ford convertible and I was having a pretty good time for a guy with no skills.

When I left the Sahara I went to work at Allen and Hanson's men's clothing store at 4th and Fremont, selling clothes for owners Felix Allen and Jack

Hanson. I sold a lot of clothes to Benny Carter, the musical director at the Moulin Rouge. All those guys came in to buy from me.

With the money I bought a new blue 1955 Volkswagen from VW dealer Frankie Newman, one of the first Volkswagens to be sold in Las Vegas. One night we all got drunk at the men's store, thought we could break some kind of world record, and crammed eight guys in that little bug. Then for a lark we drove it from downtown Fremont Street out to the Flamingo Hotel—not on the street but on the center median of the famous Las Vegas Strip—and never got busted.

Billy has a Drink at the Thunderbird

While I was having fun with cars, my dad was having fun with horses. He belonged to the Sheriff's Posse, along with Oscar Bryan, the Lindeman Brothers—Bud and Bill, and the owner of the Thunderbird Hotel, Joe Wells. These were tough cowboys, but nice people. My mother had them all out to the house to dinner. They were polite and respectful.

Dad's first horse, Billy, came from Doc Sorensen, a popular stock supplier up in Idaho. Doc's daughter, Berva Dawn married Casey Tibbs, the number one cowboy at that time. Dad kept Billy in the back yard of our Del Monte house.

One day he and his Sheriff Posse buddies had been out doing something, dressed in their cowboy clothes, riding and drinking. They ended up in the bar at the Thunderbird, where my dad extolled the virtues of Billy.

"That's the smartest horse in the world," he said.

I think the other guys were tired of hearing him say that. One of them said, "Well, if he's that good, Al, why don't you bring him in for a drink?"

"Stay right there," my dad said. He went out to the parking lot where they'd left their horses in trailers and got Billy. He rode that horse right in the front door of the Thunderbird and through the casino to the bar.

Security didn't do anything because of the presence of Joe Wells.

I heard about this the next day when I went to work at Allen and Hanson.

"Boy," one of the guys said, "your dad's got some balls."

Now what?

I was selling clothes, paying rent to my parents, and having a nice relationship with Marie. Then I decided I wanted to go into acting and get into theater. I wanted to be a musician. I wanted to get into show business. I wanted to go on to radio and television. I wanted to do all of those things.

At Wyler Boys Academy, I had been in the marching drum and bugle corps. I even took some piano lessons and did pretty well. In his college years, my father had been a drummer, but he decided to quit "because I can't make a living." He was right, to a degree, except that the 1920s was a great period in America for music, especially jazz. But he quit and became a bookkeeper.

I had no formal musical training at Las Vegas High or Manogue. I didn't start to seriously study the drums as an instrument until I got out of the navy. I found a great teacher named Phil Arabia, but he got busted for pot by Las Vegas Constable Woody Cole. How unfortunate, when marijuana is a drug that Queen Victoria took for menstrual cramps.

Discouraged, I decided to move to L.A., take advantage of the GI Bill, and perhaps go to radio and television school.

A Jazz Drummer or a Comic?

My dad had bought my first drum set while I was still at Las Vegas High. He had a good friend, Bud Crouch, a drummer with the Thunderbird house band. Bud was always trading cars at Ford. A good sight reader and accomplished musician, Bud always had a pair of drum sticks in his back pocket. When he needed some money, he said to my dad, "Al, I have this drum set and I'd like to get rid of it."

In those days a guy would give you ten dollars if you needed it. Nobody starved to death in Vegas. You'd think, well, this guy's an ass, but he needs some money and he's got a wife and two kids, okay, here's ten dollars, which is like a hundred now.

"Let me see it," my dad said. He didn't know much about drums. The set was basically the same kind of set they were playing in the 1920s, with a few refinements. I think he gave Bud fifty dollars. Then he brought the set home to me and said, "You owe me fifty dollars."

"Okay," I said. And I paid him back.

I started practicing and, of course, I drove everybody crazy. I had left that drum set behind when I went to Manogue, but in Reno I began to make it a point to watch a lot of great players. In a sense I taught myself by going to watch other drummers with bands like Woody Herman's. I liked a drummer named Gene Riddle. Guy Mitchell was popular, and I went to watch him. I had poked my nose into show business.

I had the rudiments down and I had the time; I mean if you can go ding, ding, ding, a ding, ding, ding, the rest is fluff. If you can't keep time, you can't play. It doesn't matter how good or how flashy you are—twirling drum sticks and all that. I never dreamed I'd ever get the self-confidence to be a jazz drummer or a comic. Those are people on the other side of the moon. I was probably going to be a laborer, I'd told myself.

But the seed had been planted. I knew I wanted to play music. I just didn't know how to get from point A to point B.

Drum City

By the end of 1955 I'd landed in L.A. and found a pad to share with two other guys: James McDaniel, who later designed Las Vegas' Judy Bayley Theater and Fleur De Lis Apartments and Dick Ohrn, who later would have a successful Las Vegas sheet metal business. Jimmy was a great guy, studying architecture at Southern California University. His theme project for his graduate degree involved designing what I believe was the hippest uniform Bonanza Airlines ever had. Dick was attending Los Angeles Trade Technical College, and I was starting at Don Martin's Radio and Television school at Cherokee and Hollywood Boulevard.

The three of us lived off the Hollywood Freeway in a garage belonging to the famous silent screen actor, Richard Dix. If you don't think that was a zoo; girls were coming and going, like that garage was a lazy susan. I got into theater, where I met young starlets. They were all cute with great breasts and sculpted little buns and they all wanted to come over and listen to music. It was heaven in Hollywood.

When I arrived in L.A., I had the GI Bill, which paid about $100 a month. While I was going to school, I took all kinds of weird jobs. I drove a freight truck. I worked for Gilfillan and Brothers down on Jefferson as a wire stamper for aircraft. I worked on the freight docks at 10th and Alameda for Southern Cal Freight unloading thousands of batteries.

One of the jobs I did was to paint the interior of a music store called Drum City on Santa Monica half a block east of Vine and a block from the garage where Jim and Dick and I lived.

Everybody came into Drum City. You could see the great players and recording stars. Drummers Shelly Manne and Mel Lewis gave me lessons. I was a two-time high school dropout who wanted to be a drummer. I didn't have time to study eight hours a day and practice and their advice was, "Go get a gig somewhere and play on the job." So I started taking any kind of a gig. Everybody knew I wanted to play. I drove them crazy with questions and asking, "Where are you working tonight?"

Two good drummers and co-managers of the store, Chuck Molinari and Bob Yeager, were working at a strip club, so I went there at night to see them.

Owners Roy Harte and Remo Belli had just invented the Remo Plastic Drum Head. Most drum heads were unborn calf, and if you were in a humid environment the head turned to melted cheese. Sometimes with bongos and conga you had to bring a little portable heater to set them on. The heat would radiate and tighten the heads. They'd be good until it rained.

Remo wanted to test his new plastic heads. He got guys to play on the plastic heads for about fourteen days, non-stop. He got all the great drummers, Larry Bunker, Sid Balkin, left-handed Stan Levy, and Hal Blaine, who played with the Mamas and the Papas and Sinatra. And me.

I hung out at Drum City for hours almost every day of the week. When Remo and Roy wanted to remodel, I volunteered to work as their painter. I was on a ladder, painting the walls by hand. I don't think paint rollers had been invented yet. I traded the work out for my first professional drum set, an Aristocrat designed by John Grey and made in London. It was the most beautiful drum set I'd ever seen, black pearl with drumheads of unborn calf. It cost $350. It seemed like I painted that store forever to pay for it.

My Mind is an Open Mouth: A Life Behind the Mic

Those Black Spots

Latin percussion teacher, Mike Pacheco, who had been the congero and bongo player with the Stan Kenton band, taught me to play bongos. I had a difficult time reading the music because of my then-unknown dyslexia. I couldn't figure it out. I didn't think it had anything to do with IQ or brain cells—I just couldn't figure out those little dog droppings on the sheet music.

"What are all these little spots? What do they mean?"

Mike said, "That's a dotted eighth note and this is a sixteenth and you play this and then that."

If I heard it three times, I could play it. My brain would go, oh, we can do that, but trying to read it and keep the high hat going in two and the bass drum going in four was shear madness. It's almost gymnastic. You have to be pretty athletic to be a good drummer.

But I would continue to see stuff backward, and write stuff backward.

"God, what's the matter with you?" Mike asked.

"I don't know. I can play all the shit, I just can't translate those black spots."

Shelley's Manne Hole

While I was going to Don Martin's, I worked on the construction of a coffee house on Cahuenga between Selma and Hollywood Boulevard. It opened as the International and upstairs was a little broadcast booth for KBIG, a Santa Catalina Island a.m. radio station. I got a job for a few months playing jazz out of that booth from 10 p.m. to midnight. Jazz musician Shelly Manne took it over later in the fifties and it became the successful jazz club, Shelly's Manne Hole.

Deadly Legacy

I'd stayed friends with Jimmy Nelson and now that I was in L.A., we started to hang out. Jimmy had a 1948 Jaguar, and we decided to drive it to Utah to visit the set of the movie, *Genghis Khan*. His father, Sam Nelson—neé Van Falkinburg—was an active first assistant director at Columbia Pictures. He'd worked with Frank Capra, Orson Welles, and Robert Rossen on *Dirigible*, *Lady From Shanghai*, and *All the King's Men*, respectively. Sam made the arrangements for us.

Genghis Kahn would be the last film produced by Howard Hughes and it left a deadly legacy. Located in the canyon lands around St. George, Utah, the set was not far from Yucca Flat, the notorious Nevada bomb testing site of the 1950s. No less than eleven atomic bombs had been tested in 1953 alone, and clouds of fallout hung around Snow Canyon, a major filming site. For thirteen weeks everybody inhaled the dusty air and then Hughes shipped sixty tons of the dirt back to Hollywood for the set where the retakes would be made.

Actor Pedro Armendáriz was the first victim, developing terminal kidney cancer four years after the filming and then committing suicide. Director Dick Powell and actors John Wayne, Agnes Moorehead, and Susan Hayward all subsequently died of cancer, believed by many to have been caused by their exposure to the radioactive fallout. Everybody knew about the fallout at the time, but it wasn't taken seriously as any health threat.

Jimmy and I never thought twice about it. We went on the set, met all the stars, watched some of the shooting, and then headed back to L.A.

Outside of Baker the Jag blew a fan belt. Hard to find anything in Baker, but there was one all-night gas station. We measured the broken belt and at the station we must have gone through 500 fan belts before we found one that fit on a Nash Rambler. Close enough. I knew the old trick where you put a screwdriver in between the belt and the pulley, tick the starter, it slides into the groove, and you're done.

The gas station owner came out and said, "What are you boys doing?"

I said, "We're looking for a fan belt."

"Well, did you look in the book?"

I said, "There are no Jaguars in that book."

The Proposition

One late night I smoked a joint and stopped by the Hollywood Ranch Market on Vine Street to pick up something to eat. A lot of musicians hung out there because it was open 24/7. I was at the snack bar perusing greasy burgers I could smell a mile away.

Behind me I heard, "Do you like to fuck?"

I turned around to see a good-looking, light-complected black guy with a mustache.

"Girls," I said.

He grinned. "You ought to try me." He put his hand on my shoulder and made an overt gesture.

I decked him, right in the sternum. He took a step back, tripped, and went down. I think I surprised him. I don't think he expected to get punched. Next thing I knew the cops were there. The market manager had been watching and had called some of them who habitually hung out in front of the market. They let me go with the understanding that I would report the next day to the Hollywood police department "to give a statement."

"He propositioned me," I said.

The cop didn't even raise an eyebrow. "So?"

"Well, he shouldn't have put his hands on me."

Nobody witnessed it except the market manager who didn't want any trouble, so the incident went no further. That was the first time a guy had ever hit on me and I found it left me with an awkward, uncomfortable feeling.

A Usable Screen Type

I went down to Los Angeles assuming I was going to break into show business, and I did.

One weekend I came home to my parents' place in Las Vegas. While in town, I ran into Geraldine Solomon, a girl who was two years older than me and who had been a cheerleader at Vegas High. She'd been married and divorced and had two kids, but she was beautiful and had huge pom-poms. We went out a few times and when I asked her to come to L.A. to visit me, she agreed.

I was waiting for her in the Harvey House at the L.A. train depot, reading a *Life* magazine. Rock Hudson, wearing a blue chambray work shirt, was on the cover.

"I see that you are reading about a client of mine," I heard a lispy voice say. I looked up to see this ghoulish-looking man in a gray, cheap-looking suit smiling at me.

"Are you a lawyer?" I asked.

He handed me his card, "Henry Willson," with a phone number. "So," he said, "have you acted?"

"I've been acting pretty funny since I was born."

"I'd like to manage you," he said. "I think you could have a great career in movies."

I didn't know this guy managed Rock Hudson and Tab Hunter and Sal Mineo, among others. I didn't know how powerful this guy was as an agent in the studios. Right away I knew this creepy guy was gay, so I didn't get excited. I didn't jump and say, *can you make me a star?* But I did follow up and let him manage me. I dropped out of the Don Martin's Radio and Television School because I wanted to be an actor, and I didn't think the school was moving me along as fast as I wanted.

Even though he was flamingly gay, Henry Willson was well respected. And his client, Rock Hudson, was the heir apparent, the guy who was going to replace Cary Grant as the top male romantic lead, gay or not.

Henry sent me to Harvey Easton's gym to work out. He sent me to Lester Luther, a voice coach, who gave me vocal exercises where I would hold my nose and make certain sounds. I had a lot of resonance, which I never use. I don't do that deep voice, "Hello, I'm Edward R. Murrow and you're not."

The first time I was mentioned in *Variety*, the movie industry publication, was Tuesday, November 29, 1955. Bill Willard wrote in his column reporting on the Las Vegas Strip: "Corky Proctor, son of local Ford Thunderbird salesman Al Proctor, is in the agent Henry Willson stable and up for tests this week."

Henry sent me to Estelle Harmon, one of the biggest acting coaches in L.A. In January 1956 she wrote an evaluation on me for Henry:

> *"Cork is an easy-going, appealing young actor who seems to be potentially an interesting screen personality.*
>
> *"Despite a lack of previous experience and training he quickly learned to perform with pretty fair naturalness and relaxation. His work has become steadily more honest and believable. He has already improved his freedom in the use of personal business, is*

working with more authority, and is reading his lines with more color. His final performance of 'Death of a Salesman', indicated that Cork can be quite interesting and compelling when he is strongly concentrated.

"In his coming training, Cork must work for a clearer understanding of each character and a definition of the character's basic objective. He must strive to overcome his habit of keeping his eyes on the floor and his tendency to speak his lines somewhat too glibly and without thought. He must learn to think between his lines and to listen and react truthfully. Lastly though Cork now appears to have an intellectual understanding of play structure, he has not yet made use of this understanding in the design of his scenes.

"Cork is a very useable screen type and with proper training and guidance should gain a stronger knowledge of acting technique fairly quickly. This knowledge plus experience performing before groups should give him the confidence and relaxation that will enable his own natural easy charm to be used before a camera effectively."

Henry also sent me to a woman who took a real interest in me, Helena Sorrell, who had been the New Talent Coordinator for years at Universal Studios.

"You're naturally funny," she said. "You should get into comedy immediately." It would take me another twenty years to get the self-confidence to do it.

After Henry put me through all that shit, I realized his entire stable was queer. Everybody he represented was gay. One time he had me out to his house in Bel Air for dinner. We had a lot to drink and he made his move on me.

"I don't do that," I told him.

He said, "I would never let sex stand in the way of a career."

"I'm not going to do that, Henry," I said. "That's not who I am."

I had been exposed to the best and the worst, and I found I couldn't handle the feeling of being the property of a guy as slimy as Rock Hudson's agent. I lost the zest for the whole movie industry. It was too seamy. It's like when you walk into an apartment and it stinks, you see a mouse run by, you see mouse turds on the floor, the kitchen sink is dirty, the toilet is dirty and you think, I don't care if this chick gives the greatest head in the world, I'm leaving, right now. Goodbye, here's the wine, see ya. The whole industry affected me that way, and I'm not sure that it's gotten any better. There is still that sleazy, slimy element.

Yes, once you become a Tom Cruise or Tom Hanks you can pick and choose, but I was young and naïve. When I would go for a reading I would hear guys snicker behind my back. "His name is Cork." Snicker, snicker. I thought, this is all bullshit. They're not taking me seriously, and they're not taking this fag agent seriously, so why don't I get up and leave?

I had been serious. I had taken all the classes and paid for everything—the gym, the voice coaching, the acting lessons. You do all of these stupid Hollywood things and then some kid falls out of the sky—some kid who hasn't done anything at all—and becomes a star.

Disillusioned, I parted ways with Henry Willson.

Able-bodied Seamen go to Europe

Through the connections at Drum City, I met Harry Babasin, a wonderful bass player from New York. He was also a recording engineer and spent a lot of time showing me recording techniques that takes two different choruses from two different recordings and splices them together, assuming the time is the same. Today that would be done with computer technology.

Jim and Dick had graduated and moved out, so I moved from the Dix garage into Harry's basement, where I lived for six months. My romantic affair with Geraldine Solomon had faded after a few months. We drifted apart because I was in L.A. and she was with her kids in Vegas.

In the summer of 1956, I took a job selling insurance and met Louise, this beautiful Scandinavian girl, except that she smoked. As a non-smoker, turned off by my parents' habit, that bothered me, but we got by it. We developed a wonderful relationship; Louise and I became a hot item.

A great job came along as an extrusion hand former at McDonnell Douglas. I had hired on and completed all the paperwork when my friend John MacRill, a guy I was in the navy and boot camp with, called. His father worked for Sunkist Oranges, and did John and I want to go to Europe?

"Yes."

I never notified McDonnell Douglas. I blew off the job and would regret it later. I gave up the apartment in Harry Babasin's basement. I borrowed some money from my parents and only had $250 when I left. Not a lot of money to go to Europe, but I was going.

John's father wired a great deal for us with the biggest merchant marine in the world, the Westfal-Larsen Line out of Bergen, Norway. What the hell, I was twenty-two-years old, still kind of naïve, and I got the chance to go to Italy and Spain and Germany and hang out and have fun. I didn't have any money. My parents said, "Well, we only have a couple of hundred."

"Good, I'll take that."

Given passage as "able-bodied seamen," John and I left the 4th of July, 1956, on a Norwegian tanker, the *Moldanger.* We didn't get paid, but we worked and we ate and we slept and we drank beer. How exciting to go through the Panama Canal. Once the tanker ran over a whale and the entire ass end of the ship lifted six feet.

The captain was cool. The bosun's mate was out every night jumping rope. The guy was ripped—we could see every muscle in his abdomen. Those Norwegians were tough guys. Most of them spoke English, but when they wanted to have a private conversation it was in Dutch or Norwegian.

After a week, they decided they liked John and me because we didn't stir up any shit. We cleaned the cabins and never touched anything; nothing ever went missing. We cleaned the bathrooms. John and I got in there and burned for six hours. We used a case of Comet and everything gleamed. When the Norwegians saw it they said, "You work too hard."

On Wednesday the breakfast fare was spaghetti and eggs. We got constipated, felt near death. They gave us citrate of magnesia, and I thought this ought to work. Wrong. I think we went about two weeks without a bowel movement. I guess it was the food and the excitement and the Dutch beer.

We got off at LaHavre, France, and headed for Frankfurt am Main, Germany, to visit my uncle Bill, who was the Champion spark plug representative there. The Germans were installing Champion plugs into Volkswagens.

Uncle Bill loaned us his new gun metal gray Porsche to drive for a few days. When John and I pulled up to the Holland border, the Porsche, with its German plates, attracted some attention. That's when I first felt resentment. After all, it wasn't that long after the war. The border guard glared at us.

"Hello," I said, showing him my passport.

His face morphed into all smiles. "Ah, Amerikaners!"

I said, "Where can we get a good bottle of wine, some bread, and some Gouda cheese?"

"Go up the road two kilometers, you see a small building, you pull in there." He smiled and waved us through.

In a bar called the Flying Dutchman we saw a jazz pianist from the United States, Pia Beck. She had a drummer named Ed Thigpen, who later recorded with Oscar Peterson. For the price of a few beers, we got to listen to some great jazz.

When we returned the Porsche to Uncle Bill, we rented a VW and drove all over Holland. One afternoon we were drinking wine, half in the bag and speeding. We came around a corner and a few yards in front of us crawled a horse-drawn funeral procession, taking up the whole road. Talk about turning that car every which way but on its nose. I back-shifted and the car squealed to a stop. All these people, dressed in black, gave us laser looks.

In Paris, we had lunch at the Eiffel Tower. We took a train from Paris to Madrid, and halfway we stopped to spend the night at a seacoast town in Spain called San Sebastian. Somehow, our luggage got lost and we had to stay there a few days. All the fishing nets were drying in the sun—postcard beautiful.

In Madrid we went to the Museo Nacional del Prado. For two young guys who didn't know anything, we did a lot of shit. In a little bar in Spain I asked for frijoles con queso.

"That's a Mexican dish," John said. "We're in Spain."

I was given a plate of green beans and a cheese sandwich.

We were in Europe for six, maybe eight weeks. That trip was one of the best things I ever did. I've always been sorry I wasn't able to take more trips on the Westfal-Larsen Line. I recommend travel for any young person. Go somewhere. I don't care if it's the Canary Islands to study birds, go somewhere. We get too comfortable here in America. We go to point B and come back like army ants.

The Scandinavian Girl

In Los Angeles, Louise was waiting for me. We were beyond lovers; we had become soul mates. Then she got pregnant. I loved her and it never occurred to me not to "do the right thing."

I didn't have any money. Louise's mom and dad couldn't even afford to come down from Washington State, which was sad. I called my mom and dad. "I'm going to marry Louise. Do you want to participate?"

We got married in Las Vegas by Judge Russell Taylor at my parents' home. John MacRill—a lawyer by then—stood up for us. Louise looked gorgeous. In the wedding pictures I look twelve, in a suit I bought at Allen & Hanson. Afterward, we had a reception at the Thunderbird Hotel in a beautiful room with an open bar and a few friends.

It was fun, but I was terrified. I wanted to be a musician and an actor and there I was married with a kid coming. Boy, that straightened me right up. Between that and the navy, there would be no more monkey business in my life.

In Los Angeles, Louise and I got a small apartment on Afton Place, near the Hollywood Ranch Market on Vine Street. I approached McDonnell Douglas about that great job I'd blown off, and they did everything but laugh in my face. Not a chance now. So I went back to working at the freight dock.

Keeping Time

Though some of my show biz activities were curtailed, I was able to return to Don Martin's Radio and Television School. I made time to hang out in jazz clubs, listen to guys play, trying to learn all I could about jazz. Even though she was pregnant, sometimes Louise went with me.

I was applying for any kind of work, but I wanted to play. So every night I was at the Hillcrest Club on West Washington Boulevard listening to Dexter Gordon, Dave Pike, Billy Higgins, Ornette Coleman, and all those wonderful, young, gifted black musicians. They played jazz in toilets for $20. They all had albums, but that didn't mean anything. You can have ten albums and still be starving to death. They were true to their craft. These avant guard guys were creating all this new music. Ahead of their time, they played what they wanted. But there was a theme and some chord changes. I didn't know exactly what I was hearing, but I knew it was great. I felt it in my gut. I thought, boy, something was going on there.

A lot of the time they were paid in heroin or some other kind of dope, none of which appealed to me, especially not the thought of sticking a needle in my arm.

I started working with black rhythm and blues bands, keeping time, one, two, three, four, two, two. I started learning what a drummer is not supposed to do, not what he is supposed to do.

I heard them say, "It's not what you play sometimes, it's what you don't play. Stay out of the way. If there is a vocalist, you want to be quiet." I learned that if the band is doing a shout course, you can wail your ass off, but when somebody is singing, the band should be subdued. The vocalist should be on top and the band should be way down at the bottom.

The swing bands of the time were Count Basie and Duke Ellington. Benny Goodman was the King of Swing. Paul Whiteman was a dance band. My parents thought pudgy Paul Whiteman was the king of swing. When I became a jazz musician I told my mother, "Paul Whiteman couldn't swing his fat ass for two bars if he had to."

Survival in L.A.

I wanted to dress well and I had no money, so what to do? I went to thrift stores and bought whatever I could.

Kathy was born on the 31st of July, 1957. We moved to a nice little house down on Jefferson Boulevard where Kathy could play in the fenced backyard. Louise got a good job for *Encyclopedia Americana* and supported me through this rough time. Every night I went out to listen to jazz musicians; during the day I'd try to do something to hustle some money. I don't think we even had a TV. Louise stayed home at night with Kathy and read.

I got a job driving a freight truck for Southern Cal Freight in a rough, industrial area in downtown L.A. I went to school at seven in the morning at Don Martin's, finished at one and by two I was on the freight dock. Originally, I went down there to apply as an office person because I could type pretty well—70, 80 words a minute—but they didn't hire me for that. A guy named Layton said they were looking for dock workers, guys who would move trucks around in the yard at night. I took the job because I had a work ethic and I had to work somewhere. I lasted seven months, probably the longest I ever held a job in my life.

The Don Martin program was two years. This two-time high school dropout actually finished and got an Associate of Arts degree in radio and television. But I had almost no self-esteem. In the school, people kept telling me how funny I was. I didn't feel that way, and there was nowhere to get up and be funny, no such thing as "open-mic nights" anywhere. Around L.A. there were poetry reading nights. The jazz nights, I could go sit in and work on my chops as a drummer, but there was nothing for comedy. I never believed I was going to be a comedian. I didn't have that kind of vision to see it as a talent. So what if I was funny? I didn't know how to direct it, collate it, what to do with it.

A Liar and Deceitful Man

Louise and I were destitute, scuffling. I was taking anything. If there was a job to be had, I was there.

A friend I'd met at the musicians' union, Kip Walton, after I got out of the navy worked with Art Linkletter and his partner and producer, John Guedel. Linkletter had successfully transferred his longtime popular TV variety/talk show, *Art Linkletter's House Party*, from CBS Radio to CBS television in 1952. Guedel designed a format that gave Linkletter complete freedom to be creative and spontaneous. Guedel had all sorts of ideas for the show that included musical groups, humorous Linkletter monologues, and audience participation to win prizes. A game show was devised where a single young man and single young woman were hooked up to play a quiz for money. The show took place at the Art Linkletter Playhouse on Santa Monica—later the Steve Allen Theater—half a block from where Louise and Kathy and I lived at 1122 N. Vine Street. I could just walk out the front door and go over there.

My friend Kip got me an audition for the show, where for money I became a liar and a deceitful man.

"Are you married?"

"No, I'm not married."

They paired me with a single lady named Barbara and we went on together as a pair. She lived in Long Beach. I felt bad lying about not being married, but short of stealing with a gun, I was on my rear end financially.

I told Louise the truth. I could make a minimum of a thousand bucks, a lot of money in 1957.

One day in the makeup room I met Mr. Linkletter. "Gee, it's good to be here, Mr. Linkletter," I said, "and it's so nice to meet you."

"That's a nice thing to say." He looked surprised. "Most of the people here are cranky and yelling about something they didn't get, and they thought they needed this and should have had that."

"Oh, no. I'm thrilled to be here."

The producers got me aside after the first few shows and told me, "Be careful. You look too professional."

Can you imagine? Twenty-five-years-old—how could I look too professional? Linkletter was cool. He let it run. He didn't say, "Hey, stop that. We don't want you to upstage us." Upstage meaning that I looked too slick, like a ringer. How could I be a ringer? I looked eighteen. I had blonde hair and a tan, like one of those beach kids. But I guess I was young and attractive and maybe looked a little overpowering.

I lasted on the show for three consecutive weeks, during which I took Barbara out for a dinner date. The Linkletter people gave me fifty dollars, and we went to a nice restaurant. Then we talked about the "date" on the show. Barbara was a lovely little twenty-two-year-old girl they picked out of the list of people. She never knew I wasn't available, because I didn't divulge anything.

My Mind is an Open Mouth: A Life Behind the Mic

Barbara and I were going for $10,000. In one of the games they showed a silly, little film of a baby pushing a red and white ball. We were being filmed watching the film. This was before video, when they used 16mm film. We were in front of a live audience, who rooted for us and waved in the background.

Afterward, the host questioned us about what we saw. A visual challenge.

"How many times did the baby touch the ball?"

"How many people did she throw it to?"

Barbara and I conferred, and we blew the answer.

We couldn't remember that the baby touched the ball four times and then pushed it to three people.

We were so close. We were up to eight grand and because we blew the answer we were off the show, so we only got half of that. We split it, each walking with $2,000.

My friend from the musicians' union and I were the only ones who knew I lied, that I wasn't single. I didn't care. I earned the money because I was entertaining. I didn't know why I was getting laughs, but I was getting them.

A week later the check came in the mail and Louise said, "Well, we're a couple of grand better off than we were last week."

Jazz as a Pedestrian Obstruction

After I graduated from radio and television school, I looked for a radio job. I applied at stations all over Southern California. There were only a fraction of the number of stations there are today and only so many morning guys who were funny. I wanted to be the morning jock, work from six to ten, play the music and act crazy.

Dick Moreland, a disc jockey who worked with me at KRLA—now a big talk station in L.A.—played the bongos. One night the two of us headed off to the Caprice, a tiny jazz night club on Peck Road in El Monte. In the back of the car, I had a new drum set I'd somehow finagled to buy. Usually, it was sell the car, buy drums, sell drums, buy a car. That went on for years.

Being the crazy bastard I am, on our way back from the Caprice I got the idea to stop before the Santa Monica off ramp. We pulled off the freeway, got the drums out, set them up, and started playing. Soon the cops arrived in their big 1958 Rocket 88 Oldsmobile.

"What are you doing?" they asked.

"We're playing jazz." They probably thought we were heroin addicts.

The cop looked puzzled. "I don't know what to cite you for, so I guess we'll write it as a pedestrian obstruction."

The September 20, 1958, headline in the *Los Angeles Times* read, "Early Morning Music Men Recreate Their Freeway Concert."

We got a bigger story and picture on the front page of the *Times* than Sammy Davis did getting his divorce the same day from Loray White. The story also appeared in *The Mirror News*.

I happily paid the fine.

Fleeing L.A.

Louise and I moved again, this time down to Rodeo Drive—not in the Beverly Hills section—but in the predominantly black neighborhood off Jefferson Boulevard.

We were broke and it was January 1959, the middle of winter. I called my old friend in Reno, Jerry Poncia, who was now getting established as an architect.

"Jerry, I have a wife and a kid, and I'm dying on my ass down here."

"Come on up," he said. "I'll help you if I can."

The day I was supposed to start a job with Sav-On Drugs, we left town.

In the flurry of packing, we discovered that Kathy, now twenty-months-old, may have swallowed a box of thumbtacks. We quickly drove her to the nearest hospital.

The emergency room nurse was hesitant. "You know," she said, "The doctor is black."

I said, "I don't care what color he is. Can we get an x-ray and see what's in her tummy?"

It turned out that she hadn't swallowed any of the missing thumb tacks. The doctor was extremely sympathetic and wouldn't even charge me. I think we paid three dollars for the x-rays.

The place we'd been living in belonged to an old vaudeville performer, Jed Dooley. He was a sweet man, and I felt bad because we moved out in the middle of the night, owing him a month's rent, $60. But we didn't leave the place a mess. We left a brand new electric fry pan on the counter and a Morris chair, the early version of today's recliner, which today would be worth a few thousand dollars. The arm rests, mahogany or oak, were six inches wide and could hold a cup of coffee or a snack or a tray.

When I talked to Jerry I found out there was a radio job available and voiceover work for Channel 8 TV in Reno. I sent them my on-air check and a copy of my Don Martin diploma. They wrote back saying, "The minute you get to town, come in and we'll talk to you." That was encouraging. You couldn't get hired over the phone. You had to be there.

We drove our 1951 Ford from L.A. to Vegas, where Louise and Kathy stayed with my parents while I drove to Reno hauling a trailer. Along the way I fried the motor, a brand new engine I had put in in L.A. It took me six hours to get to Beatty, not even halfway. People drove along the road, saw me and passed. Finally a guy named Phil came by in a cleaning truck and loaned me five gallons of water. What a nightmare trip.

Survival in Reno

Everything in Reno seemed to start off on the wrong foot. It was a brutally cold winter, the air dry and freezing. We weren't at all prepared. I didn't even own a topcoat. I had a pair of blue suede chukka boots and a three-button suit that I had bought to wear on jazz gigs in L.A. The first three weeks I stayed with Jerry and his father hired me to work at the Sierra Sport's Book on Commercial Row. For three dollars an hour, I went in each morning and washed the race results off the blackboards—nine bucks a day.

At the Book I ran into an old Manogue classmate, Jack Callahan. I mentioned that I needed a place for my family to live.

Jack said, "My aunt owns a ranch out on the Mt. Rose Highway with some cabins." Mt. Rose Highway was the road to Lake Tahoe.

Jack's aunt, Nora Callahan, rented one of the little cabins to me for $60 a month. Louise came from Vegas with Kathy on the LTR (Las Vegas Transit

Reno) bus. It was a twelve-hour trip because the bus stopped everywhere—Tonopah, Walker Lake, Hawthorne, etc.

In Reno they say that when the bugs are really black, it's going to be an extra cold winter. That winter those bugs were midnight, darker than Nat Cole. The only heat in the cabin was from a fireplace where every day I built a fire. There was no store of firewood so I scrounged it around the ranch. Nora never came out to the ranch and there was beginning construction of a two-car garage. Every day I'd go out and knock out a few 2 x 4s to burn in the fireplace. If the guys running the ranch for Nora figured out what I was doing, they never said anything. By the time we left most of the garage materials were gone.

It was "Dr. Zhivago" cold and Kathy, now two and a half, got sick. Green stuff running out of her nose, crying all night. We took her to a doctor.

"She's had pneumonia," he said, "but the fever's broken. She'll be fine. Take her home, give her some oil of eucalyptus and keep her warm." We did, and she bounced right back.

After freezing for three months at the Callahan Ranch we moved to Sparks to share the home of Leo and Maryann Scalf. Leo and I had been in radio school together and he worked at a station in Reno. We lived with Leo and Maryann four or five months.

We were so destitute I felt like there was a cloud over me. Like I was the little guy in the "Li'l Abner" cartoon who couldn't do anything right. I thought, *boy, why me?* A voice said, *why not? It's your turn. You need some karma. What doesn't kill you makes you stronger.*

Odd Casuals and Cowboy Bands

As soon as I arrived in Reno I went down to the Musicians' Union and put in my card. Rules were you had to live in Reno ninety days before you could work, but there was a shortage of available drummers; everybody was working.

At the union hall I met a talented piano player named Tom Russell—handsome, blond, great smile—who wanted to put a trio together. It would be him and me and a bass player named Chuck. I wasn't the accomplished player that I became later, but I had a good time. I could count from one to four, and I was a good brush player. I could play quiet and fast, which is a lost art even today. Tommy gave me the gig and I found a guy who would sell me a $50 tuxedo in installments.

We worked for Bill Tomerlin, a big, good-looking guy who owned Reno's Golden Hotel. We played "Rhapsody in Blue" and all kinds of classical music and timpani stuff—great training. We worked opposite an eighteen-year-old singer, Vikki Carr. From Texas, she was part of the Chet McIntyre Trio. Each time she sang "Danny Boy" she cried and got standing ovations and didn't even know why. Vikki sang from the throat instead of the stomach, which caused her trouble in later years.

When that fun gig at the Golden ended in the summer, Tommy went on the road. I stayed behind, not wanting to leave my wife and daughter.

By July, with Tommy moved on, I was working in construction, "playing" the shovel, making a living. I had a wonderful tan and my hair was again bleached blond. I looked like a chocolate bar with teeth.

I couldn't get a job as a house drummer because I couldn't read that well. If you don't read well, you can't be playing those shows. I learned that doing a short stint at Harolds Club as the show drummer with Don Conn's house band. He didn't know I couldn't read.

The show was the Wiere Brothers—a classic European musical comedy act, brothers Herbert, Harry, and Sylvester. Mildred Seymour was their accompanist. They were refined and sophisticated, but their music was all chopped with fly shit all over it. Somehow I managed to get through it. The Wiere Brothers was a visual act with movement and we had to match the guy with sound. When he fell down I would *brrrrr* and cover three drums and then when he took a pratfall, *whoomp* on the bass drum. Later, when I heard another guy play it, he didn't do that great either. He was reading his ass off and still missing stuff.

By the third night I was doing pretty well, but there was a lot to remember. I learned from Don Conn and the band, but at the end of the week, the tension was too high. I said to myself, *I've got to quit.*

When I told Don Conn, he said, "Why? You're doing great."

I said, "I can't read."

"You can't read?"

"No."

"How did we get this far?"

He thought I was just nervous. I left the Wiere Brothers and continued to do those odd casuals and cowboy bands, anything that came to town. I was working six and seven nights a week making a living; I didn't want Louise to work.

The guys at the music store, particularly the owner, Steve, liked me so they often referred me. Entertainers would come in and say, "Hey, we just got to town and we're looking for a drummer."

Steve would say, "This guy can play anything."

When you have that kind of support group, you don't feel like you're auditioning and hanging on like Frank Sinatra did in *The Man with the Golden Arm*. I never forgot that. For years I would go in and see Steve and thank him. When he died, I wrote a letter to the *Reno Evening Gazette* about how Steve had been so helpful to so many guys.

Now I had some balls. I knew I could play and I knew my time was good; if there were a few train wrecks, so what? We got through it. Second show would be better and the fourth show would be smokin'. I'd be catching stuff that they didn't believe.

Tuxedo Gal

Eulane Delmonico, a cocktail waitress at the Holiday Casino, saw me playing, subbing for a guy. Afterward she said, "My friend Kay Stevens is coming to the Riverside, and she's looking for a drummer."

"Great."

She smiled. "When she calls, I'll tell her I saw you play."

I said an old joke about when a band is looking for a drummer: they want a guy who looks like Robert Taylor, plays like Buddy Rich, wears a 42-long suit and will go on the road for $75 a week. If you could find a guy like that, you had the perfect drummer. At least at 6 feet 1½ inches and not unattractive, I got the job.

Kay was also a tuxedo gal. She wanted me to dress formally. We opened July 4, 1959, at The Riverside, working for Mert Wertheimer and his partners. At the end of the second night, we all went out for breakfast. Tommy Amato, the bass player and Kay's husband, shook his car keys at two poodles on the road. Goofing around, I was acting faggy. I said, "Listen," kicked my foot high in the air, "Okay, boy dancers." My foot met his hand. He didn't even see the kick coming, and his keys flew into the Truckee River.

Six o'clock in the morning and I was in the Truckee River with my tuxedo pants rolled up to my cajones, looking for Tommy's keys. We never found them. They may still be on the riverbed bottom. Tommy didn't have a backup set of keys, his Cadillac was locked, and he had to call a locksmith.

I thought, what a way to start the job.

Tuxedo Bandit

The night the police thought I robbed the Cavalier Motel, I nearly got shot.

I was late to work with Kay Stevens at the Riverside, down the street from the Cavalier. The six-foot-tall robber wore a dark jacket and dark pants, white shirt open at the neck. Guess what I was wearing? As I ran, I had my hand in the pocket of my tuxedo pants, holding my little snap-on tuxedo tie.

The cop hit me with a body block, shoving me into the side entrance of the Riverside so hard it took skin off my cheek. He almost knocked me out.

His hand holding the gun he pointed at me shook. "Stand still, or I'll blow your ass off!"

"Gee, I heard that once before when I was stealing a car. I don't want to hear it again."

Buck, a big Riverside security guard appeared from the back door. "Cork, what are you doing?"

The cop had me against the wall, that gun shoved right into my heart from my back. "We got him, we got him," he yelled to the other cop,

"You got what?" I said

He said, "What are you doing?"

"I'm running to work. I'm late. I'm a musician. I work in here and I'm starting in ten minutes."

"Yeah, likely story." He pulled my hand out of my pocket, and there was my bowtie.

The side of my face burned from being scraped against the bricks. I was so angry with this stupid kid, I didn't give a shit.

"Buck, tell this schmuck who I am."

He told him my name and that I was a musician. "He's due on stage in ten minutes."

The cop stepped back and let me go.

I glared at him. "What? No apology?"

I wiped the blood off my cheek as best I could and raced inside. The first song was, "Things look swell, things look great, you can have the whole world on a plate." My adrenalin was racing so fast I picked up the tempo to match.

"What's the matter with you, anyway?" Kay said. "What are you on, crank or crystal meth?"

That young cop had scared the shit out of me. He had the hammer back on that gun. One false move and he'd have killed the wrong guy. Luckily in my anger I didn't open my mouth and say what I'd been thinking: *Do most guys rob a hotel with a pair of tuxedo pants on? Hello, how long you been a cop? Can I go to work now or do you want to follow me inside and pistol whip me?*

That night two guys had robbed the Tropic Lodge and at the same time two other two guys had hit the Cavalier Motel. The Metro cops were going one way and the Sheriff's department was going the other way. Right inside the Tropic Lodge, they shot one of the guys with a .357 magnum. The other guy ran out the back and they caught him in a dumpster. One of the Cavalier robbers got away in a car, long gone with the money. And how much could you get from a motel? Maybe $300? Wow—enough to carry you for the next ten years if you lived in a storm drain and ate garbage.

The 1960s

Kathy Disappears

Louise was pregnant with our second child the day Kathy disappeared. We had moved from Leo and Maryann's to an apartment at 1520 Holcomb, half a block east of Virginia. I had bought a new 1960 four-door Ford station wagon. It was a nice summer morning and I was doing something with the car in the driveway while Louise was busy in the apartment.

I went inside and said, "Where's Kathy?"

"I thought she was with you," Louise said, suddenly alarmed.

I jumped into the car and criss-crossed all the streets in the neighborhood, frantically searching for a little pigtailed three-year-old in a burgundy jumpsuit on a red tricycle.

Back at the apartment I said to Louise, "We can't wait. We've got to call the cops."

I took a picture of Kathy down to the Channel 8 television station. I knew the guys there because I'd been doing some voiceover work. They broke the shows with a news flash, "There's a little girl lost between Virginia and Kietzke Lane."

The hours agonized by. Louise wept. Guilt flooded my mind along with terrible pictures of what may have happened to my little daughter.

It was three in the afternoon—nearly five hours later—when we got the call that the police had her.

A woman had seen her picture on television and remembered the little girl she'd just spoken to on the sidewalk in front of her house.

She'd gone out and asked, "Where do you live?"

Kathy had said, "I live right here."

The woman called the police and they came and picked up Kathy and her red tricycle.

When we got her back, I smacked her twice on the ass and hugged her and said, "Don't ever do that again. You scared us to death." I hated the helpless panic I'd felt, like being imprisoned in a horrible nightmare.

But what did she know? She was three-years-old.

Louise took her inside, undressed her to examine her body, and reported that she was fine.

We never could figure out how our little three-year-old traveled due east three miles on Colorado Boulevard and crossed busy Kietzke Lane, to be found in front of the Channel 4 television studio on the other side of that major thoroughfare.

Later I talked to Reno's chief of police, Elmer Briscoe.

"Someone picked her up," he concluded, "and then changed their minds."

Kathy says she has no memory of what happened during those five hours. I don't even want to think about it.

My Downfall

Often, two lounge acts would alternate, back-to-back. We'd go on when the show in the main room broke. The hotels would schedule a strong lounge act to attract people and keep them from scooting from the main showroom out the front door.

One evening during my 45-minute set break I went over to catch a band called the Buddymars, appearing in the 7th floor Harolds Club Fun room.

A great little showroom—only seated about one hundred people—it also featured Petula Clark, Trini Lopez, and Matt Monro. It was so popular that you had to kiss the maitre'd's ring to get in. But I knew everybody because I'd worked there.

In the middle of the act the Buddymars brought out this incredible-looking Puerto Rican dancer named Elanita Padilla. A beauty contest winner who looked like she was carved out of mocha chocolate, she was an exciting dancer. Her hair was pulled back in a bun. It was like watching Lilly Christine, the cat woman at the El Rancho Vegas when I was young and parking cars. My heart stopped. She looked at me and I went ditsy. I was 170 pounds, twenty-five-years-old, and horny as a two-peckered billy goat in a tux.

The next night after her show she came down to see our group and sat at the bar.

I want to clarify here that this is not about a conquest. This is about falling in love, falling in lust—whatever—when you're married. This unimaginable passion. God knows, if I wanted to see a beautiful, perfectly proportioned body, I had Louise, so it wasn't about, gee, my wife is no longer as attractive as she was when I married her.

For the eight weeks the Buddymars were at Harolds Club Elanita and I carried on every night and every afternoon. When she left town, I was like a little kid who'd just had his lollipop stolen. Elanita, knowing I was married, went back to Philly.

That was the beginning of my downfall. I guess if you're going to chippy, get a good one. If you're going to steal a car, don't steal a Yugo—steal a Mercedes. You'll do the same amount of time.

It's interesting how infidelity starts. Whenever I watch a TV show or a movie like *Fatal Attraction*, I recognize the fact that it's overpowering. It's beyond hormone imbalance. It's, man, I've got to have her, or vice-versa. It spoils you. Not only the great sensuality of the sex or flash-fire, but the time frame. You're married, you've got kids. You can't have a matinee with your wife with kids running all over the house.

On the Road

When Kay Stevens left the Riverside and went on the road, I went with her. We traveled to California and worked places like the Java Lanes in Long Beach and the Gay Doll Room at Winchester. I was driving a '52 Cadillac Coupe de Ville. I was playing pretty well by then, but I wasn't making much money, $140 a week. Most of it I sent home to Louise, who was okay with that. There wasn't much work in Reno because I didn't have any credibility, and this was better than sitting around.

I stayed with Kay eight months. But she was a bitch, an angry woman, critical of everything. My playing improved a great deal, as did my attitude and self-confidence. Within two years, I was able to return to Reno and get $300 a week. One day, fed up with Kay's bitchy criticisms and without another gig in sight, I quit.

Short Gigs

Back in Reno, I worked short gigs, anything and everything, scuffling and starving. I took hillbilly gigs out on West 2nd Street. Those cowboys were great guys. The music was three chords but it was fun, just keeping time. Periodically I would get a jazz gig for twenty-five bucks. Once I drove to Lovelock, over one hundred miles, for fifty dollars. I needed the money and if you want to do something you love, the money will come. Now I believe that more than ever.

I was building a reputation for being a better-than-average player. The majority of bands didn't have music written down. They had "head arrangements" like some of the jazz tunes. You learned the tunes and when you went to sit in, they called it out in a certain key. To the drummer it doesn't matter what key the song is in, unless he's going to sing. I loved it because I didn't have to rehearse anything.

I was out every night looking for work. I would go to Lake Tahoe and hang out, tell everybody I was looking for a gig. I would hear, "Oh, yeah, we heard about you."

Louise was the drum widow, home alone four, five, six nights a week because I was trying to get a gig. I had to get out and see people. There weren't many day jobs, even though Harrah's had a tremendous amount of day entertainment. At one time Reno had as much or more than Vegas did, and high caliber stars: Rickles, Sammy, Cosby, Dick Shawn.

The King's Four

In April 1960 I was introduced to Bill Kay, with a group called the King's Four. Billy was Jewish and funny and I liked him immediately. We had the same kind of whacko sense of humor.

Bill told me, "Stan is going to leave the band."

Stan Worth played piano with one hand and drums with the other. I was intimidated, not only by his musicianship, but the fact that some of the band's arrangements were intricate. Stan had created some busy stuff. The bass player was Stan's brother, George. Tenor sax and clarinet player Frank Ciculla, George, Stan, and Billy Kay had all been in the air force, stationed at El Mirage together when they started the band.

They all came across the street to see me where I was filling in with another group. Later, Bill came back and said, "We like the way you play. Would you be interested in joining us?"

"Yes." The money offered was $225 a week. I might have gotten more, but I didn't know how to negotiate.

The last week Stan was with them there was a lot of tension in the band. They had me come and watch for three nights, but like a fight, you just have to get into it. Finally, I got a few nights playing with Stan and I stepped all over my dick because I wasn't paying attention.

Stan felt his career wasn't going anywhere with the group. He wanted to go back to L.A. and arrange, which he was more than capable of doing. He had a tremendous jazz flare and he sang well. Perhaps some of the tension came from leaving his brother behind—they were really tight. And Stan had been listening to too many people who told him, "Fuck the band. You should be a star." When Stan left, that relieved a lot of tension.

Gold Cuff Links

The King's Four was booked at the Commercial Hotel in Elko, Nevada. Our friend Frankie Fanelli, a wonderful singer who had a bunch of hits, worked up the street. We all were hanging out one night at O'Carroll's Bar in Lamoille, a little town seventeen miles east of Elko. I sat down to talk to a beautiful girl who was having dinner there, Abby Lazano. When I asked her what she did, she said, "I'm a working girl."

That was the first time I'd heard that phrase, and I learned it meant she was a hooker. She worked at a brothel in Elko called Betty's D & D. We always referred to it as, "Dine and diddle."

Abby liked me and I admit I was attracted. For three nights running, she paid out of her own pocket for me to spend an "all-night date." But I laid there, literally, semi-dressed and just cuddled and talked to her. I never touched her. She liked jazz and she was also a heroin addict. When the King's Four left Elko, Abby gave me a $150 pair of solid gold cuff links.

I made the mistake of going home and sharing this information with my wife. Louise grabbed a huge hammer, took those cufflinks out onto the back porch and went *bam*. From then on, I never confided in her.

Easy to Drink

In November 1960, I was working at Lake Tahoe with The King's Four when my second daughter, LuAnn was born. We were living in Reno at 1540 Holcomb off of south Virginia. Mom came from Vegas to take care of Louise and stayed almost a month.

Driving to Tahoe every night in the wind and the rain was arduous, not to mention dangerous. Driving that two-lane highway in snow and ice—it's a miracle I didn't get killed. I'd leave late for work and then when I was there, I drank, every night. Mediterranean stingers. Can you imagine anything more vile than Galliano and Metaxa? I didn't do drugs. I guess a lot of guys who smoked pot could sustain, but it screwed up my time. I tried it a few times while playing music, but I didn't handle it well. I didn't want to be back there with a giddy look on my face. There was a lot of pot-smoking going on, but mostly I drank. Luckily, I never got hurt, never got in a wreck. But close—a bunch of times. When you're in show business people want to buy you a drink, so it was easy to drink and I rarely paid for them.

Great Gigs

The King's Four had some great gigs. In Tucson, we worked the Saddle and Sirloin for Irene Safarnas and her husband, Jimmy. New to the band, I still had little confidence in my playing ability, felt terrified, out of my element, but I rose to the occasion and things turned out pretty well. We worked in Houston, Texas and the Dream Room in New Orleans for Walter and Sam Noto.

As I think about all the other guys over the years, I'm lucky that I haven't been sick with any respiratory diseases. In the Dream Room in New Orleans, our heads were eighteen inches from the ceiling. I don't think we even had a circulating fan, and in 1960, everyone chain-smoked. I was the only guy who didn't.

Louise and the girls went with me on the trip to New Orleans. In Elko I'd bought a new 1960 Ford country squire station wagon. To save money, I bought a six-cylinder with a stick shift, and no air conditioning—just $1,700. I took the bottom cushion out of the back seat and put a mattress on the floor big enough to go up the sides and cover the door handles. It made a nice little padded play pen for Kathy and Luann. As I drove, they could stand and look out or play or nap.

Psycho

On an off night in New Orleans, Billy Kay and his wife, Marty, and Louise and I decided to go out to see a movie, so we got a babysitter. *Psycho* was showing at a theater on Canal Street.

At the box office we had our money out, and the black cashier was giving us a funny look. At that moment, a cop on horseback approached and said, "You can't go in there. It's a black folks' theater. You have to go down the street to the white folks' theater."

So that's what we did. We were from California; what did we know?

Paying Our Dues

We once made a trip from New Orleans to Walla Walla, Washington in five days. Talk about beating yourself to death. I was learning fast and my playing was improving every day, but not the money.

At the end of a year and a half Louise and I were having a tough time financially. I had to kick our 1960 Ford Wagon off to a guy, a takeover thing where I gave him the car and he made the payments. We bought a '52 Dodge two-door for $20. One of those little green army belts was around the right hand door to keep it closed. When Louise got into that car, she wore a babushka and dark glasses.

"I don't want anybody to see me in this car," she said.

We paid our dues.

What I tried to do was maximize the time I had with every band. I tried to get as much out of it as I could; even though I didn't know what I was doing, I knew that in order to get better and better I had to go with something that challenged me. I couldn't step down. I don't know how country drummers can play that same shit night after night. I love Merle Haggard, but the drummer never gets to play. He's just back there chopping wood.

The Shopping Center

Jerry Poncia and his friend Jack Lyons came to me with a business proposition. They were partners with lawyer Don Carano and Jerry's business partner, architect Frank Merrill.

"We need $10,000 to develop this property on Odie Boulevard," Jerry said. "We're going to build some apartments and stores and stuff. Do you want in?"

"Sure."

I was making $25,000 a year, still a young guy, and I had saved some money.

Nat Casselli and Bill Paganetti, who later created the Peppermill chain, had their first bar and restaurant, Sir Loins, in our Odie Boulevard shopping center. Sir Loins, like the Peppermill after it, was famous for its cocktail lounge flame pit. We were their first landlords.

Two or three thousand dollars a year came back to us from the shopping center rents. Jerry was good to me. When they sold the property fifteen years later, I got my ten grand back, plus all the rents. The center was always full; we never had a vacancy.

Time, my Biggest Asset

By fall of 1961, I got tired of the road and the bullshit, mostly the bass player slowing down and speeding up the time every night. I became musically frustrated and it was time to go.

Accordionist Dick Contino was opening at Harrah's lounge in Reno. Dick told somebody he wanted to get a new drummer. Word spread, I heard it from Billy Kay, and I went to Harrah's to apply for the job. One of the guys Dick brought in, along with guitarist Bill Comstock, was trumpet player Lee Raymond. Lee was Dick's band leader. I introduced myself and he hired me on the spot, without hearing me play.

Though my sight reading was terrible I spent that day with Lee downstairs in the basement. He pulled out Dick's music, all chicken marks and scratched and 'go back to the coda,' etc. Lee would play the part with his trumpet. He'd go through it two times and I had it. The first show, opening night, I didn't miss a lick.

That night on the bandstand I met Dick Contino for the first time. He turned around and said, "Wow, where have you been?" Lee had told me that Dick had had a lot of terrible drummers. I knew my time was my biggest asset. I could make the tune start where it was supposed to start and finish where it was supposed to finish. It didn't slow down or speed up. Dick and I shook hands and I had the job. That was my first decent-paying job, and I had a wonderful time. Dick was a great guy to work for. We still see each other occasionally.

My reputation began to spread. Lots of people came in to see me with Dick at the Mapes. *Wow, who is this guy? Cork Proctor, and he lives in town.* It became like dominos; the phone began to ring. Now I never suffered from lack of work.

Dee Dee and Bill

I joined a musical comedy act working at Harrah's: Dee Dee and Bill. I left one band and a week later I was on this band for better money and a company car, a '62 Chevy wagon. In it I carried the props.

We drove some hellacious trips, all night long. It's 1,170 miles from Reno to Albuquerque, and I did it on automatic pilot. I don't know why I didn't get killed. I'd snap awake going eighty miles an hour in the dirt. I'd roll the window down and eat sunflower seeds. When I got to Albuquerque, there were inches of sunflower seeds on the floor of the car.

With that group I smoked a lot of dope and shot to 265 pounds. In Kansas City I found an after-hours Mexican restaurant to frequent. You smoke a joint and go there and eat 46 pounds of beans and grease. No wonder I gained weight.

Bill Greer was the first guy I ever worked with who played oboe, an instrument with a strange embouchure. Dee Dee played a little piano, sang, and was very funny. She performed an impressive tribute to Lena Horne.

The GI Loan

In 1962, Louise and I bought a little house at 630 H Street in Sparks with a GI loan for $14,750. Two bedrooms and one bath. Payment was $91 a month. Louise was ecstatic. With two babies and already tired of show business, I'm sure, she was happy to settle down in a friendly neighborhood. She raised our daughters there till our divorce in the 1970s.

A Little Excitement Around Here

Mark and Joanie Masaglia still laugh about their wedding on January 16, 1963, when I set the church on fire.

Mark was the head of the musicians union in Las Vegas and Joanie was in the singing group, tThe Sawyer Sisters. The Little Church of the West was on the grounds of the New Frontier Hotel, on the Strip in Las Vegas near the Silver Slipper. Hank Penny was supposed to stand up for Mark as best man. A few days before the wedding Mark found out that Hank was detained in LA. So he asked me to do it. The wedding was scheduled for 1:30 in the afternoon and I'd been drinking. In fact, I may have been drunk. Everyone was at the church and Joan was late, hung-up by a drunk hairdresser. Mark stood at the altar, and I was throwing out some lines to pass the time.

None of us can remember exactly how it happened, but there were candles, drapes around a stage area, a cigarette lighter, and then flames three feet high. I was lighting the candles and I guess I got a little cavalier. I remember saying,

"We need a little excitement around here," before those old raggedy-ass curtains caught fire.

I didn't do it deliberately. I've done some stupid things but that certainly wasn't my objective. I think somebody said something, I turned around and boom, that's all it took.

Scary.

Jack Kent, the drummer, helped me jerk down the drapes and everybody stomped on them to smother the fire.

Then, from the back of the chapel, here comes the bride.

Throwing Lines from the Drums

It's lonely on the road. In Tucson at Mike's Troop's Townhouse—there was a plexiglass floor where you could see fish swimming around beneath it—I fell in love with Dee Dee. We began a tremendous affair. I seriously thought about leaving Louise. But then I would think of Kathy and Luann and the financial disaster it would have been because Louise didn't work.

Dee Dee talked me out of it. "You can't do that," she said. "You have two children, and they will never forgive you."

She was right.

Dee Dee also pushed me into comedy. Watching her and Bill night after night after night, I learned a lot about comedy. I was writing jokes for them, little bits, nothing impressive. They had a good writer, Mort Greene, a rigid guy who wrote both songs and comedy lines. I don't think he ever managed Dee Dee and Bill as well as he should have. He kept them at a C level, though they were funny, a double A act.

Bill was drunk a lot, hanging out with The Characters—Freddie and Carmen—and Jimmy Vincent from The Goofers. It was a whole medley of drunks.

Bill fired me once because he suspected I had been with his girlfriend, but he never really knew. He hired me back.

With Dee Dee and Bill I drove all over the country like I had with the King's Four. I was throwing a lot of lines from the drums, and that pissed off their songwriter/manager, Mort Greene.

"Stop doing that," he said, "You're upstaging Bill and Dee Dee."

So there was no more room for me in their group. I'd been with them for a year and a half. I couldn't go any further with them. The affair with Dee Dee still threatened my marriage. My relationships with both Bill and Mort were strained, which made it easy to leave.

We were working the Riviera Hotel in Las Vegas when Pete Mateo came in. He had a band called Susie and the Night Owls. He saw me and said he was looking for a drummer who could do stand-up and sing. I sang okay. At least, I sang in tune. I thought this was a wonderful opportunity to leave Dee Dee and maybe save my marriage. Just cut this off, and that's what I did.

I'll never forget the shock in her face when I told her and Bill together that I'd be leaving in two weeks. It was painful to see, like breaking your arm. She was upset with me for leaving, but she didn't get in the way. "It's a career move and you gotta do what you gotta do," she said. I replaced myself with another drummer and was gone.

Drums and Comedy

Susie and the Night Owls was a spin-off band of Joy and the Boys, a hot vocal comedy group in Seattle during the 1962 World's Fair. The chance to both play drums and officially do comedy was irresistible.

As soon as I saw Susie's real initials on her suitcase, I knew it was a mistake to join that band. Her name was Edna Grace Overshire, EGO. I should have said, "I don't want anything to do with this. I know what's coming."

Susie/Edna was a reformed whatever. If I said, "I don't want to sit down in my pants because I'll wrinkle my crotch," she'd cover her ears, and this was a woman with a lot of miles on her. If she were a tire, we'd call her a retread.

But I took that job with Susie and the Night Owls so I could do some comedy. There I got to know Pete Matteo, a wonderful jazz piano player from Philadelphia with a Jimmy Durante nose, and Tony Austin, a guitar and banjo player. There we were, great players with this hokey band.

Susie and the Night Owls worked the Thunderbird in Las Vegas and for Davey Victorson, entertainment director at the Sands. We were getting some serious money. I made $425 a week in 1963 and 1964. I began to stand up and sing parts. I was moving more and more toward comedy. I wanted that mic. I wanted those laughs and I wasn't sure how to get there. You know the old joke—it's only three feet from the drum to the microphone, but it's a million miles.

We had a lot of differences of opinion on Susie and the Night Owls. Pete would never rehearse. He would yell shit at us. 'Don't do that—we're playing in front of four hundred people in the audience—stop that. I told you not to do that.' It was hilarious. After a while, it got to be, 'okay, shut up Pete, we know what we're doing.'

We went to Seattle for an eight-month appearance at Rossellini's 410, a great supper club in the White-Henry-Stuart Building at 410 University. It was run by Governor Albert Rossellini's cousin, Victor Rossellini. In Seattle I started eating regularly in a place called the Red Ramen. I had a little steak every day with sliced tomatoes, onions, and salad—no dressing—and cereal in the morning and lost forty pounds. I met a lady named Lori Thompson, who owned a wig and hair salon called Periwigs by Lori, and we had one of those wham, bam, you're both drunk and there you go.

But I sent money home every week to Louise, and when I appeared at the end of the Rossellini's run with a 36-inch waist, she said, "My god, look at you!"

I stayed with Susie and the Night Owls for a year, until the end of 1964.

The Rudy Rodarte Trio

With Dee Dee and Bill at Eddie's Club at 13th and Baltimore in Kansas City, I'd met a bass player named Brian Bee. He showed up in Reno looking to get something going. He played okay, sang, and did a lot of cute songs and parodies. I liked him. I think in Kansas City we'd gotten high together a few times.

Now he was in Reno, with a number in the phone book. He didn't even know I was in town. I called him.

"Hello, is this Brian Bee, the bass player?"

"Yeah."

"Are you good?"

"Real good."

"Are you working tonight?"

"No."

"Do you want to go to a movie?"

He said, "Who the fuck is this?"

I said, "It's Cork."

He asked what I was doing and I told him, "I live here. I just got off the road. I hear through the grapevine that you're putting something together." He asked if I was interested. "Sure."

Brian went to Rudy Rodarte, whom I had met and played with through the musicians' union. Rudy never got any identity and never recorded; he was an alcoholic who plodded along, but he was one of the greatest vibraphonist and marimba players in the world.

Rudy and Brian and I rehearsed as a trio for a few days. Then we went out as the Rudy Rodarte Trio to look for work. Some gigs we appeared alone and on some we backed up entertainers like husband-and-wife singing duo Art and Dotty Todd, and Alvino Rey.

Born in Oakland, California as Alvin McBurney, Rey changed his name during the craze for Latin music. He also knew a lot about electronics; at fifteen he figured out how to attach an amplifier to his guitar. He was the first musician to do that, became known as the "wizard of the steel pedal guitar," and was wildly popular for his steel and Spanish guitar playing. He was married to one of the four King Sisters, a popular vocal group. We worked with him at the Winthrop Hotel in Tacoma.

At a supper club called the SS Princess Elaine in Blaine, Washington, I got us fired. Blaine is on the border between Canada and Washington state. We heard that this guy Colman Steel, who had a successful restaurant at the top of the Space Needle during the 1962 Seattle World's Fair, had the Princess Elaine, an old ferry converted into a restaurant moored at the garbage dump in Blaine, Washington. They needed a trio so we went in there and I started acting silly.

Now this was a dinner salon on the boat. We were a little trio playing jazz, making $600 a week—less commission to Jack Belmont, the agent in Spokane. A good, fun gig.

Once on our day off Brian and I drove in his '62 Ford convertible into the gorgeous countryside to see what was there. We stopped along the road to pick wild blackberries. Then we were driving and hit a pheasant. We took her home, wrung her neck, and cooked her with two potatoes topped with Marie Calendar pie pans. Just put them on top of the grill on your stove top and bake.

I began doing bits from the stage. I'd pick up the local newspaper and see who was indicted, kind of like what Mort Sahl was doing, but I would go into a local story and trash these people.

One time I put on a yachting hat and announced, "This is your captain speaking. Unfortunately, we won't be able to get under way tonight for our back bay cruise, leaving from the beautiful garbage dump at Blaine where the seagulls poop on everything. At noon Seaboard Finance came out and repossessed both motors. So we're just going to walk around the deck and get drunk and throw up and be somebody."

The bit came into my head out of nowhere. Somebody called Colman Steel and said I was making fun of the supper club. We didn't know the joint was in Chapter 11 bankruptcy. Man, Steel went airborne, infuriated. I began to realize how thin-skinned people are. That kind of thing happened so many times that I began to wonder if I had ESP, if I was picking up vibes.

We were supposed to be in Blaine for a month and this happened two weeks in. Jack Belmont called and spoke to Rudy. "What are you guys doing?"

"Man, we're having fun. We're just playing."

But we got fired, paid off, and left early.

Years later, Colman Steel came into Harolds Club's Silver Dollar Bar in Reno. Rudy and Brian said to me, "Aren't you going to say hello?"

I said, "I'm not going to say anything to him. We didn't know he was going into bankruptcy. We didn't mean to beat him up, and what's the big deal? I told the truth and if he can't handle it, screw him. He fired us because he was an asshole. I'm not even looking at him."

In the interim, I think he'd also lost the Space Needle Restaurant.

That was one of my early firings. My mouth managed to get us in lots of trouble.

We're the Winners

Through emceeing for charity at the Reno Air Races, I'd met Roy Powers, director of marketing, advertising, and publicity at Harolds Club in Reno. I camped in Roy's office for three days. Finally, he showed up.

"Hey tiger, how're you doing?" he asked.

I told him about the new trio.

He said, "Well, we need a relief group." That meant the nights the other bands were off we could work. It would mean four nights for us. "How about we try it for a week and see how it goes?"

Roy renamed us The Winners. We went into that lounge and kicked ass. We schmoozed, we shook hands, 'hey, how are you? Hey, we're The Winners and we'd really like to work here. What a great joint.'

By the end of the week we were solid gold. We stayed five years.

I Love Radio

About the same time The Winners began appearing at Harolds Club, I got my foot back into my other love, radio. Reno's KCBN had gone rock 'n roll. I think they were the first station in Reno to do that. It was a tiny little watt station—you could spit further than they could broadcast. I heard they were looking for a morning man. I went down, made an air check, and the moment I got home they called and gave me the morning drive shift, 6 to 10 a.m.

The Winners schedule at Harolds Club was: Monday, midnight to 6 a.m.; Tuesday, 5 p.m. to 11 p.m.; Wednesday, 9 p.m. to 3 a.m.; Thursday, Friday and Saturday, 2 p.m. to 7 p.m.

Tuesday mornings I would split from the trio eighteen minutes early, jump in my car, run down to the station to be on the air exactly at 6 a.m. and throw the transmitter switch. As the tubes were getting hot, I'd be saying, "Hi, it's KCBN, good morning, it's six o'clock. How are you doing out there? Let's wake up. Let's rock."

Half drunk, I'd throw something on the turntable. I'd been up all night playing with the greatest jazz players in the world. I did crazy shit. I'd say anything, make up stuff, like, "Today we're going to do something different. We're going to hook the Associated Press machine up and have a rock 'n' roll funeral with the Beach Boys." For four months I did four hours, six days a week, at KCBN for $125 a week.

I took a tape of that to KFSO in San Francisco. Their number one disk jockey, Don Sherman, was leaving and the manager wanted to hire me for the breakfast show. But then he said, "I'd love to hire you, but you're too crazy. You'd make a great morning man, but I feel like you're a loose cannon. I'd be waiting for my bosses to come in and knock me out. But you've got great ideas."

Don Sherman had a strange, eclectic career. It was dying and then he ran into the chief of police's sister with his car and killed her—all of a sudden he was back on morning radio, bigger than ever.

I almost got the job, which would have changed my life drastically because I loved radio. I started in radio and still love it.

Louise and I were finally getting on our feet and she volunteered to go to work, but I never let her. I worked two and three jobs. I also chippied a great deal in between, but I was proud of the fact that she never had to go to work.

The Silver Dollar Bar

The room The Winners worked in at Harolds Club was called the Silver Dollar Bar. It probably held less than fifty people. The half-moon-shaped bar had real Carson City mint silver dollars embedded in the bar top. Two bartenders and a bar back worked in the moat between the bar and the stage. Every night for five years we had to lift an eight-foot Deagan rosewood marimba on and off that little stage behind the bar.

A colorful Reno resident, an old man everyone knew as "Alabama," came into the Silver Dollar. He had a long white beard and he was drunk. He also didn't particularly like me. When he tried to light his pipe, he accidentally set his beard on fire. Flames came up the side of his head. I threw a drink on him. He got mad and the next thing I knew we were on the ground, me trying to put out the fire with him fighting me off.

In December 1966, the end of our first year, we bought a full-page ad on the back page of the entertainment section of the *Reno Gazette*.

The ad read, "The Winners build themselves as one of America's best known unknown groups. 'This year's been a gas', referring to their year-long engagement at the Silver Dollar Room at Harolds Club where their lively sets have become prime favorites for those who like the spontaneous groups who never perform the same act twice."

That's what we were known for. Also, we were one of the better dressed unknown groups, so Roy had the idea to dress us for the photo half-nude in barrels. We each wore a barrel, with top-hats and socks with our toes sticking out. Brian and Rudy were against buying the ad. "Why are we doing this?" they protested. "We should buy an ad in *Variety*."

"Screw *Variety*," I said. "We're not on the road. We're in Reno."

It turned out that I had some good marketing skills. I didn't know what I was doing, but I knew it felt right. We sent out 750 Christmas cards to Harolds Club employees. I got a working list—which you could never do now—of all the employees with their home addresses. Brian and Rudy mumbled that they didn't want to do all that work, so we corraled a bunch of our close friends, got some wine and booze, and stayed up all night addressing those cards.

Boy, don't you think we were a hit. The employees came to work saying, "God, can you believe it? Those Winners sent me a Christmas card!"

"Me, too, and they all personally signed it."

Now we were the hottest shit in town. We were playing great. We were having fun. It's wasn't a perfect band, but when you're spontaneous, it's like comedy. It's never perfect—if it's perfect, it's a sitcom.

The Power of Television

Five nights a week I also hosted the Late Movie on KOLO TV Channel 8 in Reno, with occasional "surprise" guests, like Joe Conforti, the famous whore master from the Mustang Ranch. Another time Evel Knievel rode in the back door of Channel 8 on his bike. I taped two shows on one day that they could broadcast on Tuesday night and Wednesday night while I was working with The Winners. I promoted The Winners a lot on the show.

The prisoners at the Minimum Security Prison in Susanville, California, eighty miles from Reno, could pick up the station. Several of them wrote to me, asking us to come there and perform. On the air on the late movie I would read their letters. I learned that there were 1,200 guys out in logging camps in the Susanville prison. There are no fences, no nothing, but if you split, you're back to do hard time. Nobody runs away, maybe one idiot in a thousand, because it's beautiful. It's like a country club out in the woods.

The Winners did a lot of benefits, good promotion for us and for Harolds Club. We went to Susanville three or four times. We took a great jazz singer from Reno, Carol Moore, and Joe Cadena, the lead trombonist for years with Harry James and a lot of local guys. The prisoners were receptive, and we had a great time. Once I even took my daughters, Kathy and Luann. It was a good experience for them, sitting in a predominantly black and Latino audience.

I not only got letters from the prisoners but also invitations from women saying things like, "My husband works from midnight to six if you want to come by," and "I'm home alone and I saw you tonight and I'm touching myself and here's my number." They would send pictures of themselves, pretty scary shit. I'd go home and show that stuff to Louise, which was probably a mistake because I'm sure it didn't make her feel very good.

You don't realize the power of television until you're sitting in the chair, hosting a show.

Halcyon Days

At the top of the Mapes Hotel was a famous showroom called the Sky Room. All the top entertainers appeared there. I saw comedians Dick Shawn, Milton Berle, and Larry Storch, the comic who was on *F Troop*. The Mapes had a new act every week and there would always be a comic. I saw Buddy Greco there the first time in 1960. I met them all. Some would come down and hang out in the Silver Dollar Bar. The guys in the Harry James band would come and sit in at Harold's Club.

Harvey's Wagon Wheel at Lake Tahoe also hired acts like Shecky Green to perform in what they called the Quonset hut, a dome over the driveway. Harrah's had the great stars, Sammy and Vikki Carr and Bobbie Gentry and Cosby. For great entertainment, Reno was happening.

I'd walk into the Harrah's Lounge at four in the afternoon and see Matt Dennis, who wrote "Angel Eyes" and a bunch of great songs. That was one of the first places to have an air curtain between the casino and the street—no door—so you could walk in and out any time, twenty-four hours a day. They had killer acts in the lounge like Billy Eckstine and Dick Contino. I think some of the lounge acts were better, maybe, than the big room acts. And it was cheap. For seventy-five cents, you got a drink and free entertainment. Harrah's always had a good policy.

Those were the halcyon days of my career because every night was like going to school.

Casino Giants

Bill Harrah and Harold Smith and Harvey Gross were the three casino giants in northern Nevada. They were "the" gamblers. Harvey Gross had Harvey's Wagon Wheel at Lake Tahoe.

I was doing all the Chrysler commercials for Modern Classic Motors, which Bill Harrah owned. He had all these exotic cars lumped into the showroom there on South Virginia Street. They were also a sponsor on my Late Movie five nights a week on KOLO.

I don't know of anyone else who ever worked for both Bill Harrah and Harold Smith at the same time. I was advertising Bill Harrah's car collection while performing at Harolds Club.

A Husband with a Gun

After I left KCBN I got a radio job on KOLO-AM—afternoon shift, three to six, broadcasting out of the second floor booth of Reno's El Cortez Hotel on the corner of 2nd and Sierra.

Clark "Click" Slocum, the morning guy, was the hottest thing on radio in all of Nevada. He had a wonderful stentorian voice, "Hello, this is the Clicker." Nine to noon was the mooch, Pete Carruthers, who never did know how to tip. Dave Cooper, who would later form Cooper, Burch and Howe Advertising in Las Vegas, broadcast from noon to three.

One afternoon in the middle of the 5:30 p.m. sports hour, a guy came in and threatened to kill me.

"You've been f---ing my wife," he screamed, waving a loaded .45.

We never locked the doors and I was alone in the studio. Everybody had gone home at five, and my relief didn't come in till six.

94   *My Mind is an Open Mouth: A Life Behind the Mic*

"I don't even know your wife," I said, "Who are we talking about?"

He told me her name and I had no idea who she was. Besides, when did I have time to screw around? It was all I could do to get from job to job and a nap. I was working with The Winners at Harolds Club and still doing the late night movie. Maybe that's where this woman saw me and decided to make her husband jealous.

"You know I'm on the air here," I said, "and if I flip this switch, this conversation is going to go out to thirty thousand people. So let's get your wife on the phone and let me talk to her."

"I'm not gonna do that."

I got pissed. "You're going to come in here with a loaded gun and threaten my life, and we're not going to the source?"

He waved the gun higher. "Well, you better be careful."

"Here's the phone. Call her." He mumbled something, and I said, "I'm not the guy you're looking for. I think we're done here. I'm going live now."

He turned and left. I didn't realize how scared I'd been till after he was gone. I never called the cops, but I told Dave Cooper. After that we locked the doors. Five months later I ran out of gas and quit. Between the heat in the Silver Dollar Bar and being exhausted, I was starting to get recurring bouts of strep throat. I was so exhausted I had to give up something.

Comedy Inspirations

There were great comedy inspirations in the '50s and '60s. We all thought Bob Hope and Jack Benny and George Burns were great. There is nothing you can say bad about those guys. Myron Cohen and Alan King, with his wisecracking wit, and Danny Thomas were wonderful social monologists who never said "hell." They came out and did this wonderful litany, this body of material that consisted of wonderful stories that were hilarious. Then, Fat Jack Leonard, Shecky Greene. I loved Johnny Carson. He was funny when he did his stand-up. I played drums in the Sahara showroom between him and Buddy Rich for a show. I was called to fill in for Ralph Pollack, who had been called to fill in for Santo Savino in Jack Eglash's house band.

"I don't know if Jack trusts me," I said.

Ralph just laughed. "There's nothing to know, just play a few bars."

There was a full house that night, 800 people. Buddy's band opened and then Johnny came on. I knew Buddy from Reno when he was with Harry James. He could be a bastard, but he was cordial with me. His daughter was also named Kathy. Johnny Carson had two security guards walk him out onto the stage. Cold as ice, he was afraid of everybody and everything.

I played the intro and that was it. But I managed to screw it up, and luckily the guys caught it. The bandleader said, "Next time wait till I put the baton up."

Blue Language Laws

You could get away with a certain amount of innuendo, but you had to be careful. At the Lake at Harrah's, they had edicts—man, you couldn't say anything bad, anything vulgar, anything out of context. If you said "hell" or "damn," you got fired. You could do risqué things that were borderline, but you couldn't do any outright beaver jokes or boob jokes or anything like that. If the songs were reworded so that they were cute, they would let them slide.

In some clubs, like Harolds, there was a little more latitude. Paul Gilbert, whose daughter Melissa was later on *Little House on the Prairie*, was a wonderful comedian, creative, bright. He used to walk on and say, "It's all bullshit." That was his opening line, but that was at Harolds Club where Harold, Jr. and Sr.—crazy people—were drinking all the time. All the bands in there were crazy, too. If you said "shit" in Harolds Club, nobody thought anything about it because it was that kind of rough, bust-out joint. If you got crude they would say, 'hey, lighten up.'

The Winners were there for five years, and I don't think we ever had an issue over language. I might say "shit" but it was in context. It wasn't just to throw around the room and see if I could knock people off their chairs. If I said it, it was a joke and that was the punch line or something. As long as it makes sense and you're not abusing it and beating it to death, then I think it's acceptable.

I just tell the truth. I never got to the point of an Andrew Dice Clay or Pryor or any of those guys. First, it was unacceptable and second, I wasn't

My Mind is an Open Mouth: A Life Behind the Mic

comfortable doing that because I knew if you said two or three of those words to an audience, they would soon disappear. I feel the same way about Dennis Miller who is a brilliant comedian, but I don't think you need all those words. He's funny without all that stuff.

So that's the way we all started out, the Jack Carters and Charlie Callas and some of the early, early guys who were here working. Cosby never did blue language. Pat Cooper couldn't say anything offensive or vulgar. Harrah's in Reno and Lake Tahoe was rigid, man. They posted those blue language laws on the walls in the dressing rooms and backstage. Everywhere Harrah's could post one they did. When I worked with Dee Dee and Bill, and Dick Lane was entertainment director for Harrah's, he had a live patch, what we call a line patch, to a speaker right in his office. He kept it on whenever he was at work, in case he heard somebody slip with a "kiss my ass" or something. He couldn't do anything with Prima, though, because Prima was too strong. They had to give Louie a lot of latitude. Louie and Keely went *zooma, zooma* and made all these references about pubic hair and a lot of other stuff in jokes. Sam would do a tune called "French Poodle." I took a hold of her French Poodle and the innuendo was I grabbed her by the pubic hair, but Harrah's didn't say anything.

The Smothers Brothers were on stage at Harrah's Reno. At the time Bobbie Gentry was married to Bill Harrah and I was in the audience this particular night. Tom, with the quizzical look on his face, his yo yo man look said, "Dickie, where do babies come from?"

Dick said, "What?"

"Where do babies come from?"

"Tom, babies come from the stork."

There was a count of one-two, and Tommy says, "Well, who fucked the stork?"

Bill Harrah, this pious man, loved it. Thirty years later, Dick Smothers was at the Bootlegger Restaurant in Las Vegas and I got up and I did the bit with him. I played Tommy's part. They were great guys and certainly a welcome addition to show business.

The 1970s

The Heat of the Moment

The Winners appeared at Harolds Club from 1965 to 1970. I was the embodiment of the old joke I made earlier about my father: "He was good to his family; he never came home." It was true. Like my father, I had also become a chippy. I was exposed to everything cute, and I had girlfriends on the side. I tried to keep my extracurricular activities to a minimum because I knew it was eroding my marriage. When I got to Harolds Club in 1965, it was just too much of too much. It was the sixties, and everyone—guys and girls—was looking for a good time.

I'd be on stage six nights a week with a dealer standing in the pit with a great-looking fanny. I'd throw out a line like, "Boy, if I had a rear end like that, I'd be making a million a year."

Sometimes I could just say, "Hey, want to go half on a baby?"

She'd say, "Sure, meet me at 11:30," and it was a done deal.

They made it too easy. Now that I look back, I can see that it was debilitating. Some guys manage to hide it, but a lot of guys were very visible. There were guys I know who I don't think ever looked at another woman. Not many guys, but some. The temptation is always there. You know you're doing the wrong thing, but you brush the knowledge aside in the heat of the moment.

Frank Rueckle, the doctor who performed my vasectomy in 1969, was the number one OB/GYN in Winnemucca where there were a number of brothels. He became an expert in sexually transmitted diseases, which luckily I never contracted.

When his nurse shaved my balls I got half a hard-on. What is it about nurses that turn guys on?

Rueckle showed me a drawing he'd made of my balls and where he was going to cut the vas deferens. He gave me a local anesthetic, and as he was cutting, he said, "Tell me a funny joke."

"You're cutting the vas deferens," I said, "so after you've had a vasectomy, your activities will have a vast difference."

"That'll be $100," he said.

I went to work that night in the Silver Dollar Bar and talked about my vasectomy experience on stage using that line.

A few days later they opened the new McDonald's on Wells Avenue and for $100 I was Ronald McDonald for four hours. Kids move quick and fast; onstage I quipped, "They jumped up and down on Ronald's McNuggets."

I learned that from Shecky Green; when shit happens, take it right on stage.

A week later, it was time to remove the stitches. Dr. Rueckle had told me, "Your wife can take the stitches out. Just be careful she doesn't pull the knotted end through the wound. And put some alcohol on it."

Louise and I went into our bedroom and closed the door. I took off my clothes. Completely naked, I stood with one leg raised on a chair. Louise, seated on the edge of the bed, closed in with the tweezers.

The door opened and in walked Kathy.

We never locked our bedroom door and had told the girls to knock before they came in, but she'd forgotten.

Louise was cool. She said, "Kathy, go to your room. I'll be there in a minute."

My Mind is an Open Mouth: A Life Behind the Mic

Christmas Eve at the Mustang Ranch

Joe Conforte, owner of the Mustang Ranch brothel, and Oscar Bonavena, the boxing champ of South America who was later murdered there, used to come to see us at Harolds Club.

Louise wasn't wild about it when I was invited to go to the Mustang Ranch to perform on Christmas Eve. I conned two friends, Harolds Club entertainers Jackie Curtiss and Ray Malus, into going with me.

"We're going to work for crippled children," I said. They weren't from Reno and didn't know the Mustang Ranch was a brothel.

The "ranch" consisted of nice, clean mobile homes connected into one big compound. Serious chain-link fencing surrounded the place, with a dog run adjacent to the main entrance gate. Two shepherds, attack-trained in German, barked and ran up and down the line of the fence. Menacing-looking, they let the customers know there'd be no monkey business.

After ringing a bell on the outer fence a guy came out and put the dogs on hold so we could pass through the run to the front door. Inside was a bar and a restaurant. I always wondered, who'd want to go to a whore house and eat?

Imagine Jackie and Ray's surprise to pass the dogs and see twenty-five pretty girls in cotton flannel pajamas.

"This is not a children's place," Ray said.

"Well, they were children," I said, "before they became hookers."

Jackie and Ray sang and I was the comedy emcee. We drank and then we all sang. In came a string of Oriental customers. When we'd see them we'd sing, "Oh, Come to the Church in the Wildwood" or "Oh, Come All Ye Faithful." Pretty soon, we turned it into a medley.

Between puffs on a huge Cuban cigar, Joe told us, "Take anything you want, eat, drink—it's on me," and then he left.

By 4:30 in the morning, the three of us were completely trashed. We'd been there for hours, singing, cavorting, drinking, and acting nuts.

In walked a customer, all by himself.

"Hey," I called, "This is your life."

I thought he'd have a cardiac seizure. I think he thought he was on that TV show of the same name. He turned around and ran back out the door.

My daughters now think this was pretty funny, because when they asked Louise, "Where's Daddy?" she told them, "He's out with crippled children."

Winners no more

Joking around with The Winners was great preparation for doing comedy, but I still wasn't ready to step out on my own. I knew I could do it but I had a family, a wife and two kids. Going out cold as a stand-up comic is brutal. And I'd be leaving my drum experience, all my musical ability behind.

The Winners worked everything. In early 1968, I had heard through the grapevine that the Easter Seal Society in Reno was looking for a rehab therapy tub which cost $750, a standard, stainless steel tub with a Jacuzzi pump. We bought one and donated it. We gave a girl named Rosemary a $750 journalism scholarship.

In 1970, when I decided to leave and take the plunge into stand-up comedy, Brian and Rudy hired my old drum teacher, Mark Barnett.

"Get a guy who's multi-flexible," I told them. "Get a guy who can sing." I recommended a talented guy, Les Thompson, who later went with the Nitty Gritty Dirt Band.

"We don't want somebody telling us what to do," they said. They were so chicken-shit.

"You're shooting yourself in the foot," I said. "Forget what I think. I know how the Smith family thinks. I got us the job. Remember me, the guy who sat in the office for three days? I know how they think. They are going to come and cross-reference what I did with the new guy you get. If the new guy is just a good drummer, it won't mean anything because it won't be funny. You guys are going to be arguing about who does the lines and the jokes and the setups and calls the tunes."

But, no, they hired Mark. The three of them scuffled and stumbled around on the stage and two weeks later Harold Smith called them into his office.

"You boys have been great," he said, "but we're going to make some changes." He gave them their notice.

Mark was devastated because he had been a production drummer in the Sands Copa Room band with musical conductor Antonio Morelli, backing up the Rat Pack, and now, all of a sudden, he was out of a job. He had moved to Reno to be in the band. Luckily he and his singer wife, Colleen, had kept their home in Las Vegas.

L.A. One More Time

I longed to go to L.A. and get a comedy thing started. Three years earlier, Stan Rutherford, business agent of Reno's local 368 musicians union, had introduced me to L.A. TV producer Herm Saunders. The *F Troop* producer, along with Ken Barry, Larry Storch, and Forrest Tucker, had come in to see The Winners, and I got to hang out with all of them.

"Man, you're great," Saunders told me. He immediately wanted me to leave the band and go to L.A., but with a wife and kids, it wasn't realistic. I couldn't leave.

We had kept in touch, and now Herm encouraged me to come back to Southern California and give it another try. It was January 1, 1970, the beginning of a new year, new career, new everything. I was going to do a single comedy act. I thought I was going to go to L.A. and kick everybody's ass. That lasted about an hour. I got down there and it was a nightmare.

Herm, who produced *Adam 12* and *Dragnet* and *F Troop*, tried to help me, but I was dumb and naïve. When he suggested things like signing a contract to give him 25 percent, I said no. I didn't recognize the power he had in the industry. Somebody should have slapped me in the face and said, *do you realize who this guy is?*

Elda Stein, a Keno writer I'd met at Harolds Club, had moved to Huntington Beach. We were having an affair, and she said I could live with her. I had $3,200 that should have gone to the IRS but I chose to live on it while I tried to get my comedy act going. I commuted to L.A. from Huntington Beach.

Jackie Gayle told me they were looking for a comic at a nightclub off Fairfax and Beverly Boulevard owned by some Japanese guys, so I went there and got up. Lenny Bruce's mother, Sally Mar, was in the audience and somebody introduced us. Her advice was, "You gotta put some more shit in your act."

I did this bit about how I wanted to buy my sixty-five-year-old mother a Christmas gift from Fredericks of Hollywood but Sally Mar said I needed more jokes—joke, laugh, joke, laugh, joke, laugh—in a shorter amount of time. I was still relying on improvisation and wit instead of writing. I was working too hip, way too inside, and everything that could be wrong was wrong. Plus, I didn't look funny. I had all my hair, all my teeth, all my digits, no impairments.

Because of my affair with Elda, I wasn't working on my career. I was playing chase Mr. Woody around L.A. Louise thought I was "on the road." She may have suspected funny business, but my mother had loaned me some money and I was sending money home.

I had no personal direction toward anything. I asked myself, *do I really want to do this?* I was running out of money, I hadn't paid any taxes for a year and a half, and the IRS was closing in. *Should I go back to playing?*

Four months of fun later I fled back to Reno, back to playing the drums.

The Continental Lodge

At that point the marriage was still cooking along pretty well. The kids were doing fine in school. No problems.

In the sixties The Winners had worked opposite The Craig Evans Trio. Evans was a good singer and piano player and I teamed up with him. I got us a gig at the Royal Inn at 7th and Keystone. I walked in and said to the manager, "I don't know you and you don't know me, but I think we could do something here." I told him about our act.

The guy said, "Okay, let's try it out."

Craig and I went in for $250 a week. The next week we got $300, and the money rose from there.

Down the street was the Continental Lodge, owned by Joe and Gilbert, a Swiss and Italian who didn't know what to do with it. Piano bars weren't hip and their lounge was dying. They hired a man named Tom Yarbrough to take it over. Tom and his lawyer, Bob Berry, came in to the Royal Inn. They watched Craig and me do two sets. It was one of those magic nights when we were rocking the joint. They came back three nights in a row before Tom finally introduced himself.

"We leased the Continental Lodge," he said. "Would you guys be interested in working there?"

By then I knew to check out the room before committing. "First we have to go look at the room," I told him.

Well, the room was crap, depressing. It was laid out wrong. Everything in there was wrong. So I found a handyman construction guy and went in there and tore out everything. We built a new, wide piano bar, fashioned after a breakfast bar. We redid the lights, cheap ones we put on a dimmer. Two banks of three 150-watt spots. I bought some heat proof paint and painted two of them pink and one of them blue, so when Craig sang a ballad we had the right lighting. We put in a sound system and we opened.

I was back playing drums and doing comedy and we turned that place into a political watering hole. Every politician in northern Nevada made the Continental Lodge the place to come because we had all the political election posters and bumper stickers on the wall.

Craig and I were on a roll and they couldn't hold us back. Yarbrough gave me carte blanche—I could do anything I wanted. We started 'Cork Proctor's Sunday Afternoon Jazz Concerts.'

Abby Schwartz, the bartender said, "You won't break $500." The first Sunday we did $900. We were having fun, and we got the best local players to come in and play. Sometimes there would be somebody from out of town we would pay and/or get him a room.

For a year and a half Craig and I did well, but we worked our asses off. We worked 9 p.m. to 3 a.m., two-hour sets with twenty-minute breaks. I wore white Levis and a Hawaiian shirt and at the end of the six hours I was dead. My clothes were soaking wet. We didn't even have a place to change.

People coming through the front door had to walk in front of me there on the bandstand with a mic.

"Oh, nice outfit," I would quip. "Your mama dressed you funny tonight."

I slammed everybody from Bob List, the governor, on down to Randy Capurro, the second youngest state assemblyman to ever get elected. The DA came in and I said, "How did you get the job? You're incompetent. People don't even think you finished law school." If they came through that bar I hammered them. Every night was New Year's Eve.

Las Vegas Sun newspaper journalist Ruthe Deskin, in town for a UNLV/UNR basketball game, wrote a glowing column about me. She told me I was the freshest thing she'd seen in thirty years.

Meanwhile in the daytime I worked in construction. I wallpapered a place at 9th and Virginia called The Library, owned by Bill Galt, owner of Galt's Chicken Farm out on Pyramid Way. I took a bunch of old books and ripped the pages out and wallpapered the whole joint, the bathroom, everything.

Then the atmosphere at the Continental Lodge shifted. Yarbrough and Berry and the Italian guys were having a falling out, business-wise. There was a whole bunch of shit going on, and I got wind that they planned to sell the joint. Around that time I had a beef with Craig. I went to Tom and gave him an ultimatum. "Either he goes or I do."

Tom said, "You're done, Craig. Nice having you here."

I hired Simon Ferrell, a singer and keyboard and tenor saxophone player. A good entertainer, Simon came and sat in with the Winners, doing "Night Train" on his sax, and people screamed and yelled. So I knew he was a good choice to replace Craig.

We worked together there for another year.

Wanted for Murder

I did a lot of club dates for the Reno Chamber of Commerce and any benefit where I could to get the mic in my hand.

I was scheduled to appear at a luncheon in a meeting room at the Sparks Nugget for the Law Enforcement Intelligence Unit (LEIU). Early in the morning on the day of the luncheon I went to check out the place where I would perform. They were doing a run-through of their program, which included slides of "people of interest" in unsolved crimes all over the country. Their idea was to provide a cross-reference of suspects from all over the U.S. who they felt might have come to Nevada.

While I was standing there a slide appeared of a guy wanted for a murder in New York's Central Park. It was Simon Ferrell, only they were calling him Frank Dellasandro. I thought, *wow, I've been working with this guy.*

That night at the Continental Lodge I said, "Simon, I've got to tell you something. These guys are on to you. My lips are sealed, but they're looking for you in conjunction with a murder."

Simon was a junkie and probably did snuff somebody. But I knew him as a great partner and a decent human being, even though he was a tough guy. Like a lot of heroin addicts, he had his demons, but we got along great. When I had to go on the road, I gave him the job to book whoever he wanted. I'd get a drummer to sub and put Simon in charge.

He'd say, "But I don't know what to say. I don't know what to do."

"Sure you do, Simon," I said. "Just keep talking to the audience. These are your friends. They've been coming to see you for a year. They love you, man. They don't know if you're playing the right changes or the wrong changes on the Hammond. They're coming in here to have fun."

The chief of police, Jim Parker—he'd been at the LEIU luncheon—came in with his wife every Friday and Saturday night to drink and dance at the Continental Lodge. Parker never recognized Simon.

The Elegant Wagon

Jerry Poncia came to me and said, "We're building a nightclub on Peckham Lane and Moana and it's going to be something. Do you want in?"

The joint would be in a shopping center called Moana West, at Moana and Lakeside. "We" would be Jerry, Don Carano, Bill Gadda, Leon Nightingale, and a couple of other guys.

"Yes," I said, "but only if I can do comedy."

I would be a lesser partner with 15 percent of the net. But there was never any net. I learned the hard way that you have to get your percentage on the gross.

Reno contractor Lud Corrao, hired by Jerry to build out the nightclub, said, "We'll graze the wood with a blowtorch."

"No, we won't," I said. "I'm taking down all these barns. We're going to make this rustic." I found the wood in the middle of winter in a snowstorm. In an old cabin I took down, I found a dead cat, ossified, under the floor. As a joke I nailed him on the wall. Jerry, who'd been drinking, looked at him and said, "He looks good, leave him."

We got Senator Pat McCarran's sister, a nun, to give us a freight wagon from their family ranch. We recessed it into the concrete, made it the stage and called the club The Elegant Wagon. We bought a Hammond B3 organ with a Leslie speaker for $2,800. There would be dancing, and I offered the job to Simon Ferrill, but he turned it down, preferring to stay at the Continental Lodge. I hired Bill Anderson, a favorite northern Nevada pianist of jazz singer Joe Williams.

A nightmare escalated. Aside from the usual opening turmoil, Don Carano's kids began coming in every night, getting drunk and raising hell, to the extent that customers began to complain. Don's ex-wife, Patty, would come in and order drinks and food and refuse to pay for anything.

"Screw Don," she'd say. "Put it on a city ledger."

"You're not on the ledger, Patty," I said, but there was nothing I could do.

Even though the food was great, Jerry and Don and the others continuously changed menus. Customers returned expecting what they ate before, and when they couldn't get it, they became upset.

Ninety days in I was ready to trash the whole project. I was drinking a half a bottle of Courvoisier a day, had gained forty pounds, and at night was screwing the cocktail waitresses and any other girl who showed up for a drink. I had the keys and power to close the joint when it was personally convenient.

Some nights I locked the door to have my way with somebody. At midnight, I'd be in there playing records—we had a great sound system—and sitting at the bar drinking alone. A chick would show up who wanted to stick around and "get to know me." Hey, here's a girl I know from Harolds. *Hi, how are you? Come on in. Have a drink.*

There might be one bartender, and I'd blow the guy out for the rest of the evening, saying "You're done. Clean up, get your money, go home." If there were customers, I'd say, "We've got to clean in the kitchen, goodnight." We were supposed to close at two a.m. but it might be five after one. I'd shoo everybody out and lock the door behind them.

Hey, what do you think of this carpet? Would you like to lie down and look up for a while? After three Courvoisiers and coffee, we were naked on the floor.

Hey, it's my club, isn't it? I thought. I was getting screwed from both sides. I did whatever I could to flaunt my partners. I didn't want anything to do with them. Jerry had so many projects going; he and Don were both on their way to becoming multi-millionaires.

The Animal

A woman I recognized from the Continental Lodge came into the Elegant Wagon to dance. Soon she became a regular. I was happy to learn that Arlene Bath was long divorced from husband Steve because I never fooled around with married women.

Of Spanish heritage, her maiden name was Illesques. A beautiful woman with a great smile, fun to be with, she had that something and we became a clandestine item.

At age fifteen Arlene had given birth to twin boys, then had three more kids. She loved them but they almost ruined her life. When they were sixteen, the twins, Rick and Ray, had gone to Truckee Meadows, drunk and driving their mother's car, hit another car and crippled a passenger for life.

Arlene couldn't handle alcohol. Three glasses of wine and she was an animal. That's what my friends nicknamed her, "the animal." My friend Carme, a wonderful Italian singer, would say, "Where's the animal?" and I'd say, "She'll be here." Twice in one night Jerry Poncia and I got Arlene out of jail for drunk driving. We got her out, and four blocks later they busted her again. She was still drunk, they put her back in jail, and we bailed her out again.

Arlene was a creative self-starter. When they finally pulled her driver's license, she went to a cemetery in San Ysidro, California, found a woman named Arlene who had died eight months earlier, found the woman's social security number, got a driver's license, and continued to drive illegally. They never caught her.

I Quit

On Saturday nights after the job I'd take my eighteen-foot ski boat, *Helio Trollop*, and my family to Lake Lahonton water skiing. Sometimes we'd sleep over. One Sunday I was exhausted, we'd been skiing all day and I'd been drinking. I was fairly strong and as a joke I picked up ten-year-old Luann and threw her twenty feet into the water. She came out, rubbed water out of her eye, and said, "Daddy, you're drinking too much."

Louie Cartinella, manager of The Elegant Wagon, was honest and helped as much as he could. Together, we tried to keep the joint alive, but there were too many egos, too many Italians. Between the goofy-ass Carano kids and the ex-wife, the menu changes, the Courvoisier, and the chicks, I stressed to the point where I didn't even care if I had a job. The pressure of trying to please all these people turned into an overpowering nightmare. I was probably on the brink of a heart attack. Our systems can't take that kind of abuse. I also recognized that my marriage was going down the toilet about a hundred miles an hour.

I went home and told Louise, "There's too much shit going on out there, and I'm out of control."

"Then you better quit," she said.

Almost six months to the day we opened, I had a meeting with all my partners. I laid the keys down on the table and said, "I quit."

"What's the problem?" Leon asked.

I was angry, but I tried not to be melodramatic. "The problem is that we're not doing what we agreed to do. I came here to be a comic. I don't want to be a drummer and I don't want to play dance music. The deal we made was, I come, initially we make some music and then, eventually, I get up from the drums and I do comedy. It's never happened. And I can't deal with Carano's kids."

Don said, "That's your job."

"It's not my job. Those are your kids. Why don't you train your children to act like gentlemen?" I got irate. "I can't deal with the bull, and I can't have you guys micro-screwing with everything every night. We're done."

I didn't speak to Jerry again for ten years.

Fatal Attraction

Finally, it got to the point with Arlene where it was near fatal attraction. I had to shut it off. I honestly believe if I had said to her, "I want you to take care of

Louise," she would have. She loved me, man, right down to my shoes and I, in turn, was married with my emotions running amok. Also, I was bothered by her serious drinking.

It was a difficult time because I broke Louise's heart. Louise could have been in the yellow pages under fiduciary loyalty. I know guys hit on her when I was out of town. She told me that some musicians would ask, "What do you do when Cork's not around?"

Still, my affair with Arlene lingered on.

Out from Behind the Drums

I wanted to do comedy. Even though I wasn't a real stand-up, I was starting to get comedy gigs. People were saying, "Get Cork. He's a good emcee." They would give me a facts sheet, a little cheat sheet, I'd memorize some stuff, and get some information about the guy who was running the golf tournament or whatever. Then in my routine I'd blow him right out of the water.

I began to get a reputation for being the fastest mouth in the west. I started getting phone calls and things were moving.

One day Roy Powers called. "Do you want to come in and work?"

"Roy, I don't want to go back to the drums."

He agreed that I could do comedy. October 13, 1972, was the night of my first official stand-up gig. I hired a piano player named Sam, and I paid him a lot of money. I was making $500 a week. Sam was a nice kid, but stupid. He didn't know any tunes. He had a fake book, and he couldn't even read that, so I got rid of him. I hired pianist Bill Anderson again.

While I was still with The Winners, comic Fat Jack Leonard worked the Silver Dollar Bar. He was nice to all the young comics. Paul Gilbert had told me, "Man, get off your ass, get out from that drum set, and go be funny. You can step up with the big dogs. You're not going to get killed. You'll be fine. You've got more chops than a lot of guys that have been doing this for ten years." It was through the support of guys like that that I got back to doing what I do best.

For six months I did comedy shows at 5, 6, 8, and 10 p.m. in the Silver Dollar Bar. I stayed six months and Louise and I got pretty straight, paid a lot of bills.

Hooker's Nook

Jack Piper, general manager of the Frontier, called and asked me to work in the Winner's Circle Lounge at the Frontier Hotel in Las Vegas. He offered a five-week contract, $750/week. He would have paid me more. *Now* I know I could have gotten $2,750 or even $3,000 a week, but at that time I still didn't know how to negotiate.

This was my first job in Las Vegas. Arlene, with her advertising connections, bought a big billboard out by the airport. "The Amazing Cork Proctor is at the Frontier." She paid a Reno artist, Michael Smalley, $30 to draw a little cartoon guy of me with a mic in my hand, which she put on the billboard. I used that cartoon logo for another twenty years.

The first week I stayed with Billy Kay. After that I paid a friend and former classmate from Las Vegas High, Tony Malone, $300 to share his Vegas Valley Drive condo for the remaining four weeks.

May 5, 1973, the night before I arrived at the Frontier, they busted the bar where I was to work, the Winner's Circle Lounge—known locally as "hooker's nook." George Cavanaugh, the bar manager, had coined the phrase "hooker's nook" to describe the Frontier's place to get laid. People came into the bar and sat down and girls appeared. The police had hauled almost thirty hookers out of the bar, and George told me not to make any reference to it. Naturally, I went out and opened with, "You shoulda been here last night, etc. etc."

George, who'd been getting kickbacks from the bellmen for other "arrangements," said, "Ah, I thought you wouldn't say anything." He didn't know me.

I appeared at 10:30 p.m., 12:30, 2:30, and 3:30 a.m. with piano player Bill Anderson. We worked opposite Billy Kay. In his group, Billy Kay and Chapter One, were two girl singers; he subsequently blew his marriage off to marry one, and the other girl, Baby Rae Littlechief, later married Sheriff Ralph Lamb.

Billy Kay was such a strong act, it was a challenge to follow him.

We called the stage in the Winner's Circle Lounge, "the raft," because it was twenty inches high, about six by eight feet and had this terrible old sound system. On the raft at the Frontier I got strong because there was so much going on in there, so many distractions that I had to get good.

One week Roy Clark was appearing in the main showroom. I was onstage doing my shtick, when Billy came up, indicated he wanted to say something, and took the mic out of my hand. I didn't know what he was going to do, but I trusted him.

"Hey folks," he said, "Any of you who'd like to go see Roy Clark right now, you can go into the showroom for free."

Half the people in my audience rose and walked out.

"What?" I was devastated. Even Billy's own band couldn't believe he did that.

Later I learned that Roy Clark was nearly full, and the hotel wanted him to break Wayne Newton's attendance record.

A Helmet and a Groin Protector

By the time I returned five weeks later to Harolds Club, I'd developed some balls. I'd gained a lot professionally and comedically. I would take on anybody in the audience. You want to heckle me? You better get a helmet and a groin protector because this is my job.

But then I recognized you can't beat everybody. As the great, late, Buddy Lester used to say, "You go out and do the best you can and if you beat them, you beat them and ignore them." Hecklers don't know anything—all they do is screw up the continuity. When that happens, you've lost your audience. I look at it this way: I'm out there trying to do my job, just me and the mic and the audience. I don't need any help. If I'm bad the audience will let me know. They don't have to say anything if it ain't working. I've worked with a lot of comics, and we've had this discussion about hecklers.

After one show, a guy said to me, "Man, that's the strongest I've ever heard you."

"You know what? I wasn't in the mood for any crap from a heckler tonight. I've had kind of a strenuous day, and I just wanted to be funny. Is that so bad?"

"Boy, you took her head off right at the pubic bone."

"Yes, and that's the way it should be."

It was said that Buddy Hackett had a rule that for the width of the stage and back three rows: there could be nobody over fifty-five, nobody under five, no smokers, and no hecklers. The maitre'd, if he knew the customers were regulars, would usher them down front and say, "Now don't be talking to Buddy." Buddy didn't want to put up with any crap from anybody. It destroys your thought process. When you're sewing and the grandkids come in and pour coke on the machine or one of them grabs the material you say, *hey, I'm trying to make something here*—same thing.

That summer of 1973 I was back and forth a lot between Reno and Las Vegas. Six weeks in the Winner's Circle at the Frontier in Vegas, down to San Diego in July to emcee a benefit at the Pan Pacific Auditorium for the Mexican American Chicano Fund, up to Virginia City in September to emcee the World Championship Camel Races.

From the September 7, 1973 *Reno Gazette*: "Cork Proctor will emcee the derby and comfort bedraggled camel jockeys." From Ellie's *Virginia City* column: "Caught Corky's early show at Harolds Club and presented him with an official 1973 camel button."

Mr. Woody Goes for a Ride

I had a lot of shots, lots of chances to take my career to a higher level. But I was always more concerned with taking Mr. Woody for a ride than I was thinking about my career. I think the biggest problem was, truthfully, my immaturity. It also cost me my marriage to Louise.

During that five-year period between '65 and '70 when I was working at Harolds Club, I was in my 30s, fairly good-looking, nuts, and I guess the humor was attractive. It was too easy to make a conquest. I was like a guy in a candy store. Forget about romance. It wasn't about scoring. It was recreation, interaction. We knew so many women at Harolds Club—three floors of pretty dealers and cocktail waitresses. They weren't all available, but many were divorced or widowed and willing.

I went to a psychiatrist, Dr. Richard Brown, and I asked him why I was obsessed with sexuality. He knew I was married. He told me, "You have a case of arrested development. You're still trying to get square things in a round hole, and you'll keep doing this until you figure it out. I can't do anything about that. You've chosen that road, infidelity."

The girls were a rope ladder to some kind of self-esteem. I sleep with a beautiful dancer or singer and all of a sudden I'm king of the world. I wake in the morning and there's this animal taking a shower and I'm shaking my head thinking, *my God, how did this happen?* I heard voices that said, *come on, you're not going to get her.* It became a challenge, when somebody said I couldn't do that, I thought, *watch me.*

The night of Kay Starr's birthday party at the Bonanza Club on the Carson City Highway, Harold Smith, Jr.'s secretary, Judy Nicora, said to Louise, "Boy, we all admire you. Everybody knows that Cork screws everything in sight, but you're so cool with it."

Talk about a cheap shot. Why don't you just pull her ovaries out? That hurt Louise.

She confronted me. "What's she talking about?"

I wasn't going to lie. I said, "You know what, Louise, I'm always around women. I'm always going to be around women, and I'm a guy who's probably going to be looking for the rest of his life, if not doing."

She accepted it that time. She didn't leave. Maybe she looked at it from the viewpoint of, he's a decent guy, he doesn't beat me, he's the father of my children, he brings home money, everything is paid for, and we have a nice car. It was a crappy way to look at a marriage, and I still have regrets. I will say one thing on my own behalf. I never abused any of those women. I never took their money, wrecked their cars, smoked their dope, or stole their underwear.

At the end of that five-year period I decided that I had to get out of Harolds, because I knew something bad was going to happen. Louise was getting phone calls. A woman would call and tell her, "I saw Cork out with so-and-so."

When Louise confronted me again, I'd say, "No, I wasn't with her." I wouldn't tell her I was really with someone else. Finally I couldn't dance around the questions any more. She had me.

"I don't want to do any more damage than I've done," I told her. "If I step out of the picture, people won't call you."

"I'll forgive you, if you won't do it anymore," she said.

But I knew the trust would never be there again. "Every time I go out the door you'll be suspicious of where I say I'm going and who I'm with."

I moved three blocks away into the house of my friend Al James, an entertainment agent. When we started the divorce proceedings, it was cool. I got Louise a respected lawyer named Oliver Custer, an old southern gentleman, one of Nevada's first lawyers. Nothing was contested, and I volunteered to pay $500 a month child support for Luann and Kathy.

"That's a lot of money," Louise said.

"You better take all you can get," was my flip retort.

Thirty years ago it was a lot of bread. There aren't too many dads who can step up and say, I paid it every month. Sometimes I slept in my car, but I paid it.

To celebrate the divorce, I had my jeweler friend Tom Newton make Louise a ring, a little Pisces with a diamond chip in each eye of the fish. Then I took her on a "divorce cruise" down the Mexican Riviera. Ironically, we sailed on Princess' *Spirit of London*, which later was featured on at least one episode of the *Love Boat*.

Reno was a small town where everybody knew everybody. I knew it would be awkward for Louise if I stayed there, so a few months later I announced, "I'm gonna move to Vegas."

"I'm going with you," Kathy said. "I don't want to be around to see what's going to happen to Mom." At seventeen, she only had three months left before she graduated.

"You son-of-a-bitch!" Luann cried. "What have you done to my mother?" Boy, that hurt. She was fifteen and didn't speak to me for the next two years.

Lost Focus

By February 1974 I had been a comic for a year and a half. Not the best time to get a divorce. It also was not the best time to separate your children, but that's what happened. Kathy went with me to Vegas, where she finished her senior year at Clark High School. We lived at the Hacienda for six weeks, and then realtor Jack Clark, a Vegas High friend, found us a house to lease

My Mind is an Open Mouth: A Life Behind the Mic

near Decatur at National and Lemon that was turn-the-key—TV, curtains, bedspreads, linen, everything. A beautiful joint with a lease/buy option, and I gave the owner $2,500. We stayed there a year, and then Kathy graduated and went back to Reno. The owner wanted me to buy the house, but I didn't have enough money. He gave me my earnest money back and I moved into a little apartment at Third and Bonneville in a building owned by attorney George Cromer, behind his law office. The apartment was so small it had one single light bulb hanging from the ceiling. I slept with WWII army blankets on the bed. Most of the money I made went to pay child support.

Now making $500 a week working at the Union Plaza, I started dating frivolously, singers, dancers—it was a good time. Some people saw me and said, "We ought to get you a TV show."

I'd say, "Yeah, sure, call me some time," and blow them off.

I'd lost my focus, and I wasn't listening. My receptors were turned off. Looking back, I could have had a career like a Jerry Seinfeld or Ray Romano. I had the skills, I was funny, but the problem was the little demons inside of me saying, *you're not good enough for that—you're just okay to work some toilet on the Strip.*

The Royal Inn

When Michael Gaughan and Frank Toti opened the Royal Inn, man, they had a gold mine. It was an exciting place, stuff always going on. The Dixie Band worked there. Comedian Peter Anthony. Hammond organ and tenor sax player Lee Ferrell with Ronnie Fabre and Ed Grell in a band called, "Pride and Joy." Today, Lee's the keyboard player with Bill Medley and father of comedy actor Will Ferrell.

Cal Savoy, a sweet man, was the Royal Inn's entertainment director, but he looked like death warmed over, thinner than thin. He looked like somebody put a suit on a skeleton. I wanted to work at the Royal Inn, but apparently Cal couldn't seem to make up his mind to hire me. So I called the governor.

During the sixteen years I lived in Reno, I'd done a lot of work with the Democratic and Republican parties. I emceed roasts, wrote comedy for guys, worked for the installation of Judge Rose. Governors Bob List and Grant

Sawyer and Mike O'Callaghan became friends. I could go to the legislative sessions in Carson City, hang out, and listen to things. Then I'd go to work that night and talk about how screwed up the Assembly was, or why they couldn't get a consensus on a bill they wanted to get through.

In those days, I could call the governor's mansion and Mike or his wife Carolyn would answer the phone. Bob and Sandy Miller also answered the phone themselves.

I called Mike and said, "I'm trying to get into the Royal Inn. The guy, Michael Gaughan, is thinking about me, but he's not sure."

The governor said, "Oh, I know Mike. What do you want me to tell him?"

"Tell him to put me to work, that you think I'm worthy and I'm dependable."

Boom, that was it, the magic touch.

He said, "Hello, Mike; this is Mike O'Callaghan."

"Oh, Governor, how are you?"

Understand, I'm paraphrasing, but this is pretty much the way it went down because Michael Gaughan told me later.

He said, "I understand you've been thinking about hiring a friend of mine, Cork Proctor."

"Yeah, as a matter of fact Frank and I have talked about it."

"I want to give him high marks. He's done a lot of political things, fundraisers and stuff like that. He's always funny and he shows up on time."

That's gubernatorial juice. Next day I had the job.

The contract was for two weeks, working midnight, two and four a.m., a horrible schedule, $500 a week, and I was so glad to get it. It was like God looked down and whatever She was thinking that day said, "I'm going to give you this one."

When I opened on March 21, 1974, I got a newspaper column mention: "Cork Proctor, Reno's answer to Peter Anthony, will make his eagerly-awaited return Las Vegas appearance when he steps into the Royal Inn lounge for a two-week engagement beginning March 21. At last count, Proctor was two benefit performances ahead of Anthony for the year, but Peter claims 'foul', saying Cork counted a special New Year's Eve benefit gig at Joe Conforte's 'Trailer Park' in both 1973 and 1974 since it was 'an all-night affair.'"

Center Stage commented: "Opens March 21 at the Royal Inn in Las Vegas and announces that subjects bearing his scrutiny will be: foot fetishes, satyrs, Certs, soul brothers, nuclear warheads, poodles, religion, dope, Dr. Spock, KKK, UFO's, IRS, GSA, fondling and fondue."

Panorama quoted: "Cork Proctor told us about the teenaged girl who was trying to run away from home, but every time she got to the door she had to go back and answer the phone."

The food was great—ninety-nine cent breakfast. Drinks, fifty cents. I'm surprised that I still have a liver. There I was, young, broke, semi-depressed trying to do comedy, and from the stage I could smell that gin and that vodka and those lemons and Metaxa. Fifty cents? *Set 'em up for everybody.* People in the parking lot were drinking on me, homeless people, gypsies driving around the building getting a drink. Got it to go.

Jim Parker, aka the Vegas Vampire often quoted my lines in his *Panorama* column:

"Look at that striped shirt! It's either a referee or a giant bumblebee going through menopause."

"There is nothing that equals the tender qualities of a hard-boiled egg who's scrambling for re-election."

"When you're nearsighted and sitting in the back, those bare bosoms look like knotty pine paneling."

When Jim's *Vegas Vampire* TV show was cancelled, I told him, "Remember Jim, every knock is a boost. You know who said that? Evel Knievel when he broke his back flying over eighteen cars and a garbage can."

When Peter Anthony worked there I watched him and got up with him. After I got the job, he came and got up with me. Carme would come and drummers would get up and soon it was like an after-midnight comedy jam session.

My daughter Kathy came in one time, and from the stage I said to her, "Well, now you know how your father is able to pay that child support."

My act was a break for the band. Pride and Joy would finish their set and leave the stage. I'd go up, pick up the mic and start to talk. No introduction, no finesse, no nothing. We performed on a little teeny, semi-circular stage over a bartender and a ramp, like at Harolds Club in Reno.

The Royal Inn employees were pretty laid back. Everyone wore those silly little buttons that said, "We're Glad You're Here." But it was tough, because one of the bartenders was stealing and Johnny Peters, the shift manager, was trying to catch him, so there was a great deal of tension all the time, both on the stage and off.

A Joke Out of Everything

A month later, I got to come back to The Royal Inn. Opening night I walked out on that tiny stage, picked up the mic, and said, "Hey, we're going to have a great time tonight!"

Bang.

Gunshot. In the pit, Dale, one of the pit bosses, dropped.

I went straight ahead. "Well, maybe we're not going to have a such great time."

Two other pit bosses jumped the shooter.

"Right in this corner," I continued, "Ladies and gentlemen, the pit boss has a stranglehold on the unsuspecting player. The next sound you hear will be the patrol car."

Security came, and police and medics were called. Though he'd been shot, Dale hadn't been hurt badly and was able to walk.

I made a joke out of everything.

So many people came to see me night after night that I had to be creative; I couldn't do the same material every night.

Through These Portals

I had no car and walked from George's Bonneville apartment to work at the hotel on Convention Center Drive. My father finally bought me a '64 Ford wagon, so I had transportation. I was okay and Lydia was impressed, so that's all that counted.

Lydia Farrington, my new girlfriend, was a tall, 6-foot 2-inch showgirl in the Tropicana's *Les Folies Bergère*. Comedy magician Berri Lee introduced us. Berri had jobs up and down the Strip, where he would often double. He'd do a show at the MGM, then run over to the Stardust and take somebody's place who got sick. He had a Rolls Royce and a plane, and he'd take girls up and do nasty things to them at 12,000 feet. One morning he'd planned to take Lydia flying, and had told her, "Before we go I want you to meet this crazy guy working down the street, Cork Proctor," and he brought her to the Royal Inn.

In the car on our way for the first time to the Bonneville apartment, she said, "My God, where are we going; to the ghetto?"

"I got a divorce," I said. "This is where I live."

Shortly after we began dating, comedian and vegetarian Peter Anthony invited us to his house for dinner. Peter and his wife, Bonnie, lived in the little Francisco Park homes in the neighborhood of Desert Inn and Eastern. Peter made green spaghetti sauce, which gave us the worst flatulence in the world. We were drinking wine and acting silly when Bonnie looked at the wall separating the tiny dining room from the dark living room and said, "You know, I hate this wall."

"Hey," I said, "we can take care of that."

I went right out to the wagon, where I always had a bunch of tools, got a sledge hammer and brought it into the house.

I thought Peter was going to crap his pants. His eyes got the size of silver dollars when I said, "You really want to take this out?"

Bonnie said, "Yes."

I went outside and found the 100-amp breaker box. It looked like all the wires from the breaker box were going through the wall that she wanted out. Luckily, the wall was decorative, not a load-bearing wall. With my usual, cavalier, arrogant attitude I went back inside and said, "Bonnie, we can do this."

"Let's go," she said.

We moved some furniture and rugs. "Stand back." With that twenty-pound sledge hammer I knocked the wall out. The whole reconstruction took a week. Friends, like Jim Parker, the Vegas Vampire, came in and out to help. We kept drinking and eating spaghetti. We made a gothic arch on one side of a support beam and on the other side we made a Spanish arch. I redid the electrical switch and moved it higher under the header. We cleaned up as we went along.

The party must have consumed piles of that vegetarian spaghetti. Everybody walked in there and said, "What's that odor?" Man, it was green spaghetti sauce with garlic, courtesy of Peter Anthony Laureno. When it was time to paint we wrote on the walls over the arches, "Through these portals pass the greatest farters in the world."

That was a fun week—I had a great time—and it took my mind off the divorce.

The Mouse Pack

From 3rd and Bonneville, in my gig suit—pants, tie, coat—I walked each night to the Royal Las Vegas, behind the Copa Lounge. It took forty-two minutes. By the time I got to work I was adrenaline pumped. I'd walk in the front door, have a cup of coffee, hit the stage, ready to go.

I was tired, but at the end of the night I would go to other hotels to see comedians Peter Anthony and Berri Lee and Carme, who was in a Ray Binney review. We were all working, but nobody was making any big money. Peter and Berri and Carme and Billy Kay and I became a little cadre. The rat pack was big in Las Vegas, so we called ourselves, "The Mouse Pack."

Peter was at the Sahara, his first time opening in a lounge. Opening night he came out in his silk tuxedo to find 300 people with newspapers in front of their faces, like they were reading them. It was hilarious, and Peter was overwhelmed. It was a set up—Herb Kaufman's idea, probably the last funny thing Herb ever did. Herb owned the shopping mart, Vegas Village, and was a big fan of Peter's.

Each of us had some el stinko nights when the voice in our head says, *What are you doing up here? Where did you get the balls to think you could get up here and entertain these people? You should be driving a garbage truck.* Those little voices kick your psyche around. Once you get over them, when you get older, you look at it like, *hey, maybe they'll like me and maybe they won't.*

Buddy Hackett used to say, "If you don't like me, that's one thing, but if you don't like the material, I can change the jokes." Buddy was a genius, brilliant. I had great respect for him. The first time I became aware of Buddy was probably in that Dean Jones movie, *Herbie the Love Bug.* Over the years I saw Buddy many times. He was never afraid to go out and do fifteen minutes off the top of his head. Shecky Greene was even more direct. I don't say he was better because it's apples and oranges. Shecky would walk right out on the stage and talk about something he saw on the way to work. It was always hilarious and clean.

Good Things Come to Those Who Work for Them

May 4th and 5th I was back in Reno, emceeing "Law Enforcement Open House" at the Pioneer Theater Auditorium from noon til 5 Saturday and Sunday for the Greater Reno Chamber of Commerce, Reno Police Department and Washoe Planning & Allocation Committee.

Through May Advertising I did voiceovers, ten thirty-second spots at $10 each for the Reef Resort Inn, and one for Western Slenderizing that billed $29.

In June I opened for singer Louis Jordan in Harolds Club's 'newly improved Silver Dollar Bar' for two weeks, show times 9 and 11 p.m. and 1 a.m.

I wrote an article about my history with the Silver Dollar Bar that was published in *The Reno Gazette*:

Good Things Come To Those Who Work For Them
By Cork Proctor

About nine and a half years ago, Harolds Club was looking for a group to handle all the relief entertainment chores. This particular job was highly sought after and some groups had worked the club for a few weeks and then moved on; most were disenchanted with the vacillating hours. The basic schedule for six nights was as follows: Monday, midnight to 6 a.m.; Tuesday, 5 p.m. to 11 p.m.; Wednesday, 9 p.m. to 3 a.m.; Thursday, 2 p.m. to 7 p.m.; and Friday and Saturday were just as exciting as Thursday. The hours were a challenge in themselves.

About six months after going to work in Harolds, another room opened across the alley, this room was called the "Arch Lounge." A grand opening party was held, and yours truly was the master of ceremonies for the evening. Harold Smith Sr. was there in all his splendor and carnival attire.

For those of you reading this article who never knew the Smith family, or for that matter, chose to gamble some other place, you may have missed one of the great frontier spirited and perhaps the

last of the bizarre gambling groups to open and run the casinos
prior to the corporate investments arriving here. Suffice it to say,
the Smiths were respected if not revered by gamblers from all over
the world. The signs have come down now and newspaper ads
will I suppose do the same job of calling the public's attention to the
Harolds Club or Bust slogan, but the magic is gone.

My relationship with the Smiths, including Pappy, Harold Sr., and of course, his son, Harold Junior, was great.

We had a group called "The Winners" and working those hours for the club soon became a game to see who could get the most sleep on Tuesday, since that was the worst day for rest. At this point the schedule went to hell and we were doubling in both rooms, the "Arch Lounge" and the "Silver Dollar Bar."

By this I mean we might work Monday in the Arch and Tuesday in the Silver Dollar and then double back to do a party for Kay Starr or some other friend of the family.

These were exciting times for the group. We learned to do the job and stay away from social partying with the immediate Smith family.

Harold Sr. has a brother named Raymond who was also our boss, in effect; however, he was out of the limelight, so to speak, part of the family. I don't believe we said ten words to Raymond in the five years we stayed at the club. Perhaps that is one of the reasons we stayed five years.

I wanted to touch on some of the highlights of the old Harolds before pressing on to the new aspects.

A funny sight to behold was Harold Sr. in full leathers and helmet back from a hair-raising ride on the red Harley to Pyramid Lake with Freddy Cogswell in tow and shouting hellos from the floor of the Silver Dollar Bar while we exchanged obscene remarks (all in good taste, of course) and threw in an occasional finger gesture to make a point.

During all these years of loose conduct, we never missed a day of work, nor did the family have to worry about our consistency on the stage. We worked hard and loved the club, the employees, and had a great run.

Picture a group of four completely different personalities thrown together in a tiny room, in a corner, a Scopitone machine that played music and showed

My Mind is an Open Mouth: A Life Behind the Mic

pictures at the same time, oft-times while we were in the middle of a song or gag. Plus, add a Keno board to give the latest results on the big games, one or two bartenders, a noisy blender, a barboy dropping glasses, bottles and syrup cans at random, a paging system that announced such statements as "Al Lazzarone please dial 656," and of course a never-ending stream of folks trying to find the restroom or have their bus ticket validated for the trip back to Lodi.

That picture of the club is overshadowed only by the unique musicianship and stage personalities called The Winners. Roy Powers gave us that name and we are beholden to him for not only the name but a lot of encouragement and help as well. The group consisted of a Mexican-American marimba player, Rudy Rodarte, probably the best anywhere, a pseudo-Polish guitar player named Ken Dotson from Michigan, a hip Okie named Bryan Bee who played bass and some trombone when his nocturnal activities didn't fray his lips, and myself, an A.S.P. (Anglo Saxon Protestant) who played some time on the drums and did a little talking and some light comedy.

Got the picture? Weird mix but the magic was there and the music and comedy got better with each year.

·A fire on the fourth floor, directly above the broiler pit, destroyed our nine-suit-each wardrobe, all the personal belongings, including tape recorder, electric razors, cuff links, pictures, etc. The Smiths made sure we were reimbursed to the penny for our losses. Now that's class.

Having worked for this amazing family for five years, and since the sale of the club to the Hughes Corporation, I have had the chance to see many types of people come and go from Harolds. The club still has most of the intimacy that made it famous. The guns are remounted and framed, the carpets are still wild and plush, new lights have been added to reduce energy and yet soften the usual glare to the customers' eyes, and more changes are under way, but the biggest bonus for me was to return to work on May 27, 1974, and find the Silver Dollar Bar made into a cozy, warm (in terms of intimacy) exciting showroom, without the noise of blenders, waitresses trying to scream in their orders to shell-shocked bartenders (who became that way from watching a living deity named Sonny King knock down the ceiling with a mic stand) and people merely looking for a place to sit down and rest. Even though the Smiths are gone from Harolds, I feel certain they would be proud of the appearance of the club today.

They would appreciate anybody like me, who after a long wait, is now in a room built strictly for entertainment. To all those who said, "Don't quit, kid; you'll find a room where everything will work for you," you were right. I found it in the Silver Dollar Bar at Harolds in Reno, and waiting was the best part. I only wish everybody could get this lucky. Now that I have the tools to do my job, I better take care of business.

Tough Guys

After that stint at Harolds Club, it was back to Vegas to open producer Dick Francisco's show *Bare Minimum* in the mini-showroom at the Royal Las Vegas. *The Hollywood Reporter* wrote, "Comedy newcomer Cork Proctor … giving the *Bare Minimum* revue the maximum attendance …" 10 p.m., 12:15 a.m., and 2:30 a.m. for $3, including two drinks.

Producer Dick Francisco hired me to be the featured comic in the show, and because he was a relatively new producer in Las Vegas, the budget wasn't much. I was there for three months, three shows a night, six nights, making $500 a week. I didn't give a shit; I just wanted to work. That was good money for a recently divorced guy.

One night Bobby Vinton came in with his manager and some friends. Sitting at the table in front of his were two guys. One of them was drunk, and apparently I said something from the stage that pissed him off. He flipped a lighted cigarette in my face. It bounced off my forehead. God damn, I was mad. I don't normally get that crazy, but I wanted to kick the guy's ass. They were sitting close enough to the stage that I could have drop-kicked him right in the face.

Bobby grabbed the guy's arm. He was gonna punch him, but his manager said, "No, don't hit him."

I thought, *No, the show's closing, and I don't want to cause Dick any problems.*

Afterward in the lobby I saw the guy.

"You better get out of here before I lose my patience," I told him.

He sneered. "Oh yeah, you think you're tough?"

"I know I'm tough."

A month later I walked into the Riviera and recognized him. He was a pit boss there. I tapped him on the shoulder and said, "Not so tough tonight? Not enough liquor?"

He couldn't do or say a thing to me because he was working.

The Merv Griffin Show

Vegas talent agent Donna Taylor got me an audition one Sunday afternoon with Merv Griffin, who was broadcasting a daytime show out of Caesars Palace. He had a wonderful band that included trumpet player Jack Sheldon, guitarist Mundell Lowe, and drummer Nick Ceroli.

Caesars had given Griffin's talent coordinator, Don Kane, a little space in the hotel's business offices. When Donna and I walked in for my appointment, there was a football game on television, the volume up loud. Kane and two other guys were watching the game and bullshitting. They all impressed me as not only light in the loafers, but able to leap tall buildings in a single bound.

I went in wearing a three-piece suit, my balls in my mouth, to try to be funny for these guys. I introduced myself.

"Tell us what you do," Kane said.

"I interact with the audience."

I started doing a hunk of comedy that I had been working on. In the middle of it the phone rang.

"Mr. Kane, Mr. Kane—long distance."

I made a quantum mistake. TV on, phone ringing—no one was paying any attention. I should have said, "Excuse me, I'm wasting your time, and I'm sure as hell wasting mine. I'll come back sometime when you can pay attention, so you can see how funny I really am, because right now, you don't give a rat's ass about how funny I am."

Instead I did twelve minutes. I sweated like I was in the line-up for a rape case, and came out of there soaking wet.

Donna said, "I thought you did pretty well."

"I sucked," I said. "Kane didn't hear anything."

That's the dangerous part of show business, when the power is vested in one man. Don Kane was obviously not sincere about doing diligence to the industry, or bringing somebody out of relative obscurity, which is what I tried to do later on in my job at the Orleans as entertainment director.

Lonnie Shore and all those guys would suck up to Don Kane. Once you got on the show, you were in. Once you did well with Merv, he'd have you back. He used guys like Pete Barbutti and Johnny Dark because they were safe. They weren't vulgar, didn't get in trouble. I could have been there, but I sure as hell couldn't do it from that position. I lost heart.

I told Donna, "I'm not going to keep doing this."

I wished I could have gone over and slapped the shit out of Don Kane and the rest of them and said, "You know what? You don't deserve to have talent here. You don't understand the value of talent and shame on Merv Griffin for letting an old fag like you have this kind of power." I wished I'd risen to my height of 6 feet 1½ inches and said, "I thought you wanted to hear if I could be funny or not. You don't, so see you later."

I've always been sorry I didn't do that. It didn't matter because I wasn't going to get on anyway. I never got to meet Merv Griffin, and he didn't care either. He was a multi-millionaire. He made so much money with *Jeopardy*, he didn't care about that daytime show. It was his play thing.

Meanwhile guys are dying, kissing ass, doing anything to get a shot. I felt bad for Donna, who did the best she could for me.

Sweat Equity

The previous December the MGM Grand Hotel opened with *Hallelujah Hollywood*, their version of the *Folies Bergère*. I had become lovers with a lady named Kathy Jacoby, who played Fanny Brice in the production.

One night we were both loaded—I think we'd been smoking dope or drinking too much—and went to the El Jardin for dinner.

"I bought a condo at the University Biltmore," she told me, "for sweat equity."

I knew that meant that you didn't have to put up any money. They used your rent money—three or four hundred a month—for five months as your down payment, while you made improvements.

The University Biltmore was at Harmon and University Streets. I didn't know you could buy something like that on that kind of squeak-in, if-come deal. I liked it and bought a unit myself, with the same arrangement.

Besides Kathy, my neighbors were advertising guy Ron Bell, and Jeff Harmon, the good Harmon Mortgage twin.

The condos were two stories, and I had two German shepherds, one of which had been given to me by Bobbie Gentry's drummer, Bobby Gill. Two shepherds in a condo didn't work out too well, and I wanted to keep them. I discovered I couldn't stand the C, C & R's—all those rules and regulations— so after a year or so I decided to move. The University Biltmore wasn't well-constructed, and I couldn't stand the noise from other units, either. Today they look cheap. Anything over thirty, forty years in this town, get the bulldozer.

Crock Proctor

By fall, 1974, I was back in Reno working the Silver Dollar Bar again, 8, 10, and midnight. This time the Harolds Club marquee spelled my name in two-foot letters, "Crock Proctor." The *Sparks Tribune* commented, "It was a mistake loyal Cork Proctor fans could well appreciate."

January 1975, back to Vegas to appear opposite The Jets in the Hacienda Sombrero Room. *Daily Variety* writes: "Proctor's sessions are heavy, heady raps if one could follow all the verbal mazes, or they can be light, amusing trips. You have your choice, but none can ignore his skilled and yockworthy palaver delivered nonstop for one full hour, an unusual comedic tour-de-force."

February, back to Reno to work at Harolds Club with The Lancers. The 28th of that month I did the roast for Senator Alan Bible, former Storey County District Attorney, at the Eldorado Convention Center. The *Reno Evening Gazette* reported: "Tales were told Thursday night as retired Senator Bible was roasted and toasted by friends and acquaintances." Bible served Nevada for twenty years in the Senate. The article described how the evening "ended with a champagne toast and a presentation of the distinguished citizens award by the Greater Reno Chamber of Commerce, which sponsored the gathering." About me, they wrote, "Comedian Cork Proctor satirized Gov. Mike O'Callaghan as 'a guy too damn cheap to buy a hair piece,' and introduced a fake letter from Reno Mayor Sam Dibitonto explaining, "I wish I could be there tonight, but I'm playing with my trains." Then they called me, "the mouth of the Truckee." Maybe because I said of the Eldorado, "It's certainly nice to be here in the world's first high-rise Denny's."

In those years I did a lot of fundraising benefits. I did the Reno Association of Legal Secretaries Boss of the Year event. I did the Barristers Club down on Lake Street—all guys who had been lawyers and judges, including Mills Lane, the famous boxing referee who went on to have his own TV show. I was the master of ceremonies for the United Way of Northern Nevada Kick-Off Dinner at Harrahs' Convention Center. If there was anything going on in Reno, I was there. I emceed the Judges Association Baseball Game, at that ballpark where you get on the freeway by City Hall. Bobbie Gentry made a featured appearance at the game.

Benefits would lead to paying gigs.

I began working golf tournaments for Western Nevada Supply, a gig that would last for twenty-five years. The first one I did for nothing, and the last ones paid me $2,000 a night. They were great guys to work for.

Schwann's Ice Cream paid me $750. I got referrals from the Convention Authority; the phone rang and someone would say, "Hey, we've heard about you and …"

There were no tapes, no video then. I got a lot of referrals. "So-and-so called and said that you did a really good job." I had letters of credibility. Henry Rose, an agent who had previously been a piano player at the Thunderbird, got me gigs. I did a lot of benefits in Las Vegas as well, like St. Jude's Night of Stars.

I never used a cheat sheet; I never walked out with a piece of paper. I figured I'd commit this to memory; I'll go out there and if I have A, B, C, D, E, F, G, H, I and J, I'll find stuff in between and that will stretch the thirty or forty-five minutes.

Every time I could get the mic in my hand, I took advantage of it. I tell young people: get as much chops, as much experience as you can. Get out there and make your mistakes. It's all right because when you're doing something like a benefit, if you goof, they're not paying for it anyway. They are lucky to get an emcee. My opening line would often be, "All right, how many of you people don't like me already? Let's see a show of hands. Well, I'm not too impressed with you either. You're not my favorite group. If you ever get a chance to be a crowd, pass it up." You shake the temples when you do that, but usually you'll see people start smiling, and they realize the whole thing is stupid anyway. Here's a guy beating himself to death, trying to be funny. It was always a marathon. But hey, I had the mic in my hand. I was being funny and getting my feet wet.

Today, when Gwen Castaldi was interviewing Pete Barbutti, he said, "For comedians there is nowhere to train, nowhere to rehearse, no place to woodshed." You take the mic, you go out there and win, lose or die, you are on your own. That's the way you get strong, running the gauntlet.

The Ten Most Wanted

By March 1975, I had returned to Vegas for a sixteen-week engagement at the Hacienda. It stretched out and I was still there in August when *Love Affair* opened in the Mirage Showroom of the new Marina Hotel.

Tom Weisner and Mel Kennedy built the 714-room Marina on the northeast corner of Tropicana and the Strip (years later Kirk Kirkorian would morph it into the construction of the present MGM Grand). Weisner and Kennedy leased out the hotel's Mirage Showroom to Allen Glick's Argent Corporation. Glick, along with Frank "Lefty" Rosenthal, opened the nude review, *Love Affair* in August and gave Paul Lowden credit as producer. Ron Andrews, a bass player, had the band with Joe Lano on guitar, Vinny Falcone on piano, John Pesci on drums, and keyboard player Danny Skee.

They hired me to be the featured comic in the show, and for the three months it ran, I doubled. After the Marina show I ran over to do shows at the Hacienda. With different days off, it meant I worked seven nights a week.

In *Love Affair* I did a piece of business I called "The Ten Most Wanted Criminals." Before showtime I videotaped the audience through a little hole in the curtain. I would come out onstage and introduce myself as a detective from Metro.

"Good evening. I have this video tape I'd like to show you. These are some of the most wanted people in America. They have aliases. They wear disguises.

They use cars with stolen license plates, and it's possible one of them may be sitting right amongst you."

Boom, we'd hit the tape. It was black and white, stark. One time I caught a guy in a booth in the back of the room, his smiling face, and the back of some girl's head bobbing up and down in his lap. When we projected it, the guy freaked. After the show he ran backstage.

"The tape," he cried. "I gotta have that tape!"

I said, "It's too late."

His mottled face reflected his desperation. "You don't understand. I'm in a federal prosecution case right now."

I laughed. "Don't worry, it's already been erased."

Each night there would be a few in the audience acting silly—picking their nose or something—and I'd zero right in on them. Pretty soon, they'd be looking around the room and realize they were on the tape. You'd see the wife elbowing her husband, *look at you, picking your nose. What's the matter with you?*

In *his newspaper column, On The Town*, Charles Supin reviewed it: "Cork Proctor is imaginative, and his routine with the hidden cameras is hilarious, as is most of his stand-up stint later in the show. But there is such a thin line dividing love for an audience and contempt for it. Jerry Lewis lost fans because he couldn't figure out which is which, Don Rickles has become excessively defensive out of this same fear. Cork Proctor, as talented as these stars, will have to be extra careful because he has a great future; if."

Dick Clark's Good Old Rock 'n Roll Show was over at the Hilton for a week. For six nights in a row, Dick Clark, along with his dad, came into the Marina to see me.

Finally he asked, "Would you be interested in doing any television?"
Sure!

That was one busy fall. Besides appearing at two hotels at the same time I was dating Linda Hart, a singer/piano player appearing in a country and western show at the Landmark.

I got so goofy from running around that one night I walked in to work one of the rooms and a tech guy said, "What are you doing here? We're dark tonight."

My Mind is an Open Mouth: A Life Behind the Mic

Almost Lounge Star of the Year

The *Nevada State Journal* quoted one of my comedy lines: "Nice suit you have on, sir. Somewhere there's a '51 Chevy going around without seat covers."

In his column "Vegas Vibrations," Jim Parker wrote: "He tore up his Hacienda crowd the other night, when he quipped, 'Ronald McDonald was arrested today in Downey, California for exposing his quarter pounder.'"

That year I was nominated by the Las Vegas Academy of Variety and Cabaret Artists as Lounge Star of the Year. They sent me a letter of nomination, but after that I didn't hear anything, so I figured I didn't win.

The 1970s saw the height of the lounge era. At the Holiday Casino they had Giselle McKenzie and then the Trio Sneed, three Swiss yodelers. I played with them, screwed up their act. I knew how to make them look bad in America. At the Hilton the Treniers would get me up to do ten or fifteen minutes of comedy. I must have worked with everybody—Freddy Bell and the Bellboys, Billy Ward's Dominoes, Stan Irwin, Herb Jefferies, Sidro's Armada. There was such excitement in the lounges, so much going on.

I was lucky to be there and get to see so many of the greats, too. Steve and Edie at the Dunes, and Shirley MacLaine doing *Sweet Charity*.

My God, we will never have that again. It's over. Now we have bald-headed people jumping in and out of water in fourteen different versions of *Ka*. I don't know where they are going with this.

The Governor's Banquet

That fall I emceed the First Annual Governor's Banquet, October 16, at the Dunes Hotel in Las Vegas. The guest of honor was Governor Mike O'Callaghan. No host cocktails in the Seahorse Terrace Lounge from 7 to 8 p.m., then dinner in the Crown Jewel Room. Jerry Lewis was billed as the "entertainment" but he made a token appearance, in and out, one joke, see ya later. Other stars on the bill were Phyllis Mcguire, John Davidson, and Rich Little. $25 per person, dancing with the Jack Eglash Orchestra, with all proceeds going to the Nevada Combined Health Agencies Program. Mayor Bill Briare was honorary chairman and Culinary Union boss Al Bramlet was Ticket Chairman. I also noticed a lot of mob guys there that night.

Mini-Burlesque

I opened in the Silver Dollar Bar for jazz and blues singer Herb Jeffries. In the 1940s Herb Jeffries had a hit song, "Flamingo" that sold about thirteen million copies.

Jack Piper, who had been running Harolds Club, had gone to be general manager at the Frontier in Vegas, and in 1972 a woman named Pat Edwards had taken his place, even though she wasn't that qualified. As manager of Marketing & Public Relations and entertainment coordinator, she had an idea to produce a show she called *Mini-Burlesque*. She scheduled it to open Dec. 9, 1975, in the Silver Dollar Bar after Herb Jeffries ended. Knowing my track record, she cast me in the show, along with featured dancer Cassandra Lee, "Silver Dolls" dancers Kim Richards and Donna Hamrick, and a little, five-foot-tall singer/dancer/comedian with frosted, carrot-red hair named Sloopy. Pat's idea was that I would play "straight guy" to Sloopy's comedy. Sloopy, whose real name was Elda Myer, would be the featured comedienne.

We all had a hand in creating the ninety-minute show. We got together for a rehearsal and talked about it. We had black-outs and sketches, and I did twenty minutes of stand-up.

Sloopy was good, a fifth-generation entertainer in a vaudeville family that was friends with Bill Robinson, "Mr. Bojangles." At age four, Sloopy learned to tap dance from Sammy Davis, Jr. But, God, she was so intense. If the lines didn't go click, click, click where she wanted them, look out. She was a book comic, and if anything was done off the wall she went crazy. She could ad-lib, but she refused to. Interestingly, Harolds Club promoted "the two masters of ad-lib" and "the unpredictable humor of Sloopy and Cork." In print they attributed to me the comment, "It's the first time I've ever met anyone more uninhibited than me."

She yelled at me right on stage one time. Ad-libbing and winging it is what I do, and I couldn't stick to a comedy script. We didn't work well together.

Mini-Burlesque was not a topless review. Kim Richards had vowed never to work topless. Cassandra, a funny study and gorgeous—and no, I didn't—had worked as a stripper. We all talked about it one night. Cassandra—not her real name—had been showing her tits up and down the Strip and in Reno. She

My Mind is an Open Mouth: A Life Behind the Mic

had Gypsy on her license plate and lived way beyond her means at the Las Vegas Country Club.

I said, "Sweetheart, don't you think one of these days your parents are going to have some friends come in and see you and say, wow, we saw your daughter's hooters?"

"Oh, that'll never happen."

Well, eventually it did happen. Then she vanished. Last I saw of her, she drove off into the sunset in her white Gypsy Cadillac.

The stage in the Silver Dollar Bar for *Mini-Burlesque* was small. We had a tiny back room, the size of a broom closet, or the bathroom to change our clothes. Three dancers, a comic, the Wally Jones Trio, and a comedienne—no room for anything.

Now I was doing three shows a night—9 p.m., 11 p.m., and 1 a.m., six nights, for $900 a week—still suck money. I went to Pat and threatened to quit if she wouldn't raise the money.

She had a woody bigger than mine. "Well, we don't pay that kind of money," blah, blah, blah. She stared me down. "We can get ..." and she named three other comics.

I was paying some heavy taxes and had no money put away, so I couldn't make good on my threat. "Mini-Burlesque," originally scheduled to run for four weeks, was extended to eight weeks, and I stayed until it closed.

Two Naked Women

Arlene, who worked for an advertising agency, got a suite in the Arlington Towers comped for the closing night cast party, hors d'oeuvres, and champagne, and then we kicked everybody else out.

To explain what happened next, I have to go back to a job the month before. I'd been hired by Bill Stremmel, Reno chapter president of the Missouri Safari club, an African big game hunters club, to emcee the annual award presentation dinner at the Museum of Natural History in San Francisco's Golden Gate Park. My fee was $700 plus an additional $80 for transportation money so I could fly from Reno to San Francisco. I brought a p.a. speaker system and Arlene with me, so I gave Arlene money for gas to drive.

There were a bunch of stuffed animals in the museum, and my opening line was, "It's nice to see something you guys missed."

After the dinner a woman said to me, "Mr. Proctor, I've been coming to these dinners for thirty years, and this is the first night I ever heard anything entertaining."

Now Arlene was friends with Randi Stremmel, who was formally separated from her husband, Bill. My fantasy dream had always been to do a three-way, and here I saw the opportunity. Before the dinner I told Arlene I wanted to get together with her and Randi.

"No problem," Arlene said. She whispered in Randi's ear, and it was agreed.

After dinner, Bill Stremmel refused to pay me the $80 for transportation. "I'm not going to pay you for that," he said. "You drove down."

"That wasn't the deal we made, Bill," I said. "What difference does it make how I got here?"

He was adamant. Okay, I thought, *I'm going to fuck your wife.*

Now, a month later, Randi was formally divorced, and she was with Arlene at the closing night cast party. In this big, beautiful suite was an onyx bathtub with gold-plated fixtures that could hold six people. It was February and I had pneumonia, but when I got in that tub with two naked women, I immediately got well. For three days we smoked dope and shared each other in the biblical sense. I felt a tremendous sense of payback for Bill doing me out of the $80.

The Sombrero Room

By the end of 1975 I'd been running back and forth for almost a year and a half between the Royal Inn in Las Vegas and Harolds Club in Reno.

Band leader Ron Andrews was also entertainment director for the Fremont, the Marina, and the Hacienda. Five nights in a row he came to see me at the Royal Inn and brought with him Paul Lowden, a Hacienda partner/investor. They saw what I was doing and were high on getting me to leave the Royal Inn to work at the Hacienda.

I could continue to work Harolds Club between a few weeks or a month at the Hacienda. I still wasn't making much money, but I had back-to-back work.

Working the Sombrero Room lounge at the Hacienda was like working in a Toyota factory. Not only was it noisy, it was impersonal—no perceived value. The audience didn't pay, they didn't care. They didn't give a rat's ass if you were brilliant. The best thing I could say about the Hacienda is that it was an upholstered toilet. I was working all alone, no music, no nothing. I alternated in that lounge with entertainers like Babe Pier and Jay Orlando.

Before I started to work in the Sombrero Room, I met a minor investor in the Hacienda, Gene Fresh. He didn't have a title or a position, he just showed up one day. He was pointed out to me with the explanation, "This is one of the guys from back east." A nasty little car dealer from Chicago—he may have been connected, I don't know—Gene didn't like me.

"Are you going to be funny?" he asked.

"Why don't you sit up front, Gene? Then you can fire my ass after the first show, and you won't have to go through this question and answer."

I said it in front of the whole cast. I didn't care. Screw him.

One night his wife came into the horrible Sombrero Room and said, "I designed this lounge."

I couldn't resist saying, "Mrs. Fresh, I knew it had to be somebody who'd never told a joke, sung a song, hung a light bulb, or even been on stage because look what you've done here. You have eight booths of eight people. In my career, I've never seen eight people show up for anything. You usually get deuces. You've created a monster. Now, you have sixteen people sitting in an area that holds sixty-four."

I thought, *this dumb woman. What does she know about anything?*

It pissed her off, and Gene Fresh, too, because he knew I was right.

I walked away from her. Once again, the juice of the mob guys. Hey, give Mrs. Fresh a job—let her build something over there.

Ron Andrews and Paul Lowden had gone on the cheap, and there was almost no advertising for me or the Sombrero Room. I worked my ass off to entertain small crowds. If I had six people in that lounge I'd give them an hour. I'd get them to all come and sit down front. The drinks were cheap. People came back because they knew I had no act. Some guy would walk in wearing a Carlos Santana hat and carrying a shovel and that would be twenty minutes.

That's what they waited for. They didn't care about jokes, they wanted to see that spontaneous humor. That's what I did best.

Recessed into the wall were light boxes with little clouded glass doors, hinged at the top. If you pushed a button next to the box, the door sprang open, and the bare bulb projected the bright light into the dim room. I made a bit out of it. I could push the button to snap the door open and closed; I could work it like an SOS signal. When I was dying, I'd walk to the light, say, "Here's a message for the pit," and snap the door open and closed several times. It never failed to get laughs, and I milked it every night.

Close Shots

One night, after seeing Shecky Greene decimate the Riviera audience, Tom Warner and Marcy Carsey, producers for great TV shows like *The Cosby Show*, came in. Someone called to tell me Shecky was sending them down to see me. There were only three people in the audience.

From the stage I said to Warner and Carsey, "God, you guys, if you're reasonably perceptive, please don't put me in the category with Shecky. Look what I'm doing. Look where I'm working. I can do what you're looking for."

They stayed fifteen minutes and blew me off. Had they seen me with a full house, before seeing Shecky, I probably would have had a shot. In retrospect, what I should have done was put the mic down, gone over and introduced myself and said, "This isn't working; when can I schedule a time for you to see me under better conditions?"

Later, when Skip Stephenson followed me into the Hacienda, Bill Willard wrote a review in *Variety* on Skip: "Man, whatever you do, don't try to duplicate Cork Proctor because what he does, not everybody can do."

When it comes to off the top of your head—"Where are you from? What do you do?"— unscripted interaction with the audience, Pete Barbutti, Peter Anthony, and I are the best.

In a May 1976 column in *Variety*, Willard wrote about me, "One of the best free-formers around with lightning fast reaction to anything or anyone that trips the wire to his agile mind."

Forrest Duke, entertainment columnist in the *Review-Journal*, wrote, "Cork Proctor, Hacienda yock sparker, explains Moscow's interpretation of détente: 'What's ours is ours, what's yours is negotiable.'"

People came because I was different, I wasn't dirty, and I shot from the hip. I didn't have a set act: joke A, joke B, joke C, talk to the audience and go into joke D. I free associated. If it was in the paper that day and if it was funny, like the guy who got his penis caught in the vacuum cleaner, I'd turn it into a bit: "What are you doing with your woody out when you're vacuuming, anyway?"

If people didn't read the papers it was still okay, because I'd go to two-week old topical material they did know about.

Larry Storch from the *F Troop* show came in with his wife and Juliette Prowse's conductor/husband, John McCook. It felt good to be able to make them laugh. Larry told me, "You're too goddamned good for this place; get out of here."

Columnist and writer George Will came in, shot me live and used it on a PBS Special. I wrote and wrote and wrote the producer, Steve Glauber, and never could get a copy of the tape. I never saw the entire show, but I know there were some singers, too. I saw snippets of it with me. Somebody watched the show and only recorded me, which I thought was strange.

After I did fifty-seven weeks straight in the Sombrero Room, I began to lose my self-confidence. I was making a living, getting out of debt and able to get another car, but it was a downer because I began to question: *God, if I'm no good, what am I doing up here with a mic? If I am good, why isn't there anybody in here?*

I made friends and tried to do the best I could. It was a strange time. A guy who liked me and came in regularly gave me a little trophy for fifty-seven continuous weeks.

Allen and Lefty's Pissing Contest

Pepper Davis was a friend who had been half of a comedy team, Davis and Reese. Pepper left his comedy partner and now did the Hacienda's publicity and marketing. One afternoon we were walking out into the parking lot together when I looked up at the Hacienda marquee.

"That's it," I said. "It's over."

On the marquee along with "CORK PROCTOR" was the little caricature of me holding a mic. Two workmen were taking it down.

"Don't worry," Pepper said. "You got the job. You're going to be here."

"No, I'm done. There's something going on you and I don't know about."

That night, I'd just got off stage when I heard my name paged. I picked up the nearest house phone to answer.

It was Ron Andrews. "You know, you're chronically tardy."

"You are so chicken-shit, Ron," I said. "You know and I know that isn't true. You're the guy who got me the job. You're the guy who brought Paul Lowden to the Royal Inn every night to see me. You couldn't walk across the casino and tell me to my face? Come on, Ron, you know I was never tardy. Remember those nights when I did an hour and a half for four people?"

Till the day I die, I'll never buy his excuse for firing me. I did a lot of dumb shit, and I said a lot of dumb things, and I got fired at lot, but I was never "chronically tardy."

I have two theories for why I was let go at the Hacienda:

Power? I might have been caught in the never-ending pissing contest between Allen Glick and Lefty Rosenthal. Paul Lowden, who hired me in the first place, was Glick's man, and Rosenthal had been forced on Glick by the mob. For some reason, Rosenthal may have wanted me out and Glick and Lowden didn't. In the end, the mob pressure that Rosenthal represented prevailed.

Money? I was never approached to pay a commission or kick back to the higher-ups. I wasn't kicking back to Ron Andrews, and I had the impression that other entertainers were.

I didn't contest it. Nobody would tell me the truth. Lowden would never talk about it.

I was fired from the Hacienda on July 29, 1976. The next day was memorable, too. I had done the walk through and signed the escrow agreement for $38,000 to buy my first house in Las Vegas: 8005 Firethorn, in the Wishing Well Tract, a block off Eastern Avenue, way out past Warm Springs.

In the parking lot of the mortgage company on West Sahara, the alternator went out and my car died. I went across the street, got a cup of coffee at Dunkin' Donuts, and said to myself, *I don't care. Hey, I can get through this.*

A week later I got an official letter from Paul Lowden that said, "You are officially done and your check is at the cage."

That was my first big firing.

Firing Epilogue

I didn't see Paul Lowden for almost thirty years, until the evening Carolyn and I attended the eightieth birthday party concert for jazz bassist/music arranger/producer Johnny Pate. Many wonderful jazz artists were there, some of whom I knew.

I walked through the lobby to get a glass of wine at the bar and there was Paul Lowden. In the biggest voice I could summon, I said, "Why, Paul Lowden! I haven't seen you since July 29, 1976, when you fired me from the Hacienda."

Everybody in the lobby turned around and looked at him. He became the incredible shrinking man. He looked like he was macaroni in a microwave. He held out this dead fish handshake. "Has it been that long?"

I said, "It's okay. I forgive you."

Carolyn said, "You've been carrying that shit around for thirty years?"

I said, "Listen. Screw him. He had it coming. I didn't do anything to get fired."

What have I got to lose?

It was time to do something serious to promote myself. I decided to produce a live record album and make it a fundraiser for the Carson City Children's Home. For the venue, I picked Reno's Mandarin Restaurant on Wells Avenue. I nicknamed the owner, Mel Choy, "Ho Choy," which means "good luck" in Chinese. He loved that.

For the four nights I performed and we recorded, we charged a donation for admission. Charlie Frisch, an IRS agent who was on the board of directors of the Children's Home, ran the door. I raised $1500, a lot of money in 1976.

Mel kicked in part of the bar tab and Jay the bartender said, "I won't steal any more than I have to tonight."

It was noisy in the restaurant, glasses clinking, people talking. As soon as you walked in, you smelled the Chinese food. I did my usual ad-libs.

When a guy in the audience heckled me, I said, "Okay, stop. Let's get the whole audience to yell back at him."

I left it on the tape. There were some good things, and some not-so-good things that didn't work, but that's comedy. You never know what's going to work. I didn't have a cheat sheet. I never work with one, and I should because it helps your brain a great deal.

The liner notes I wrote for the back of the album described the place:

"If you like realism, this recording should suffice. You can hear the sounds of drinks, hecklers, a Chinese wok being scrubbed, the cocktails sloshing around and the glasses breaking, cash register popping and slamming, background conversation amongst the customers, genuine laughter, inside jokes and of course, some comedy. It took four nights to get these effects on vinyl and I am happy with the results.

"The Mandarin Room in Reno, Nevada is a different kind of place to do a comedy recording. The policy of the room has been: rock music, jazz artists and singers and now a real WASP satirist. The customers run the gamut from black pimps to hard hats and from off-duty nurses, hookers, dealers, and lay people to ex-priests, music buffs and a smattering of dopers, teetotalers, vice cops wearing ill-fitting beards and eighth grade show-and-tell disguise kits, and some good loyal friends who follow wherever we are working. Special thanks for this combined effort go to those who jumped in and helped me do it ... my rain man, Ray Bennet, who keeps me from making ethnic slurs; Mike Fitzgerald, whose efforts held the hecklers and the fights outside and in the head to a minimum; Suzy, Fern and Davi for their spirit and laughter (cocktail waitresses); JT (the bartender) whose funny powders in the drinks did the trick and got everybody loose; Don Leonard,

who suffered thru the recording and editing problems and never became cynical after listening to endless playbacks and goofs, plus putting up with my jive and inane questions. And kudos to Don Dondero, my good buddy who trekked to the joint and took the cover picture—you may have guessed, that is not a picture of a micro-oven at 7-11. This album was recorded under the worst possible conditions March 3-4-5-6, 1976, so if possible, play it on an early (circa 1948) hi-fi set and let your neighbors bitch ... or better yet, take it over to their house and play it there."

I banged that out on the typewriter off the top of my head.

I called my label, Satyr Records, after a license plate I had for ten years. If you remember your mythology, a satyr is half-man and half-goat, given to raucous merriment and lechery. One time when I had that plate I was driving a fire engine red Volkswagen with a black top to Tijuana to the Longest Bar in America. Two girls drove by in a Corvette. They were smoking a joint and motioned for me to roll the window down. I did, and they yelled, "We want to see if you have a hard-on." They were so loaded. Then they blew the horn and drove away one hundred miles an hour.

The album was entitled "What Have I Got to Lose." Kenny Laurson produced it, and Don Dondero did the cover photography of me sitting in Nevada's gas chamber. Once again, thank you, Governor O'Callaghan, for getting me in there. Boy, sitting in that chair was an eerie feeling. There was a watertight door and two chairs made with ¾ inch galvanized pipe.

To the cover photo I added phrases to look like wall graffiti:

"Who farted?"

"Take a number and be seated."

"Call Joe at Mustang."

"This chamber uses Cryopower."

"Turn out the lights when you're done."

"Space Available."

"Kleenex."

On the bottom of the chair, "Watch your step" and "Lazy Boy."

I was sitting in the chair holding an American flag in one hand and two fake cyanide capsules.

Even after my divorce from Louise and move to Las Vegas, Arlene was still hanging around, and why not? She had worked for Sig Rogich at May Advertising's office in Reno as an account executive representing high-end clients like Nevada National Bank. Besides being well-connected, she was talented. She helped me design the cover. The photo has a nauseating green tone, perfect for a gas chamber. It's the color of the cyanide when the pellets hit from the holes under the chair.

Kenny Laursen mastered it for me and took it to Glendale to be labeled and printed. It's got my little logo caricature and both sides of the vinyl inside say, "See other side."

I probably had two grand in it. It was too inside to try to mass market. It was meant to be a promotional giveaway. Out of the 500 I had printed, I still have one hundred left. Because of the gas chamber picture, that album could be a collector's item now. In the mid-70s, Nevada did away with the gas chamber and went to lethal injections.

Thievery in Comedy

I had a piece of business that came to me one day as I was driving over Highway 80 from Reno to San Francisco in the fire engine red Volkswagen convertible with the "Satyr" license plate.

This guy passed me in an old Winnebago motor home. We were both going forty because it was snowing like hell. He had a dog inside that had licked all the windows, and his antenna went *whoop, whoop, whoop*. Attached to the motor home were two rusty bicycles and a little boat.

At the summit, the Winnebago passed me. On the back I saw a whole bunch of stickers. One said, "If this vehicle's rockin', don't bother knockin." Another one said, "Honk if you love Jesus."

Well, I couldn't resist. I figured I love Jesus, so I honked. The guy leaned out the window and gave me the finger.

That incident became a bit that always got laughs.

One night Harrah's entertainment director, Dick Lane (real name, Richard Lucianni) brought Jerry Van Dyke in to see me at Harolds Club, and I did that bit. Next thing I heard, Jerry Van Dyke had done the bit verbatim on *The Merv Griffin Show*. Set up, dog, antenna, bikes, boat; every detail, verbatim.

Three guys called in one day to tell me about it. Jim Teeter, a ventriloquist friend asked, "Do you and Jerry Van Dyke have the same writer?"

"Hardly."

"Well, he did your Winnebago bit on Merv Griffin."

For years I wanted to punch Jerry out, but I got over it. After he did the bit, he could have said, "You know, Merv, if Cork Proctor ever hears about me doing that bit, he'll probably kill me." It would have taken the stink off stealing the piece. I've never forgiven Jerry for doing that. His brother is the nicest, sweetest recovering drunk in the world, but Jerry is a piece of shit. That is the best thing I can say about him.

Jerry's made a lot of enemies in the business. I've been told that there is a credo at the comedy places in L.A. and also at the Magic Castle, that if Jerry Van Dyke comes in while guys are at lunch, everybody gets up and walks out. They don't even discuss it.

The Supremes, Ford Motor Company, and the Flood

In addition to working lounges and shows, I worked what we called "club dates." There were always guys like Lenny Martin, the entertainment guy for Jimmy Tamer, Peter and Sorkis Webbe, those Lebanese guys who owned the Aladdin, who would call me to work a special event.

One day Lenny Martin called to say Ford Motor Company had leased the Aladdin's Performing Arts Theater for one night and he had hired The Supremes. Diana Ross had been gone for some years, and this group featured Mary Wilson. Lenny offered me $500 to open for them and I accepted. Hey, a gig's a gig.

The night of the gig with the Supremes, the rain was so bad—I don't think that theater at the Aladdin was ever built correctly—they had to run a three-inch hose out of a moat down below the sound mixing and light booth in front of the stage. The hose ran through a hole next to the booth into a crawl space below. The hole was two feet square with a trap door—great place to put a body, I thought. The crawl space was filling from the flood water going into the foundation. They had to keep a side exit door open six inches to accommodate the hose, a black thing like a giant radiator hose, that ran across the carpet in front of the stage and out the door. Outside you could hear the portable pump they brought in to pump the water into the gardens and driveway.

It was so obvious I had to make jokes about it. People were looking, mumbling, what's that? I said, "It's a snake. We're not done yet, but we're working on it." From the stage, I could look down into the hole and see three feet of water. They had some problems.

Tom Young, the sound tech, quipped, "I've got to go down in the moat and feed the alligators."

In my three-piece suit, I walked out on stage carrying an orange and white parachute. As I walked by Kenny Bright, a dapper trumpet player with a snow white mop of hair, I said, "Pull that D-ring" and the parachute opened. I walked to the mic with my parachute and said, "That damn Bonanza Airlines. They're always late, so I left the plane early."

Before I walked out on stage, Ford Motor Company had gone on strike. My audience, all Ford dealers, were turning their underwear a light shade of brown because they knew they were not going to have any cars to sell. I was out there doing shtick, working too hip as usual, and I could feel it was not working. I alluded to the strike, I did as well as I could, but it was in the dirt. I couldn't get them going. Some kid at the university trying to be a comedy critic reviewed my opening to The Supremes show and wrote, "It sounded like he made up the jokes when he got to work." Well, you ass, I did make up the jokes when I got to work.

I worked three consecutive nights at the Aladdin for Lenny Martin. The first night was Ford Dealers and The Supremes, the second night I opened with Frank Sinatra, Jr. for another convention group, and the third night I opened with Graham Central Station and Tower of Power for a different convention group.

It was the first and only time I worked with Frank Sinatra, Jr., which worked out great because he wasn't friendly. He was aloof. When you say hello to somebody and they fluff you, what does that tell you?

Graham Central Station was some experience. Everybody, I mean everybody in the audience was high. The dope smell in the Aladdin Theater could float you way beyond the flood.

Benny and Barney: Las Vegas Undercover

A week after I got fired from the Hacienda for supposedly being terminally tardy, I went there to read for a part in a TV movie called *Benny and Barney: Las Vegas Undercover*. When I got the part, I couldn't believe it. That's when I got my SAG card.

The story was a comedy/crime drama about two Las Vegas detectives, played by Terry Kiser and Tim Thomerson—a real rugged-looking guy—who were moonlighting as a comedy act. Their characters were always screwing up, wrecking cars or arresting the wrong guy. Once again, I was a cop. My part was as Sergeant Posi, a Metro dispatch officer relegated to giving them the cars they kept wrecking.

The movie was full of cameos: Jack Cassidy, Hugh O'Brian, Rodney Dangerfield, Marty Allen, George Gobel, Jane Seymour, Bobby Troup.

Filming my part lasted three or four days, for which I was paid scale. It was the last movie that George Gobel and Jack Cassidy ever made. They were nice, friendly guys to work with. There was no bullshit, no yelling, no screaming; everyone knew their lines, and we cranked it out.

McMillan & Wife

That same year I got a small speaking part in an episode of the TV series, *McMillan & Wife*. No cop role—this time I was a desk clerk. When I read for the part, I didn't mention the fact that I'd been previously with Rock Hudson's L.A. agent, Henry Willson.

That was two days' work at scale, $250/day. We filmed at the Aladdin registration desk. I only had a couple of lines. It went something like this:

Rock Hudson walked to the desk and said, "Are there any calls for me?"

"No, Sir."

"Are you sure?"

"Yes, Sir."

That was my big $500 part.

I could have done good things if I had gone to L.A. Some of the guys I worked with said, "Man, you're a stand-up guy. Come to L.A. and we'll help you." I thought, Oh, God, I don't want to be another one of those mooches. *Hi, how ya doing? Just got in town and I'm living in my car. Can you help me?* I couldn't do that, plus the quest of vaginal exaltation was a little too high at that moment. There were too many good ones around, and I was having too much fun. So the parts that came, I just stumbled into.

The Limeliters

In June I was back at the Aladdin, this time in the Performing Arts Theater opening for a week for Glen Yarbrough and The Original Limeliters. Jim Parker wrote in his *Panorama* column, "The package was cemented together by the acid wit of Cork Proctor."

It was a week, the money was okay, and it was prestigious. I had a fun time with Glen and Alex Hassilev and Lou Gottlieb of the Limeliters. Alex, the baritone who was handsome and spoke several languages, was interesting to hang out with. We did two shows, 8 p.m. and midnight, and afterward usually went to the bar in the Aladdin to drink or somewhere to have Chinese food.

Force of Evil with Lloyd Bridges

In 1977, Lloyd Bridges came to Las Vegas to shoot the made-for-TV movie, *Force of Evil*, about a killer who gets out of prison and sets out to get revenge on the man who testified against him in court. Through a local Las Vegas casting agency, I got a part that included a few lines. Luckily I already had my SAG card. I worked for three days. It was great to meet Lloyd Bridges, a real pro.

Natalie Needs a Nightie

Maynard Sloate was a producer at the Tropicana, working for J.K. "Ike" and Kell Houssels, the old man and the kid. Ike's father, J.K. Houssels, Sr., had one of the first gaming licenses in Nevada from the 1930s. They'd become gaming icons with the construction of the El Cortez, Showboat, and Tropicana Hotel/Casinos.

Maynard booked great jazz players like Errol Garner, Oscar Peterson, and Maynard Ferguson into the Tropicana's Blue Room.

Frank Scott, a builder/owner along with Jackie Gaughan and some lesser partners, was the mover and shaker who made the deal with Union Pacific Railroad to build a hotel/casino on their downtown railroad site, removing the train depot to put in the hotel that would become the Union Plaza. After that there was no depot facility in Las Vegas, and you had to go to Salt Lake or Kingman to board a passenger train to anywhere.

Scott got Maynard to leave the Trop to produce plays for the new Union Plaza. Maynard didn't have a big budget, but he got name actors like Shelly Berman and Gloria DeHaven and Phil Ford to star in the plays.

Maynard had the idea to take a play called *Natalie Needs a Nightie*, written in 1928 by Neil and Caroline Schaffner, and cast it with crazy people. He chose Phil Ford, Carme, Eddie Petty, Billie Bird, Gale Baker, and me. There were a couple of other girls whose names escape me, but they were actresses, not funny, and not even good comedy players. Between all of us we must have had 500 years of comedy. Billie Bird had been a comedian for fifty years; Carme had thirty years in lounges and reviews.

A review in *Variety*, October 12, 1977, described the show:

> *A farce about a soft drink salesman (played by Cork Proctor) who's offered a bonus by his boss for having a wife and family. When the boss arrives to meet the wife, the salesman has his friends Carme (as Jimmy Wilson) and Eddie Peddie (as John Watson) dress up in femme clothing. Natalie, well-endowed girlfriend of a neighbor, winds up in the wrong apartment, at the wrong time. Lots of dashing from door to closet, complications based on different wives and 3 babies—one black—lots of mugging and improv.*
>
> *"Written seriously by Iowans Neil and Caroline Schaffner, producer Maynard Sloate and director Ernest Sarracino pulled in a wild bunch of actors and began cutting, rewriting and rerouting*

action. What comes out is a very rapid 70 minutes. Audiences are
likely to laugh themselves silly with this one for months to come."

We all got Actors Equity cards. We were making $500 a week for six nights, two shows a night. Not a lot of money, but working with Phil Ford was an education. He'd come to fame as Ford and Hines with his wife with the buck teeth, Mimi Hines. With Phil, every night there'd be a new piece of business.

One night he was drunk. On the stage I bumped a table, spilling a drink. Two ice cubes rolled out, and Phil called, "Seven!"

I got completely hooked on theater.

The Plaza had shitty air conditioning, and we roasted under 20,000 watts of stage lights. Then we'd go to our dressing room where it was so cold you could hang meat. Between sweating and freezing, we all got the flu. We had a cot in there, and one of us was on it every night. We bundled up and drank tea to keep our energy for the second show, because we couldn't drop the energy level. We played to massive crowds—800 people in a 500-seat theater. All the ad-lib lines set the place on fire.

Maynard loved the ad-libs; they kept it fresh. He had given us permission to take great liberties with the script. But when we ad-libbed, stage manager Paul Szigety, who had been in a World War II Jewish internment camp, hated it and would scream at us in his broken accent from off stage, "Stick to the script! Stick to the fucking script!"

In the middle of the run we changed Natalies. Cissy Colpitts, who had two of the biggest colpitts you've ever see in your life, left and Roberta Braum came in. Roberta was a good actress, but both she and Cissy were classically trained actresses who couldn't ad-lib a fart in a chili contest.

Each night new stuff happened in the show. We kept it fresh. Maynard got the buy of the century. Though we weren't making much money, the camaraderie was like a sitcom. And we don't even have a video of that play.

No More Food for Bobby Sargent

R-J entertainment columnist Forrest Duke had a job three hours a night, five nights a week, as host in the Plaza's Back Stage Restaurant. Every day we were

My Mind is an Open Mouth: A Life Behind the Mic

either in Forrest's column or Joe Delaney's column: "Natalie Needs a Nightie sets another record."

For several years, the Page Cavanaugh Trio performed in that restaurant—nice place. In addition to being paid to be there, Forrest had a comp stamp with which he tried to be good to everybody, and it cost him the job.

Forrest was a kind, sweet man who couldn't say no to anything. A comic named Bobby Sargent came into the Back Stage every night, and Forrest started feeding him. Because he ate on the arm every night, Bobby Sargent eventually ruined the deal for everybody. Maynard got pissed off and took the comps away. Myself, I never ate there free.

Carme Goes to Emergency

Carme got huge laughs. He was a 225-pound Italian, built like a Hummer, in drag. One night he broke one of his high-heeled shoes and destroyed his ankle. Still in drag, he went over to University Medical Center.

"What's your problem?" asked the nurse.

In a high, feminine voice, Carme said, "I broke my shoe, I broke my shoe."

People in the emergency room howled. Then a bunch of black guys came in, one with a knife cut. They looked at Carme and said, "What happened to you, man?"

In unison, everyone in the room said, "He broke his shoe, he broke his shoe."

The Proposition

After the show one time, a couple caught me at the bar in the Back Stage. The husband offered to buy me a drink. I accepted and we sat at a table. The wife looked nice, pretty, with impressive cleavage.

The husband said, "I'd like to speak to you in confidence."

"Yeah, sure." The play's over, I've had three drinks, and I'm half shit-faced. I'm chilling, waiting for my late night date, a dancer from the Holiday Casino, to arrive.

He said, "My wife has taken a fancy to you. She would like to make love with you, and I'd like to watch."

No one had ever before solicited me to make love to his wife while he watched. I've done some crazy shit in my life, but never that. I don't know whether my genitalia was sticking out too much in the pants I was wearing onstage or what.

His proposition was tempting, but I didn't feel good about it. It wasn't me. If I'd have been a little younger or a little drunker and a little less experienced, maybe, but I'd already had my share of three-ways, you know, jump in a hot tub. I'd already done all of that over at my condo. I turned him down.

Carme's Trick Movie

I stayed till the end of the play, but Carme left early to do a "trick"—non-union—movie. They offered him a wonderful deal, money plus a piece of the deal. It looked good on paper and then never materialized.

I warned him. "The only guilds in America worth a rat's ass are the Masons and the Screen Actors Guild. You have a SAG card. How can you devalue that by doing a movie for cheap?"

I really beat him up about it.

They stroked him, telling him he would be the lead, and he walked out of a long running play to do it. By the time they got to wardrobe, they ran out of money and the movie was cancelled.

The Wind at Your Back

After *Natalie* closed, Union Plaza owner Frank Scott asked me, "Do you want to go back to work in the lounge?"

Hey, sure. $500 a week. They raped me—but I let them. God, I needed the gig.

To accommodate the way I worked, they built a ramp for me from the stage across the bar. Ross, a great bartender there, became my "victim," like Ramsey, the guy Don Rickles used to beat up every night at the Sahara. Ross would look up at me, and I would say, "All right, tell the audience you're gay. Get it over with. It'll help your tips."

In that toilet at the Union Plaza, it was so hot onstage that beer was a necessity. I never drink cokes; I hate colored water with sugar. Diet or not, it's still cancer. I drank Coors. I had the power of the pen and could sign for drinks. In the course of a night I would probably have six or eight bottles of Coors, but I was sweating like a pig. I thought I always dressed reasonably well. I would wear a nice sport coat with a shirt over the lapels and a pair of frontier pants or Haggar slacks, good-looking shoes. At the end of the night the coat would almost stand by itself because it would be soaking wet. I would say to Ross, "Tune me up," he'd hand me a cold beer, and I'd say to the audience, "Here's a toast: may the wind at your back always be your own."

In each show I would do this thing called 'run the room down.' After I had talked to everybody in the room, as my closing bit I would go back and review something about each person I'd talked to.

There was a wonderful black pit boss there, Mel Woods, and at the end of his swing shift at three o'clock in the morning, he would yell, "Run the room down." I'd start with the poker dealers and I'd go through the whole pit and then I'd recount all the people whom I had talked to in the lounge. *This guy's from Encinitas, California and he's gay and he came here to pick …* I'd make up the craziest shit in the world and that was my way of running the room down. Then, I'd say "thank you," put down the mic, walk, and take a break because I was on by myself, twelve, two and four. All the bands had gone home, and I was the only entertainment from four to five a.m.

I had no music. I had no accompaniment. I had nothing. It was me in the lounge and the mic and one hundred people.

The Holllywood Reporter, October 25, 1977: "Cork Proctor, 'The Oral Assassin,' the newest graduate cum laude of the Rickles/Greene/Gayle school of hilarious abuse and irreverent raillery, is pulling the crowds all the way downtown to the Union Plaza's Omaha Lounge for his thrice nightly assaults. Cork's 4 a.m. show is the rounder's rendezvous."

When the last set came, it was pretty bizarre because the dealers would come in. I knew them all. I'd slept with a third of them, without being immodest, had a great time, had fun. It wasn't about sexual proclivity or being promiscuous or anything. If you hooked up, you hooked up. It was okay. There were no questions asked. I did avoid doing that in my dressing room—once I almost got caught in there. The guy knocked to say, "You're on," opened the door and, hello. I said to myself, *I won't do that again.*

Remember, I was in an open lounge, working from the bar, twenty-two feet right into the pit. The dealers all stood there with these wonderful cute asses, right in front of me. I can't tell you what it was like trying to concentrate on being funny with all these great little buns right there.

Anyway, every night I would do a thing about Alan Abrams, the casino manager who had his thumb in his waistcoat, a derringer in his boot, and a razor haircut. I did a joke about that: "You know what a pit boss is? A gorilla with a razor cut." Alan walked around with his little watch fob with the elk's tooth and cowboy boots with risers in the heels, all that shit I hate. He wasn't a bad guy. He did have a sense of humor. It became a regular thing because I was scratching for material, reaching for everything, and the line always got a laugh.

Alan, who knew how to deal the games, pranced around in the pit. He had this righteous posture, like 'I'm the casino manager.' From the stage I would say, "Being the casino manager is like being the head leper in the colony. It doesn't mean shit." Then I'd say, "Ladies and gentlemen, in the pit, we have our distinguished casino manager who allowed me to do my show here tonight." I'd suck up. "Let's hear it." We'd all start applauding him. While they were applauding, I'd drop the mic and yell, "He's a shit heel."

In the pit Alan couldn't hear that last line. Inevitably somebody said to him, "You know what he's saying about you?"

Speaking Violation

In an open lounge, there was a Gaming Control Board rule that said you couldn't be crude. It you were working a closed lounge or in a showroom, you could say anything you wanted, but not in an open lounge. You would be subjecting the players to something they didn't want to hear.

I got called on the carpet while working at the Union Plaza. Gaming Control Board agent, Jaime Haddad, had come in at four in the morning and reported that "Cork Proctor was swearing."

His incident/complaint report stated:

> "While at the Union Plaza on the above time and date R/A
> (reporting agent) could not help but overhear the entertainer,

My Mind is an Open Mouth: A Life Behind the Mic

Cork Proctor, in the Omaha Lounge. At the 21 pit as well as throughout the rest of the casino, including the slot department, keno lounge, and poker room. R/A clearly heard that entertainer use such words as 'fuck', 'shit', and 'god damn' in his dialogue. The casino was not crowded at that time of the morning which made his conversation very distinct. It is one thing to conduct a lounge show in a private area if that type of obscene language is to be used, but to expose it to the entire casino is something else. The Omaha Lounge is directly in the casino and is not partitioned off in any form. It was R/A's opinion that the above conduct should be brought to the attention of the Board for review and also be considered a violation of Reg. 5.010 constituting an unsuitable method of operation."

At my appearance before Jeff Silver, head of the Gaming Control Board, I said, "Jeff, I honest to God don't think I said this. I don't think it was me."

A lot of times, I'd work with no mic. I'd leave the mic, go over to the edge of the stage, and say to a guy, "What are you yelling about? What did you pay for this show? Nothing, so quit bitching."

I told Jeff I thought it was somebody in the audience who swore and Haddad heard what he wanted to hear.

Jeff blew it off. "Cork, don't worry about it."

"If I did it, I'd own up to it. I don't want to get Frank Scott's license in trouble."

"Oh, don't worry about it," Jeff repeated. He was way cool, Jeff Silver.

Vega$

In January 1978 I was again nominated for an award I didn't get. "LV Entertainment Awards for 1977; Category: Lounge Star. The nominees are Peter Anthony, Jackie Gayle, Dizzy Gillespie, Billy Kay, Cork Proctor, Rip Taylor."

This is Las Vegas, February 24, 1978, reported, "Cork Proctor has been given a speaking role in the new Aaron Spelling Twentieth Century Fox film for TV, *Vegas*, in which he portrays 'a caustic, forty-year-old highway patrolman.'"

Vega$—with a dollar sign through the S—was the first TV series to be about Las Vegas and filmed entirely in Las Vegas. The star, Robert Urich, played a private detective named Dan Tanna who lived in a warehouse and drove a red 1957 Ford Thunderbird all over town solving crimes.

In a general casting call, I read for the part. They wanted a big, tall, bland-looking WASP. I was pretty much a shoe-in. In the pilot, I was a cop—I was always a cop—from Metro who discovered the murdered girl in the yellow Corvette. Ken Ing, who later became my martial arts teacher, played the coroner. He went on to play a lot on *Hawaii 5-0*. *Vega$* ran from 1978 to 1981.

A year later I did *The Siege of the Desert Inn*, where I played a security guard taken prisoner by the bad guys. Cameron Mitchell was the star. He was a fountain of information. "Just learn your lines and don't create waves with the director or the crew, be a gentlemen and you'll get along fine."

Burton Cohen, the Desert Inn's general manager, played himself. Talk about type casting: a Jew with a cigar. Every time I see him I say, "Let's talk about your notorious run as an actor on *Vega$*." He hates it.

Robert Urich was a good guy to work with, completely professional. He always hit his mark, knew his lines, and was always hospitable. The girl on the show, Barbara somebody, was kind of a bitch; nobody could get next to her. I hit on her and she fluffed me. I guess she didn't want to go out with a "cop."

In the third episode that I was on, they had a massacre in the Villa d' Este restaurant and I was one of the investigating officers. I think I had three lines, a powerful part, a moving experience. Still a cop.

They also wanted to use a lot of local cops in the series, so I think that's how Judge Paul Goldman's wife, Charlene, and Sheriff McCarthy's wife got their booking agency started.

For years I got checks for foreign distribution of the three episodes. $100 here, $40 there.

Memories of Elvis

On Friday, May 26, 1978, Forrest Duke wrote in his *R-J* column: "Absent for nearly a month, Cork Proctor is back. Last night Proctor began a four-night stint at the Silverbird for the opening of star Johnny "Elvis" Harra, then it's back to Cork's Customary Corner for Caustic Commentary, the Union Plaza Omaha Lounge. Shecky Greene ... in Reno, at the MGM Grand Hotel opening, in front of 2,500 invited dinner show guests ... the only performer Shecky singled out and introduced was Cork Proctor, and he did so with great praise and obvious sincerity."

This was when Major Riddle owned the Silverbird. The first night I got fired right out of that show with Johnny Harra. His show was called "Memories of Elvis," and he was excellent, but he was fat. He couldn't control himself. I think he started to believe he was Elvis. You couldn't keep him away from food, and he had the worst diet in the world.

I walked out on stage and opened with, "It's nice to be working here with Porky Pig in a Dracula Cape."

He also had no sense of humor. Thank you, thank you very much.

Each time I got fired, Carme took my place. He followed me in to open for Johnny Harra, and stayed with him for a year. He went on the road with him, but Carme couldn't keep him straight, either. Carme can marshal people pretty well. He's Italian—hey, get over here. He finally gave up and came home.

Roastmaster General of the United States

Henri Lewin, who ran the Hilton, was a good friend. I'm sorry that later he got in trouble with the Hilton chain, but that happens when the little head runs the big head, and he got in some monkey business on a personal basis that he shouldn't have gotten into.

Often Henri would call me for roasts. One time, he had me come in all bandaged, bleeding artificial blood, and said, "I made remarks about Allen Glick, and this is what his friends did to me." The local people in the audience laughed like hell.

The night I emceed the Nevada Congressman Jim Santini Roast in June at the Las Vegas Hilton, the special guest was the Democratic Speaker of the House Tip O'Neill. At the end of the evening Tip O'Neill and I were in the hotel elevator at the same time, both of us pretty drunk. "You know, I don't do roasts very well," he said, "but, my God, you were magnificent. I've never seen anybody beat up on Henri Lewin like that. You should be the Roast Master General of the United States."

"Thank you, your holiness."

"Call me Tip."

Jokes and Cowpokes

Around this time my father invited me to go to Southern California and entertain for the Rancheros Visitadores, the oldest trail ride in America. Started by a guy named Jack Mitchell, in the 1920s I think, it was like the Bohemian Club in San Francisco, a great place to go party. They went out on the trail on horseback for five or six days. Some of these guys were multi-millionaires. The food was great and everybody had fun. Edgar Bergen performed there; everybody of any stature was invited there at one time or another.

My dad was going to be there for a week with all his buddies, Jimmy Skylar and Frank Scott and Bert Todkill and Oscar Bryan—all the old Vegas guys, and their horses, which they trailered down from Las Vegas.

I worked the night before at the Hidden Valley Country Club for Western Nevada Supply's golf tournament dinner, and then drove down from Reno, taking the back road on 395. They'd given me a map, and I arrived at the gate at 5:30 in the morning. They were getting up and had already started drinking.

The ranch was big, with meeting halls and a sound system and a kitchen, but our stuff was cooked out in the open on a chuck wagon. The steaks were three inches thick, with all the corn and beans we could eat. We ate outside and slept in tents, which was a step up considering where I'd been living.

In the evening we sat around the campfire, and I did some comedy shit. I was working all the time, so my chops were up. I was filled with confidence. I wasn't intimidated by anybody there. It could have been the greatest or the worst. I just got up and did what I do.

That night I slept in a tent next to a guy who was prime owner of Coldwell Banker. I said, "Hi, John, how are you?" On the other side of me was a Mexican ranch hand. Being invited on the trail ride wasn't about selectivity. It wasn't about everybody there having a Hummer and a Rolex watch. There were guys from all walks of life, chicken farmers from Yuba City. You have to wait five years to be invited to join the group.

Early the next day I left. I didn't want to crowd my dad's space. They were all shit-faced, having a great time. I didn't get paid, and I didn't want any money. I wanted to have fun. Boy, did they have a bar.

That was one of the best times I ever had with my dad. I think he was proud of me, but he never said shit. He told his friends how worthwhile he thought I was. He never told me I was funny. In the ten years that I performed he never said, oh, you made me laugh. But I think he stood in awe, because the first time I showed him my 1099 from 1967, where I made $27,000, I'm sure he thought, that's a lot of friggin' money for a drummer and a two-time high school dropout with no formal education destined to go to the electric chair.

"Live Wednesday"

It had been five years since Dick Clark had first seen me in *Love Affair* at the Marina and asked if I'd like to do television. He got a network show, *Live Wednesday*, and God love him, he hired me. I'd been at the Union Plaza a year and a half, and here was my shot. I got the Plaza down to five nights—still for $500—and I'd run down to Southern California to film the show at the NBC studios in Burbank. I was the warm-up guy. I didn't get on camera till the last show.

I was getting pretty aggressive. I was doing network television, live, in front of thirteen million people. December 29, 1978's newspaper TV section: 8:00 *"Dick Clark's Live Wednesday: Scheduled: David Frye, Cork Proctor, Dar Robinson, The Marquis Chimps.*

David Frye was a brilliant impressionist and political satirist who lived for a long time in Vegas' Country Club Estates. I struck a rapport with Dar Robinson, the premier Hollywood movie stunt man—he jumped off a 100-foot cliff into a river for Steve McQueen in *Papillon*.

Live Wednesday got cancelled after thirteen weeks. But we did it, and it was a great opportunity. I met Melissa Manchester, Rick James, and Jane Fonda, who was complimentary and wondered how I could go out there and wing it for an hour and a half. "It's amazing how you do that," she said.

I was dating Neile McQueen, Steve McQueen's ex-wife, who was in the audience that night. Neile was working at the Union Plaza in a Broadway show, *Can Can*. She had come through the lounge with choreographer Jack Prince. I started talking about her, because she and Steve were on the cover of *People* Magazine for getting divorced after sixteen years.

At first she was oblivious that I was talking to her. Then she turned and asked, "Are you speaking to me?"

"I certainly am."

I invited her to come and have coffee in between my shows, and the rest, as they say …

The night after one of the Dick Clark tapings Neile invited me to go with her to the premier of the movie, *Comes a Horseman* at the Academy Theater on Sunset Boulevard. The two of us rode there with producer David Foster and his wife in his stretch Mercedes. At the party afterward I looked around at who all was there, like Lois and Jim Garner, and said to Neile, "I'm in over my head here; I'm just an old comic from Las Vegas."

"Don't worry, these people like you," she said. "They accept you as you are. You're my friend, and they think you're funny."

Still, I was intimidated and felt totally out of place.

Demeaning the Dignity of a Pit Boss

My segment of *Live Wednesday* aired in December, the last show was filmed in January. When I came back to the Omaha Lounge, I was fired. They got me when Frank Scott was out of town. I think it was a collaboration between razor hair-cut Alan Abrams and producer Maynard Sloate. Sloate wouldn't cop to it because he didn't have that kind of balls, but I'm sure he had something to do with it. When I came back, they told Frank some story about how I had been "demeaning the dignity of a pit boss."

I said, "That's an oxymoron. Pit bosses have no dignity. That's why they're pit bosses." They'd make more money if they stayed dealers, but they want to wear suits and tell you, *hey honey, we want to see more of your tits, and pull that butt thong up*. Plus, they have the power to call, "Coffee in pit two."

They told me, "You're done." No two weeks' notice. It pissed me off; I never forgave Frank Scott for letting them do it to me. He was the leader, and he never defended me. He should have said, wait a minute, the guy's professional, he's doing a good job.

"Trip 'Round the Strip"

In March 1979, I produced a convention show in the Las Vegas Hilton Grand Ballroom. It was something to do for wives who came to the Pacific Automotive Show with their husbands. I called it "Trip 'Round the Strip" and hired lounge musical acts Mickey Finn, Frankie Carr & the Novelites, The Goofers, and singer Karen Nelson. Four acts on two stages. I paid them all half the money up front.

"What does this mean?" one of them asked.

"It means you're gonna show up."

There were 750 women in attendance, and they could have had another 250, but they ran out of roses to give them. Poor planning on the part of the Hilton concierge. Then the women made so much noise, like chickens laying eggs.

"Ladies," I said, "we're doing our best here to entertain you."

But they had a great tech guy running the sound, so the show came off smooth. I produced "Trip 'Round the Strip" for ten grand and made three. I should have kept producing because I did a great job.

"Life, Love, and the Pursuit of ..."

Producers Harry Seybold and Mike Fugo and a flim-flam guy named Stan Lipton got some seed money and collected a bunch of us to produce a pilot for a television talk show called *Life, Love and the Pursuit of ...* Believe it or not, the title was my idea, since they couldn't come up with a name.

Barbara McNair, Dave Barry, and I were the hosts. The guest stars were singer J. P. Morgan, porn actress Marilyn Chambers, singer Rudy Vallee, and comedian Bernie Allen. In addition, I got a gynecologist and a urologist to come on the show and talk about sexually transmitted diseases. It was hilarious and a lot of fun to do. I think there's a tape of it floating around L.A. somewhere.

We rehearsed on May 30th and taped it in front of a live audience—tourists who all had free tickets—between 9 a.m. and 4 p.m. on May 31st at the Silverbird Hotel.

It never went anywhere. And none of us got paid, though they did buy me a suit.

"Bullshot"

In his *Las Vegas Mirror* column, Neil Hoffman wrote, "The Silver Slipper invited the press out to a feed and the opening of *Bullshot* the other night. Despite some technical problems, the show was … mildly amusing."

Bill Friedman, a Hughes executive with a tremendous track record, had taken over two Strip toilets, the run-down Castaways and The Silver Slipper. In the 1950s, when the Silver Slipper was called the Slipper Village, I'd seen Woody Herman's band play in the ballroom. My classmate and good friend Jim Reber had a black 1925 Model T that he'd left out there as part of the environment.

The Slipper had stopped their music policy, and they were using the ballroom as a showroom, which they now called the Gaiety Theatre. Hank Henry, Sparky Kaye, Bill Willard, and Allen and Rossi had worked that room years earlier.

Bill Friedman answered to Phil Hannifan, my high school classmate from Manogue—class of 50-51—who had gone to work with the Hughes Corporation and become successful. Phil was executive vice-president of several areas, with unlimited juice in every hotel in town; he could sign for everything at any Hughes property.

He had a lot of juice as to who was hired and fired. He wanted me to get the job in *Bullshot*, and he was an overseer because that was a Howard Hughes casino.

Bullshot opened on Wednesday, June 27, 1979. Showtimes 7 p.m. and 11:30 p.m., and on Friday and Saturday nights "Special Entertainers Late Show" at 2:15 a.m. "Just $4.95 or the special dinner show that includes 'the famous' Slipper Buffet, $7.95."

My Mind is an Open Mouth: A Life Behind the Mic

Famous country hit singer Hank Penny put the show together. They even built all the props, and in the process one of his guys, Tom, cut off two fingers with a chain saw. George Swift was the stage manner. We rehearsed for the better part of a week and it was fairly tight, but not a structured show. There was a lot of spontaneity, a lot of comedy. It wasn't A, B, C, joke, dancer, dancer, tits and ass, joke, dancer, dancer, joke. It was bits and pieces that we had written and put together.

The cast was the talented black singer/dancer Skip Cunningham, showgirl Cassandra Lee, me and Terry Ryan—married to Dean Martin's daughter, Deana—as musical conductor. I played drums, and then I'd do my stand-up.

I was making a lot of money; my contract was for $900 a week for performing plus $600 for playing drums and on top of that a piece of the gross.

We opened and things went into a tailspin. Everything that could go wrong went wrong. None of the music cues worked. Cassandra had beautiful music and feathers and a back set. She came out and the music didn't come on, and when it did it was the wrong music. Skip was singing taped music, and it didn't work. Terry couldn't do anything because her music was taped. It was the domino theory.

When the show was over, people went out of there like rats off a ship. Of course, it was press night. At the press party afterward, I knew *Bullshot* was doomed.

Bill Willard was there that night, and he wrote a scathing review of me for *Variety*:

> "Assembled by onetime country personality Hank Penny and four-walled by Herb Kaufman and Jimmy Dean, this disaster called 'Bullshot' has only the saving item of a $4.95 minimum to cheer Silver Slipper customers. If occasionally some quips by over-striving Cork Proctor manage to uncork laughs, the dodge may be considered a bonus .... Proctor, one of the better free-formers around the comedy bin, only has his best shot in an opening monolog, kept brief and establishing himself as a pretty fair 'where-you-from' hip-shooter. He becomes downright vicious and degrading during his commentary of customers caught with candid eye of a

closed circuit video camera. If he keeps it up with the same filthy
sludge, it will be a wonder that he fails to get socked either physi-
cally or by a lawsuit. He causes walk-outs with his remarks."

Another review of the show was little better. The headline read, "Bullshot Misses The Mark."

"Bullshot is a loose-knit series of Daily Variety performances,
divided by that standard of the burlesque and vaudeville theatre,
the black-out sketch. The evident strength of the evening lies in
the talents of its performers, from the very topical, spontaneous
stand-up comedy of Cork Proctor to the confident dance style of
Cassandra Lee. There is one rather unusual device employed in
the performance, a device that involves the audience as well as
Proctor in its humor. Loosely-related to Saturday Night Live's
technique of showing a real person in an audience and then giv-
ing him a fictionalized, satirical sub-title, Bullshot's audience is
panned before the show so that Proctor can then highlight 'Las
Vegas' Ten Most Wanted People. This is obviously a difficult trick
and eventually becomes unsatisfactorily repetitive in Proctor's
choice of comic epithets—'The heavy-set man in the red coat is
a well-known dope-dealer ... recently seen waving goodbye to
Laurence Arvey at the airport.' Even so it proved very popular
and stands to Cork Proctor's ability that it worked as well as it did.

This sequence also led to one of his funniest ad-libs of the eve-
ning—as things slowed to a standstill due to mechanical problems
with the videotape, he introduced the stage crew, adding, 'Give
them a big hand, it's their last night.' Its performers deserve the
opportunity to iron out the weak points and find the show of
which they're capable."

Bill Friedman, manager of the Silver Slipper, was in the audience, whose wife had had a goiter removed. I said to somebody in the audience, "If you don't straighten up we're going to make you sit and look at pictures of Bill Friedman's wife's goiter surgery."

My Mind is an Open Mouth: A Life Behind the Mic

Friedman went airborne. He didn't talk to me for twenty years. He's still mad at me for making fun of his wife on opening night. But it was humorous, and it was the truth. He took umbrage, and she's never forgiven me. Later she went horseback-riding with a friend of mine who said she raked me over the coals.

These people have no sense of humor. It's all nickels and dimes and how much can we get out of this guy and what whale is going to sleep here tonight.

The second night Bill Friedman fired the show. I went ahead and worked out the week by myself—from a production show to one guy—so they would have to pay me. Actually, they paid everybody off. They paid me almost five grand.

I suspect George Swift, the stage manager, deliberately screwed up Cassandra's music. To this day, I think Herb Kaufman paid off somebody, maybe George, to sabotage the show because he wanted to put Kenny Kerr and *Boylesque* back in the main room, the Gaiety Theatre. They'd put Kenny upstairs in the ballroom, and after *Bullshot* closed they put *Morris, a Tribute to Elvis* into the ballroom and brought Kenny downstairs to work the Gaiety Theatre. With all due respect to Herb Kaufman, it looked suspicious.

Bullshot was the only thing Bill Friedman didn't turn a card over and make work. What a nightmare. Hank Penny lost his ass on that show.

That was my illustrious firing from the Silver Slipper. The Hacienda, the Plaza, and the Silver Slipper; three firings, if we don't count the one-night Johnny Harra gig. And then two more that I'll get to.

A Man in Search of His Act

A writer for *OUI* magazine named Mike Price came to town. He had been here before, hosting a late night movie show, so I knew who he was, but we had never met. One day he called and said, "Hey, this is Mike Price; I'm at Circus Circus. Could I do an article on you?" I agreed and took Kathy, who was living with me at the time, to meet him.

We had dinner and he was higher than a kite. I had given Kathy a camera for her high school graduation, so when he said, "We need a picture," she took it in the front yard of my house on Firethorn.

An entire column about me appeared in the "WHO" section of the October 1979 issue of *OUI* Magazine. Entitled "A Man in Search of His Act," it featured a black and white photo of me sitting in a wheelbarrow holding my thumb out for a ride. The magazine credited Kathy as the photographer and paid her $100 for the use of it.

Mike Price summed, "He's a blazing daredevil, working with no set material, no 'savers,' and no net. All alone, Proctor's the Wallenda family of comedy. The fact that he works mostly ad-lib excites the audiences and petrifies the bosses; hence his usual introduction: "Ladies and gentlemen, the Union Plaza Hotel nervously presents Cork Proctor, a man in search of his act."

Dick Clark Turns 50

On November 20, 1979, Dick Clark turned fifty. I was back working at the Union Plaza and I invited Dick, his associate producer, Larry Klein, and their wives to dinner at the Back Stage Restaurant. Dion from the Belmonts, who went clear back to Philly with Dick, was in town, so they brought him and his wife along. I didn't ask the hotel for a comp; I paid for everybody.

Dick was uncomfortable going to a public restaurant because he didn't want any identity. I assured him that there wouldn't be any identity. "We're going to go in and sit in the back." He didn't want a Hollywood dinner where people talked pictures. Also, since he was an early riser and not a late night party person, we went to dinner before the normal crowd.

One of the many things we talked about over dinner was how good it was to be "alive at this age." Afterward, he sent me a beautiful thank-you note.

Taco Bell was Too Hip

Comedian Norm Crosby had a successful daily show on TV called *Norm Crosby's Comedy Shop*. It was taped in L.A., five shows taped in one day. I'd met Norm four or five years earlier; he'd seen me work in the Las Vegas lounges, and I'd hung out with him. Around the same time at the Hacienda I'd met a young comic named Larry Scaranno, who was also a drummer. Now he was writing with me. We had a little business: Comedy by Larry and Cork.

So when Norm Crosby called me and said, "My producer is looking for guys and I mentioned your name," I called Larry and paid him to help me write some stuff. We drove to L.A. in my truck so he could meet Norm.

For the *Norm Crosby Comedy Shop* show we wrote a whole piece of business on Taco Bell. You know, the busboy is outside rebuilding his car, a low-rider Chevy with tractor seats. Unfortunately, during the taping, Marty Allen— not my favorite human being—walked on unscheduled, and they let him do twenty-five minutes. The audience was full of old Jews who came on a bus from Woodland Hills. When Marty went out and did his shtick, he wore them out. Not that he wasn't funny—he was great. But then when I came out, they were looking at their watches. They wanted to go home.

It was tough and the Taco Bell bit was too hip, way too inside, but it was funny. It was similar to early George Carlin where he does Al Sleet the weather man. If you're not paying attention, you miss three lines, you miss the whole bit.

But I appreciated what Norm did and thanked him.

Florida Looks Good

Jimmy Fazio, who had been watching me work since 1973, said, "Hey Cork, what are you doing up there? You don't do that shit. This is ruining you. Look at the room. Look at you. You're funny. You come to Florida and work for me."

Jimmy was one of the good, broken nose guys who shook your hand and said, "You've got the job." He and a guy named Len Mercer ran Fort Lauderdale's Galt Ocean Mile Hotel, the first oceanfront hotel in an area called Galt Ocean Mile. It was named after Chicago lawyer, Arthur Galt, who first bought the land in 1913. For awhile in the 1930s, when blacks were forbidden to use public beaches in Fort Lauderdale, it was known as "the black beach." The Galt Ocean Mile Hotel had been the only Fort Lauderdale hotel with a ballroom with a bandstand and bar, and stars like Peggy Lee and the Tommy Dorsey and the Count Basie Orchestra played there.

So I called Vic Bari, a former accordion player who was now a booking agent and had seen me work many times. Disenchanted with the girl I was seeing, I told Vic, "I want to come to Florida."

He offered me a month at the Galt Ocean Mile Hotel for $750/week.

For three months I'd been dating a 21-dealer from the Union Plaza. We weren't committed, but she was screwing too many other guys, and I thought, boy, I'm going to catch something. She got an awful lot of phone calls in the middle of the night while I was with her. One evening I went to her house unannounced to return some tools, and when I walked by the bedroom window I saw her lying on the bed getting herself off while she talked on the phone.

"I'm so hot I can't wait to see you," I heard her say. "What time does your plane come in from Salt Lake?"

Bullshit—if you're going to chippy on me, I'm not going to hang around and let you hit me with a shovel in the face. All of a sudden a month in Florida sounded romantic, just what I needed to get me away from Vegas. So I called Vic back and told him I'd take the job. I bought a gray Ford station wagon from Gary Ackerman at Gaudin Ford, and two days later I drove away. That's my M.O.

The Bellingrath Gardens

Hot Springs, Arkansas, known for hosting the annual music festival, "The Valley of the Vapors," had a lot of spas and entertainment clubs. I knew Ray Binney, who ran The Vapors Club, which had illegal gambling as well as entertainment. Carme and Robert Goulet and Fay McKay—a lot of my friends—worked there, so I called Ray and told him I was coming through on my drive to Florida.

"Great, come on down," he said, and he gave me two nights' work on a Friday and Saturday for $500.

That weekend they had a party for the two lead Little Rock Channel 4 television anchors, a man and a woman. I hammered them so well for an hour that in the second show I couldn't even follow myself.

The day I arrived in Hot Springs I was unloading my stuff from the wagon when a guy asked me, "Where you going?"

"I'm on my way to Florida."

He said, "Boy, you got to stop at the Bellingrath Gardens in Mobile, Alabama. Give yourself a day to go there. It's wonderful."

I learned that the Bellingrath Gardens and mansion on a river in Theodore, Alabama, now a suburb of Mobile, are known for azaleas. The grounds, designed like formal English, French, and Italian gardens, are full of them. Mrs. Walter Bellingrath collected Boehm porcelain, and kept the largest collection of it in the world. The Bellingrath family owned the Coca Cola Bottling Company for many years.

The day I visited I met Luther, who had been the manservant with the Bellingrath family, and still worked there.

He said, "Sir, why don't you take off your shoes and walk in this nice cool, Southern sand."

That place was manicured better than Disneyland. Boehm porcelain and eighteen carat gold leaf on the dishes. Everything much like when the Bellingrath family left it and gave it to the state of Alabama.

I stayed until a quarter to six, when they finally threw me out.

"Sir, you have to leave now," Luther said. "You have to go home." I offered to tip him, but he wouldn't take the money.

Galt Ocean Mile

Friday, October 19, 1979, the *Hollywood Sun-Tattler* wrote that I was "in residence at the Galt Ocean Mile Hotel for an indefinite stay and his act is worth catching."

I stayed in the Galt Ocean Mile Hotel, though I had to pay for the room. Entertaining at the hotel was a rough job because the bar was cylindrical. The room had never been designed for entertainment.

When the mayor of Sunrise, Florida, John Lomello, came in I introduced him and said, "He'd wave, but it's hard to wave when you're in handcuffs." He was under indictment for some kind of monkey business, after which he was re-elected by a landslide.

While I worked there I met a lovely lady named Linda. She was secretary to Judge Harvey Ford, Boward County District Court Judge. She came in with her mother the first weekend and gave me her number. We dated while I was there and stayed in touch afterward.

*My mother, Kathryn Courtney Proctor, on
her wedding day June 29, 1929*

*Grandfather, Alfred I and father, Alfred II -
Summer 1934*

My parents wedding party - 1929

At two-years-old with my Granny Winifred Proctor - 1934

With Mom and Dad - 1934

My school photo in Orange, California - 1937

Orange, California - 1938

My Mind is an Open Mouth: A Life Behind the Mic

At Wyvern Wood LA with broken leg - 1940   *At Wyler Military School - 1942-45*

First house, 1320 Norman Avenue, Las Vegas - 1947

Photographs

At Navy boot camp in San Diego, California - 1953

You are cordially invited to be present
at the commissioning
of the

U. S. S. Illusive

at the

Martinolich Shipbuilding Company
2475 East Belt Street
San Diego, California

November 14, 1953 at 2:00 p.m.

Present this invitation for admission

Invitations to commissioning of the USS Illusive - 1953

The USS Illusive - 1953

Photographs

With wife Louise, daughters Kathy and Luann, New Orleans - 1961

At the Mapes Hotel in Reno with Dick Cortino - 1961

My Mind is an Open Mouth: A Life Behind the Mic

At the opening of the Arch Lounge, Harold's Club - 1965

The Winners in the Silver Dollar Bar at Harold's Club, L to R: Bryan Bee, Rudy Rodarte (died 05), Kenny Dotson (died early 90s), and me - 1966

Photographs

With Herb Jeffries at Harold's Club in Reno - early 70s

At the Frontier, my first time as a comic in Vegas – 1973

Harolds Club, Reno, with Louis Jordan – June 18, 1974. Photo courtesy of Smokey Lawrence

Harolds Club, Reno - 1974-75

My Mind is an Open Mouth: A Life Behind the Mic

Carolyn as cocktail waitress at MGM in original-themed costume - 1974

Mini Burlesque *at Harold's in Reno - 1975*

A pilot made at the Jockey Club, Las Vegas - mid 1970s

At the Frontier Hotel with Lola Falana for the Heart Association's fundraiser - 1976

My Mind is an Open Mouth: A Life Behind the Mic

With the Natalie Needs A Nightie *cast at the Union Plaza - 1977*

Taken by daughter Kathy for Oui *magazine - 1979*

Photographs

For the premiere of Bullshot *at the Silver Slipper in Las Vegas – 1979*

My Mind is an Open Mouth: A Life Behind the Mic

Cheek to Cheek *at the Marina Hotel in Las Vegas - 1980*

Club Juana Fley. as "Judge Ray Bean" 1980

Daughters Kathy and Luann Proctor - Early 1980s

My Mind is an Open Mouth: A Life Behind the Mic

The Rebels Band at Chili Cook Off, Circus Circus Hotel - 1981

Julie Miller + Me Golden Nugget in Atlantic City - 1982

The burlesque show at the Marina Hotel in Las Vegas - 1982-83

Once again, fooling RCCL into free flights - 1983

"Siege of the Desert Inn" episode of Vegas - 1985

My Mind is an Open Mouth: A Life Behind the Mic

Harrah's in Reno - 1985

At Harrah's Reno, L to R: me, Lee Greenwood, Lucy Lee, Berri Lee – 1985

At State Line Casino in Wendover, Nevada - 1987

My Mind is an Open Mouth: A Life Behind the Mic

At the Landmark in Las Vegas - 1986

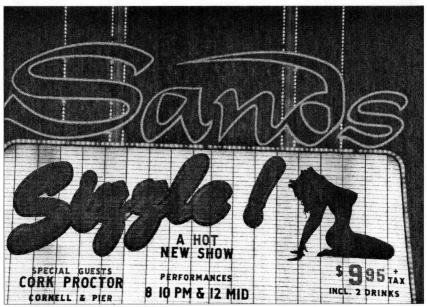

In Sizzle *at the Sands - 1986*

Gold Coast - 1988

My Mind is an Open Mouth: A Life Behind the Mic

With Carolyn – 1990. Photo courtesy of Lee McDonald

Performing in High Voltage *at the Dunes Hotel in Las Vegas - 1990*

My Mind is an Open Mouth: A Life Behind the Mic

Carolyn and I get married, gay nineties style - 1991

Comic relief for burned sign

BY BRAD TALBUTT / STAFF

Comedians Fielding West, left, Bernie Allen and Cork Proctor, right, took time Tuesday to let Strip passersby know they are performing this week at Ballys Hotel-Casino. The large marquee that would normally be used to promote their acts burned recently.

With fellow comedians Bernie Allen and Fielding West after the Catch a Rising Star sign burned - 1992

Photographs

The Mouse Pack, left–right: Barri Lee, Carme Pitrello, Peter Anthony, and Billy Kaye (with Cork Proctor, genuflecting) – about 1974

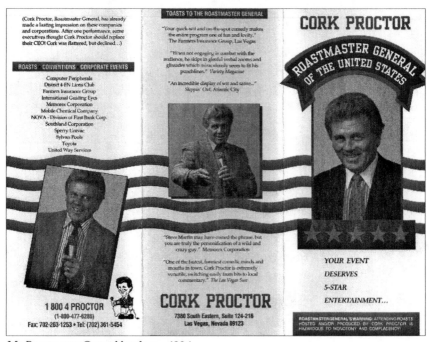

My Roastmaster General brochure - 1994

Deja Blues band with Lisa Nobomoto, Tommy Rich, Dick Greene, Eddie Maketta, Charlie McClain – circa 1996

UNITED STATES DISTRICT COURT

District of Nevada

Lloyd D. George U.S. Courthouse
333 Las Vegas Boulevard South, Room 6073
Las Vegas, Nevada 89101

September 23, 2010

Chambers of
Lloyd D. George
District Judge

Cork Proctor
7380 S. Eastern Ave.
Suite 124-216
Las Vegas, NV 89123

Dear Cork:

Thank you for the kind invitation to attend the luncheon meeting on Monday. And thank you for treating me to the lunch.

You did a marvelous job conducting that meeting and I look forward to seeing you sometime in the future.

Sincerely,

Lloyd D. George

From Federal Judge (and friend) Lloyd George – 2010

The 1980s

The Addy Awards

Back in Vegas for a short time, I agreed to emcee the Las Vegas Ad Club's annual Addy Awards for my friend, publicist Joy Hamann. The awards were to go to respected people in advertising for print, radio, television, and collateral created that year; the best visual, the funniest, etc. Winners would go on to compete regionally, and finally in the American Advertising Federation's national awards. It was Saturday, January 12, 1980, in the Terrace Room upstairs at the Desert Inn Country Club. Of course, they had to have a "star" so they got the guy who played the salesman, Herb Tarlek, on *WKRP in Cincinnati*, a hot TV sitcom that year, to come up from L.A. to "co-emcee" with me. While I worked pro bono, they paid his plane fare to Vegas, gave him a room, and a few hundred dollars.

Now most comedy actors aren't funny away from their scripts, and Frank Bonner was no exception. He wasn't funny. I also had the advantage of knowing most of the people in the room, while he didn't know anybody. He was of no help at all.

It was the usual: cocktails at 6:30, dinner at 7:30, awards program at 9. Right after we started the awards program, all the power in the Terrace Room went out. No lights, no mic. Bonner had no idea what to do, so I got up and went straight ahead—forty minutes of comedy in the dark with just the work lights. I made it work; it went as well as could be expected.

Club Juana

Back in Florida I drove my gray station wagon from Galt Ocean Mile over to Casselberry to Club Juana at the intersection of U.S. 17-92 and State Road 436. An agent and old time vaudeville guy, Roland Muse, had booked me there for a six-night gig for $750, for which I paid him a ten percent commission. I opened at Club Juana Thursday, April 21st, 1980.

I knew in advance it was a strip club. Roland said, "Hey poppa, there's gonna be a lotta girls there and a lotta pussy."

Oh good.

Club Juana owner Mike Pinter was attractive, dressed well, wore a lot of gold, and had a big knife scar on his left cheek. He was entrepreneurial and dollar driven. The club looked like a remodeled dry cleaning shop, though Mike had put a lot of money into it—mirrors, a curtain, a stage, a disc jockey. First show was 9 p.m., and the place closed at 2 a.m. It was rough. Lots of bachelor parties, drunk guys yelling, "Fuck you" before I even started. It was great training.

Linda came with her sister to see me there. I worked on and off for Mike for three years. In 2006, he finally sold his Club Juana to the Florida Department of Transportation for $3.4 million so they could build a freeway overpass.

Clearwater Beach

Jim Teter, a ventriloquist I had met at the Landmark with the Tommy Overstreet Show, was living in Orlando. While I was working at Club Juana, I visited him. When my six nights at Club Juana ended, Teter drove me over to the west coast to Clearwater Beach. He knew a guy there named Ed who owned the Clearwater Beach Hilton. The hotel had a beautiful showroom at the top called the Glass Straw, where Jim Stafford worked and Gallagher got his start.

Teter introduced me. Right away Ed put me in the lounge to replace another comic, G. David Howard, who was going on vacation.

Shortly after I started to work the room at the Clearwater Beach Hilton, a guy named Jay came to me and said I owed him a commission. He pressured me, saying he booked the room, so I paid him five percent. I should have said, "Fuck you, Jay, get it from Ed," but I didn't want to make trouble.

I got a dollar a head from the door and 40 percent of the liquor. It went well; one week I cleared almost $1,500.

During the three weeks I was there, G. David Howard came in once with his wife. Later I learned she had a tape recorder in her purse. After I left the Clearwater Beach Hilton, I went to watch David work and discovered he'd stolen 30 percent of my lines.

Another night a former maitre'd at Las Vegas' Frontier Hotel, Freddie Fredricks, came to watch me.

"When this is over, what are you gonna do?" he asked.

"I don't know."

Freddie said he had a lease-purchase option on a place called Jason's at 217 Windward Passage in Clearwater Beach.

"Why don't you come over and work for me?"

As it happened, I was supposed to do six weeks at the Clearwater Beach Hilton and got screwed out of the last three by Jay the agent. So I went to work for Freddie. I came back to the Hilton to see what kind of guy had replaced me and saw that he was dying. He was playing piano and singing.

"I thought this guy was a big draw," I said to the bartender.

"Well, he used to be."

I opened in Jason's third floor lounge—show times beginning at 9:30 p.m.—on Thursday night, April 31, 1980. Originally built by actor Chuck Connors, who'd named it the Sea Snipe, Jason's was now a terrible building with single-paned windows—in Florida!—and unfathomable air conditioning that ran all the time but always had something wrong with it. I worked for Freddie for a couple of months and got to be friends with a lot of people. I loved Clearwater Beach and Tampa and Tarpon Springs. I enjoyed the area so much I thought I might stay there and buy a house and forget about Vegas. To this day, I still love the west coast of Florida.

Working in Florida differed from working in Vegas in that you couldn't be crude. G. David Howard would do asides to oral sex, and he got away with it because people liked him. He was funny and had a hell of a following. He had set a precedent at the Clearwater Beach Hilton that was easy for me to follow, and later we became friends. He got into the Guinness Book of Records for the longest stand-up performance by reading jokes out of a book for hours on end.

Racial Remarks

In July I took a month off from Jason's to work the Lounge at Caesars Tahoe in northern Nevada, formerly the Park Hotel, for Don Severns, their marketing director.

The 4th of July weekend all the table games had a minimum of $5, and over the bar it said, "Don't forget after three o'clock, wine coolers and kamikazes—50 cents." Like a guy with five-dollar chips is going to drop everything and run to the bar and get a 50 cent drink …

The "room" was a wide open lounge—noisy. But I made the best of a bad situation. I was working opposite a good little country fiddle player, Tiger Bell, about eighteen. I was there a month.

The night of the opening, Shocky, the casino manager, was in the lounge and I made a joke to/about him. The next day in a management meeting, Shocky told everybody, "I want him fired, that son-of-a-bitch; he made fun of me."

He claimed I'd made "racial remarks" about him. Don was at the meeting and he told me about it. "Wait a minute," he told them, "I was there last night and he didn't say anything offensive."

Roger Trounday, the general manager, had gone to Reno High at the same time I attended Manogue. The next night Roger came in to watch me and brought his son. Afterward he said to Shocky, "What are you screaming about? I saw him and he was funny. He did an hour and ten minutes. What do you want me to fire him for?"

"He said it was nice to see me with a white girl."

Roger said, "That's funny, Shocky. What are you mad about? You're an East Indian. Were you with a white girl?"

"Yes."

"Then, end of discussion."

A week later Roger fired him. I loved it. There is a God.

The Mickey Finn

The week before I left I started seeing a cocktail waitress who was in the middle of a divorce from a one-armed pit boss. The day before I left, I took her to bed. That night the Park Hotel bartender—I think he was friends with the pit boss—slipped me a mickey finn.

The minute I got up in the morning I had the thin dirties, the worst case of Mickey Finnitis ever. After several trips to the bathroom, I felt like nothing was left alive in me. I had to leave at noon to drive to California for another gig, so I took every remedy I could get my hands on. Finally blackberry brandy slowed it down. But what a nightmare drive. I stopped every twenty minutes, sometimes to take a shit by the side of the road. Once I lost it in my pants while I was driving. I had no bowel control, and it was the worst experience I've ever had in my life.

Miss Nude California

From Tahoe I drove down to emcee the 1981 Miss Nude California contest at the Tree House Fun Ranch, off Glen Ellen Road as you come down the grade going into San Bernardino. The Tree House Fun Ranch was a nudist colony owned by Bill and Fran Flesher. They had all kinds of activities there, even had naked skydivers called the Buff Divers—eight skydivers in multi-colored chutes.

Jack Albertson and Dar Robinson, whom I'd previously met filming Dick Clark's *Live Wednesday*, were judges. No, we did not have to take our clothes off to judge the contest.

Dar didn't drink or smoke, and he had his kids with him. He told me he was a practicing nudist himself.

"Don't get too smarmy," he said. "These are decent people."

There were some gorgeous girls in the contest. Most of them were on the natural, and there were some who could stand a tune-up or two, but they were having a good time. I was real judicious. I mean, it was obvious that I could go for the cheap shots, but I kept it okay.

Las Vegas photographer Bob Patrick came and videotaped it. He had fabulous footage of me, once again, running around like a mad man. Unfortunately, when Bob's studio later burned to the ground, all that stuff went. No backups anywhere. Six weeks earlier he'd had a night where he took all of his outtakes and put them together and had a film festival. I'm sorry I didn't go.

Goodbye Florida

The gig at Jason's in Clearwater Beach was indefinite, subject to how I did. And I did well, but after a while I felt I wasn't being productive. G. David was opening his own club down the street, and I began to think about coming back to Vegas. I'd been in Florida eight months. I think it's true what they say; once you've lived in Las Vegas you can leave, but eventually you'll come back. I've known a lot of people who have moved away and later trickled back.

Also, I didn't feel I connected socially down there. I had a long dry spell in the dating department.

During my time in Florida, Louise had moved from Reno down to Las Vegas and lived in my house with Kathy, which was a great arrangement. I made the payments, and all they paid were the utilities. I owed Louise that anyway. She was such a good friend and a great wife. She stayed there six of the eight months.

Then on Saturday, August 23, I got a handwritten letter from Freddie on Jason's Restaurant & Lounge letterhead:

> Dear Cork,
>
> I don't think our relationship is a profitable one. Nor do I think it will work into one, as Sept. Oct, Nov, are slow months down here.
>
> Therefore I feel we should terminate next Sunday Aug 31.
>
> Also would like you to work Wed through Sunday this coming week.

If you feel I should give you two weeks notice, you are welcome
to stay on an additional week—I'll be here tomorrow at 4 p.m. if
you care to discuss it.

Fred

So Sunday, August 31, 1980, was my last night at Jason's, and I drove home to Las Vegas.

Roast at the Press Club

Before I returned I'd gotten a call to come to Vegas to roast Darrell Dreyer, State Assemblyman and News Director at Las Vegas' KNUU News Radio. The roast was at the Press Club on Charleston Boulevard in the old Fox Plaza Mall. I walked in and got the mic, and I was wired. I'd come from working three rough rooms in Florida. I had some big balls.

K-NEWS' general manager Joe McMurray was in the audience.

"You know what's good about you, Joe?" I said. "You'll never need Preparation H because you're a perfect asshole." It got a big laugh, even from Joe.

Carolyn Hamilton was in the audience that night. She sold air time for the radio station, and she had only seen me on the ill-fated press night for *Bullshot* and emceeing the Addy Awards at the Desert Inn. The photographer Chuck McManis introduced us.

Club Dates and Charity Events

I'd been out of Vegas for six years. I couldn't get arrested there, but now it was home. So I did a lot of club dates, both in Las Vegas and the surrounding region.

Flo Shrank had me come down to Phoenix and work a Christmas show for the employees at the Adams Hotel, where she was now the manager. I had dated Flo around the time I bought my house on Firethorn. She'd been managing an apartment building on Twain where my friends Murray Westgate and Elliott Crane lived. I would take anything. I didn't care. Just tell me how to get there, and when do I start?

I did a lot of appearances for fundraisers. I got a letter from Bob Miller, the Clark County District Attorney at the time, thanking me for his help. Sheriff John McCarthy wrote to thank me for some roast material:

"Without the material you so graciously provided, it would have been as humorous as a comedian out of work. Please stop by my office anytime you are in the area, but call first, so I can leave! In all seriousness, I sincerely appreciate your help and look forward to seeing you soon."

I also have a letter thanking me for my appearance on the Las Vegas *Easter Seal Telethon*. For four or five years I did the annual Circus Circus Chili Cook-off. Mel Larson, director of marketing, advertising, publicity, and whatever, ran it. Once Julia Mead, the TV star from the old *Ed Sullivan Show*, made an appearance. Bill Bennett, owner of the hotel, always came, too. It was a lot of fun.

I did the B'nai b'rith Man of the Year at the Top of the Dunes. For years I had a mic in my hand morning, noon, and night it seemed.

One Sunday at the UNLV baseball diamond I emceed the Seventh Annual Kenny Rogers Charity Celebrity/Media Softball Game, held for the Special Kids Olympics. It drew a crowd of 7,000 and raised over $15,000. Besides Kenny and Marianne Rogers, Mickey Finn, Helen Reddy, John and Jennifer Davidson, Lola Falana, Toni Tennille, Ben Vereen, Barbi Benton, and Dorothy Hamill were there.

Cheek to Cheek

Bob Brooker was the general manager of the Marina Hotel, owned in the early 80s by Tom Weisner and Mel Kennedy. I got along well with Bob, though he was always close with a buck. Betty Francisco, an excellent dancer who had been married to show producer, Dick Francisco, brought in to the Marina a review called *Cheek to Cheek*. It opened in January 1981.

Besides being a hell of a dancer, Betty had a great sense of humor. When the dancers were all saying, "Well, you've never gone topless," she said, "You want to see my tits?" She ripped her blouse off in front of everybody and said, "Are you happy now?" It was great. A chain-smoker, Betty was a charming lady who was good to me and paid me good money.

Cheek to Cheek had Kim Richards, a dancer I'd worked with in the *Mini-Burlesque* review at Harolds Club in the '70s. Kim had kept her personal commitment to herself to never work topless, and now she was in this show as assistant to comedy magician David Douglas. There were five girl dancers, Shirley LaSpina, Donna Washington, Karen Chirrick, Jane Ann Lowes, and Kathy Berry, and a male dancer, Scott Austin. $16.95 got you the 9 p.m. show including dinner in the Marina's Port of Call restaurant.

The show was supposed to stay there a few years, but Donna Washington and Shirley LaSpina and another girl wanted to strike the show for more money.

I said to them, "Do you know what you are doing? You're going to put fifteen, eighteen people out on the street!"

Shame on them. I told them they should have negotiated more money before they took the job. But they decided they were going to strike. I thought, *you bitches; you're going to put all of us out in the street.*

"It isn't about me," I said. "I'll recover, but all these other people need the gig."

We were doing pretty good business, but Bob Brooker did not want to get in harm's way, so when he saw a strike coming, he cancelled the show.

"We're done," he said. "We're not going through any litigation," and he tore up the contract. No renewal.

Those dancers put us right out of business, got the show cancelled after ninety days. I never forgave them. They were so stupid; they ruined Betty Francisco, who never recovered financially. With a start-up show like that, you have to put the money up front to buy costumes, choreography, rehearsals, sets, everything. It was probably a quarter of a million; today it's probably a million and a half. I felt so bad for Betty. It was heartrending to see that woman with such tremendous potential as a producer. It ruined her financially and emotionally. Sad and so totally unnecessary.

Roasts and Toasts

I went back to doing what I always did—single gigs and benefits, averaging four of the latter a year.

I did a lot of benefits, often with Las Vegas councilwoman Thalia Dondero or the mayor, Bill Briare, for Izzy Marion—Isadore DiMaria—who had the barber shop at the Aladdin. They called him, "Hairdresser to the Stars." I'm sure Izzy was "connected."

Izzy was always involved in things other than his beauty salons. He founded and was president of the Association of Italian Catholics. He was funny, and he produced a lot of roasts for the convention authority. On March 22, 1981, he got me to be one of the roasters, along with Nevada Lieutenant Governor Myron Leavitt, Nevada State Attorney General Richard Bryan, Judges Seymore Brown and Paul Goldman, *Valley Times* owner/editor Bob Brown, and attorney George Franklin, at the second annual dinner and roast for Congressman James Santini at the Convention Center. The Italian St. Viator Catholics sponsored it, and the master roaster was Herb Eden. Izzy Marion was a good guy who kept his word.

Peter Anthony and Pete Barbutti and I were pretty active doing whatever the community wanted. If one of them didn't do it, I did it.

After I was on a Channel 10 public television fundraiser, Frank Sinatra came over to me and said, "I watched you in the limo coming over here. You're very good."

I said, "Thank you."

By then, I was getting honed, getting my skills up, and I took no prisoners.

On November 12th at the Holiday Inn I did a Saints and Sinners roast of FBI Chief Joseph Yablonsky. I don't know that he was the greatest crime fighter since Superman, but I thought he was a charitable guy. He was wonderful to work with. It was a good night, and we raised some money.

Then on the 18th I did the St. Jude's Night of Stars at the MGM. I did several of those. *Las Vegas Sun* columnist Joe Delaney, a good friend, was active with that, and he would always call me.

December 12th and 13th I emceed the 6th annual Circus Circus-Nevada Championship Chili Cook-off in the big parking lot at Circusland RV Park from 10 a.m. to 6 p.m. There was bluegrass entertainment, and the winner took home $1,000 cash, a trophy, and a chance to represent Nevada in the World Championship Chili Cook-off in California.

Everybody there was a consummate cook. Some of those guys came from Texas with their own pots and cooking stands. I emceed it, but I also went around and sampled the chilis. They went from red hot to bland to just beans and onions. I've always been attracted to the hot, the caliente sauces, Jamaican and Haitian food— the hotter, the better. If there are tears running out of my eyes and my nose is running, I know I'm in the ballpark; this is good chili.

There were celebrity guests, and one year Julia Child came. The Lone Star Beer folks brought in a dozen live armadillos direct from Texas for armadillo races—very slow. I did the Circus Chili Cook-offs three years in a row and enjoyed them. The guys were fun. Everybody was drinking. In those days I can't remember leaving my house in my little pickup without having a Coors in my crotch. Pop the top, get in the truck, and drive. I never got stopped, and I was never drunk. I never had a DUI, but I was lucky, very lucky.

The Alabama Road Pavers

Frank Tanzer was a wonderful agent in Stone Mountain, Georgia, who became a good friend. One day Frank called and asked, "Do you want to work the Alabama Road Builders and Pavers Convention?"

"God, I don't know." I was thinking, *they're bigots*. It was in Montgomery, Alabama, and you remember what happened there.

"It pays $3,500, a plane ticket, a room, and I want 20 percent."

"Yeah, sure, Frank."

"Say anything you want," he said. "It doesn't matter because in an hour, they'll be so shit-faced, they'll be under the table."

The room at Montgomery's Downtowner Inn had a train depot décor with big rustic beams. The sound system was excellent. It was all guys, they were all stone bigots, and Frank was right: they were drunk. They were drinking 8-ounce water glasses full of vodka.

They stood and started throwing out racial slurs. These were not black jokes; these were 'nigger' jokes. I was not appalled—I knew I was going to get some of that—but then they heckled me to the point where I could hardly work, even though I had at least two guys peeing, they were laughing so hard. The heckling pissed me off. Every time one of those guys yelled, I trashed him.

"See that guy? That's what happens when you have sex using a Kleenex as a condom. Unfortunately, the best part of you is still hanging in your father's sacco de toro."

I came up with lines and kept going. It got funnier because they were drinking so much. When it was time to go, I said, "Listen, you sons-a-bitches, you're the most racist, angry, nasty people I've ever worked to in my whole life. I wouldn't come back here if you paid me double."

Guess what happened the next year? They paid me double and I went back. We are all whores.

Frank Tanzer said, "I can't believe you're going to do it."

"You know what? It's a challenge because now I've been there, and I have to come up with fresh material."

To the president of the club I said, "You tell these assholes not to yell at me, will you? Tell them up front when you have your next get-together. Just say, look, we're going to bring that same guy back, and he is funny, so give him a chance. Don't sit there and yell at him, because you are cheating the other guys who want to hear."

The second year worked pretty well.

Fun 'n Games in Atlantic City

Producer Dick Francisco (Betty's ex), and his partner, Terry James, had created a show called *Outrageous* and sold it to Bally's Park Place in Atlantic City. They had everything cast except the comic. I had worked for Dick in 1975 at the little Royal Las Vegas on Convention Center Drive, so he knew who I was.

I was out on the road, working conventions, marketing myself, making a living and doing the best I could. The story I heard later was that Ed Hillenbrand, a guy who had a comedy room in Chicago at O'Hare Airport, was in their office one day when Dick said, "Ed, we have to get a comic for the show."

Ed looked at them and said, "What's wrong with Cork Proctor?"

I guess I was the tree too close to the forest.

Dick called and asked if I would be interested. "We're going to take 20 percent."

"Yes, sure."

I wanted to go to Atlantic City; I had never worked the East coast. This was actually Dick's third edition of the award-winning *Outrageous* show with magician Higa and ventriloquist Jerry Layne.

Flo Shrank, still a good buddy, was now the general manager of the Claridge Hotel on the Boardwalk, so I stayed with her.

Outrageous III had a wonderful seven-piece band, all studio musicians from Philly. The leader, Lenny Hambro, was an alto saxophonist who'd been around New York and played studio dates with everybody.

For the first few months in Atlantic City I couldn't get a date. I couldn't score in a Polish lumber camp full of women. I'd go out each night and ask the band, "Is there anybody here that looks good?"

"They all look good."

On the back of the movable sets somebody wrote with a big spray can, "Get Cork Laid."

I started doing bits from the stage with a gal sitting in the front row. Later we had a fun date. Unfortunately, she turned out to be married. That was a shocker.

Each night I went out and did something silly. If there was a lady in the front row who was bodacious, leaning over and exposing her ample bosoms, I would say something like, "Gee, you have a lovely figure." I'd get her to stand to show off the dress. I'd have her turn around and I would say, "Boy, those are some big guns." Then she would cover them. "Did I embarrass you?"

"Oh, well, kind of."

There were 300 people in the room and I was winging it. "Lady, let me tell you something. The way you're dressed, here's an analogy. If the market's not open, don't put the fruit out on the curb." It always got a big laugh.

Upstairs in Bally's Ballroom was a show called *Roy Radin's Tribute to Vaudeville*.

On our night off a bunch of the *Outrageous III* cast decided to go see Roy Radin's show. Jackie Vernon was in it, along with Jack Jones' father, Allan Jones, Joey Bishop, and a midget. Joey was the emcee, and afterward we got to hang out with him. I had seen him in Las Vegas at the Sands singing "Cherry

Blossom Lane" and playing his mandolin. He worked clean. I enjoyed Joey Bishop's company; it was fun to be with him.

Roy Radin's Tribute to Vaudeville also had a little dance troupe in it called "Kicks." I want to tell you, I've worked a lot of topless and bottomless and strip shows, but when the lead dancer, Darlene, came out on stage in her costume, my heart stopped. And this was not a topless show, so she wasn't naked. My friend Nelson Sardelli, who was working in Atlantic City at the same time, said, "She is gorgeous, but I don't think you'll score."

"Does that mean you've tried and nothing happened?"

The next night, I saw Darlene standing at the back of the showroom watching *Outrageous*. She was so cute with these button eyes; a charming young lady.

She said, "God, you're funny."

I said, "God, you're beautiful."

That was it, HELLO and goodbye to the boyfriend. They weren't getting along that well anyway. Darlene lived near Cherry Hill outside of Philadelphia. She'd never ridden in a pickup truck, and I had my little Ford F100. We stayed off the Garden State Freeway, taking the old roads. We must have eaten at every mom and pop restaurant up and down the pikes going in and out of Atlantic City, the kind of restaurant where you walk in, smell the bread, are greeted, and the mother in an apron says, "You wanta some wine?"

"Yeah, we want a lot of wine."

The guy comes out with two liters for $3 and the mama, "Tonight I got homemade meatballs, I got pasta fasul—" She tells us the menu.

"We'll take all of that." So we're toasting and drinking, getting shit-faced.

I fell in love with Darlene, and we had this incredible relationship. There must be seven million restaurants in New Jersey on the White Horse and Black Horse Pikes. I'm sure we ate at all of them.

Shecky Greene was working at Caesars with Cathy Lee Crosby as his opening act. And of course I went to see Nelson's show, too. There was a lot to see in Atlantic City, but it was cold. That wind came off the Boardwalk, and I'm not kidding, it felt like 40 below.

I don't know who was doing what with whom, but there were a lot of heavy mob guys in Atlantic City like Philly mob boss Little Nicky Scarfo, who had a beautiful restaurant—a broken nose joint—where Darlene and I ate. It was kind of like being around Herbie Blitzstein and Tony Spilotro out in Vegas. When you saw those guys, you immediately started looking for the door because you figured there was going to be a shooting. Occasionally I'd go in with some Italian guys, and dinner would be comped. Little Nicky was a heavy hitter with the boys; he's still in prison, but he was always nice to us.

In the show I was free-forming each night and doing stuff out of the newspaper. The mayor was under indictment and ultimately went to jail. The next guy who came in was a recall election guy and went to jail, and it went on and on. I did a lot of jokes about the teamsters, but I never had any issues with the boys. I think they saw my comedy for what it was. Most of the guys know each other. You can't have a name that ends in a, i, or o, and not have somebody connected in your family. I think they liked that I joked about Governor Brendan Byrne, who was there twenty-five years ago when New Jersey got legitimate gambling.

Byrne said, and I quote, "I will not allow Atlantic City to become a haven for the mob."

"Where did he think it started?" I said. "Tucson? I mean, come on. The mob didn't come from Arizona. It came from the dock back there."

Atlantic City was scary though, because if you went a block off the main street it was like a ghetto. They converted an old building to condos that were dirt cheap. I should have bought one because right now it's probably worth a half a million.

Summer came and in their August issue *Atlantic City* magazine did a two-page spread on me, "Cork Chops," including Kathy's wheelbarrow photo. The writer said, "Tall, cordial and blessed with the ability to be spontaneously obnoxious, Cork Proctor is the most outrageous part of Bally's More Outrageous revue." He quoted some of my funny bits, like my line about the cocktail waitress: "Isn't she lovely? And she likes being tied up, too."

What Time is it Now?

All the hotels in Atlantic City had shuttle bus stops, so people parked out of town six or seven miles and used the shuttles to get around. Traffic in town was horrible, and the shuttles ran every fifteen minutes, 24/7. Since I was staying at Flo's in Pleasantville, I'd park my little blue Ford pickup truck and use the shuttle to get to the hotel. One night I went at the usual time to the shuttle lot and guess what? They were down to one bus. The other one broke down. I stood there and stood there. Then I heard a lady dealer standing nearby say, "Shit! I'm late for work!"

"What time is it?"

"It's 7:25."

WHAT?! The show was at 8 p.m. and there I was six miles away and not changed into what I wear for it. I offered her a ride and we jumped in my truck and, man, I burned the tires out of there. Luckily, a Schwartz Men's Store was on the avenue with some parking. If you knew where you were, you could park there and walk into the hotel. I had eleven minutes to make it from the truck into the hotel, up two floors of escalators, change clothes, and be onstage.

Preceding me in the show was a singer, Wayne Hermans, who did a duet with the little girl in the show. I roared up the stairs in my Levis and cowboy boots, planning to change clothes, when I heard the last eight bars of their song. On the brink of a heart attack, I ran in, threw on a sport coat and tie—had to stay in the jeans and cowboy boots.

Everybody backstage was wigging out because they hadn't seen me. If I didn't show, they'd have to reblock the show immediately to fill that sudden twenty-minute gap. I had an excuse—it wasn't my fault, but it was my fault. You're obligated to be on the job on time. How you get there is your problem. I knew they were all back there, shitting their pants.

Still running like a mad man, out of breath, I heard a drum roll and, "Now, ladies and gentlemen, the outrageous comedy of Cork Proctor."

I walked out to the mic and said, "You know what's so hard about show business? It's waiting and waiting and waiting backstage to go on." The cast broke up because they'd seen me run in.

Afterward Lenny, the bandleader said, "Where the fuck were you?"

I've never been late for a show in my life, and I'm proud of that. But that night in *Outrageous III* was waaaaay too close.

My Mind is an Open Mouth: A Life Behind the Mic

End of Atlantic City

I got upside down in my flash-fire romance with Darlene. I thought she was the best thing since high button shoes. She was fun, but there was a disparity in ages; she was twenty-two-years-old and I was fifty.

"Lock up your house," I said, "and come on out and stay with me. My house is fenced in the back, and we'll live with your cats, and maybe you'll dance in Las Vegas."

But she didn't want to come out to Vegas. One day she sent me a letter saying, "It's been great fun and so long, goodbye. I've got to run. See you later." She went on to better things, I guess.

Anyway, after eight months I got bored with the show. When I left I got Kelly McDonald the job, and he finished the year contract.

Outrageous III had won a lot of awards, and by May 1983 I was a runner-up for Featured Comedy Act of the Year in the third *Atlantic City* Magazine invitational awards show, to be held at the Claridge Hotel. Fran Freedman, the magazine's publisher, invited me to sit at her table. She liked me, so I got a lot of press. But I didn't win the award that night. It was nice to be nominated, but I think the winners were all wired in advance.

The Roy Radin show went on the road, and he came to a bad end. Later the same year his body was found in the trunk of a car in Los Angeles county with a bullet wound in the head, contract style. Apparently he was connected with some Puerto Rican guys, doing a deal to raise $35 million to finance the movie, *Cotton Club*. There was some question about who would get the commission for the introduction, and it turned out not to be Radin. He was only thirty-four years old.

The Big Room with Mel Tillis

The best gig I ever had was in 1983 opening for Mel Tillis at Harrah's in Reno. I should have quit that week, July 14th to 20th. My contract for $3,500 included "one comp room with king-size bed." That was not only the financial, but probably the professional pinnacle of my career. Finally I was able to get to the big room at Harrah's Reno where I had worked in the lounge as a drummer twenty-five years earlier.

I had met Mel when Claude Trenier's identical twin, Cliff, died back in March. When Cliff went into the Frank Sinatra Hospital in Atlantic City, they discovered he was riddled with cancer. When he died, I called Claude and said, "Would you like me to come to Atlantic City and help with the benefit?" There was going to be a benefit concert to raise money to help pay Cliff's bills and for his burial. I offered to pay my own way, and Claude said that would be great. The benefit was in the lounge of Resorts International, which was not a big room. I can't remember how much we raised, but Frank Sinatra came in and paid Cliff's hospital bill, all of it. Frank did a lot of shit that was strange, but he did a lot of noble things, too.

Sammy Shore was one of the emcees, along with a New York/Catskills comic, Stewie Stone. We traded off and when I was doing my time as a comic, Mel Tillis was waiting back stage. I did fifteen, eighteen minutes and then Mel came out.

The first time I'd met him was in the dressing room before we started. "Hi, Mel, I'm a big fan." We both had Heinekens that we shook; when beer is half flat you put your thumb over the top of the bottle and shake it a few times, and it fizzes.

After I'd done an hour—and for an emcee, that's enough—Sammy came out and took my place, and I went back to the dressing room to have another beer with Mel.

"You k-k-know what?" he said, "I l-like you b-b-because you don't d-d-do all that f-f-filthy shit."

For the first time in my life—here I am, fifty-years-old—I pressed. "Hey, Mel, if you ever have a guy fall out … I know you use Lonnie Shore, and all those guys, but if you ever get short sometime, I would love to work with you, if it worked out." I told him that I didn't have an agent or a manager and "if you offer me fair money and decent conditions, I'd love to do it."

Two weeks later, Bob Younts, Mel's bass player in the band, called to ask, "Do you want to go to Harrah's with us?" and by May the contract was finalized.

In the show I said, "Look at this. I started out here in 1959 when this was the Golden Hotel, working with a little jazz trio, I broke in as a comic across the alley at age forty and now, ten years later, I'm in the big room. It's only taken me thirty years to come sixty feet! What a career move!"

All the guys in the sound booth were going, yeah, because I knew them all.

On closing night, Kathy and her mother were in the audience. "You're not going to do anything to embarrass her, are you?" Louise asked. No.

For Kathy's birthday I had a guitar made by a little guitar maker named D'Agostino in Clearwater Beach, Florida.

Before I went out to do my time, I said to Mel, "I hate to ask you this, Mel, but my daughter is having a birthday and it'd be great if you could give her this guitar."

"M-man, where d-did you get that g-g-guitar?"

"I had it made for my daughter."

The three guitar players in the band saw it, and one said, "Man, this is beautiful." I handed it to him, and he played it and passed it to the two others.

"Look at this narrow finger board. It resonates."

It was a D'Agostino electric guitar, but when you strummed it, *brrrrring*. It had this nice resonance. A lot of time you just get a flat sound.

After I left the stage, Mel came out to the thrust, that round portion of the stage that sticks out, and began to play the D'Agostino guitar. My daughter spotted it immediately. I had sent her a brochure, but I didn't say I was going to get her one. I'd said, "Maybe one day if we get to Clearwater again."

Then she got up to go to the restroom. Mel was almost done but he hadn't given her the guitar yet. Finally, he said, "We've g-got a b-birthday girl in the audience t-t-tonight. K-kathy, where are you?"

Returning from the bathroom, she was wide-eyed, a deer in the headlights.

I was standing to the side of the stage. Mel said, "I want your d-dad to c-come out here." I walked out, and he took the guitar off and handed it down to her. "Y-you know, if you p-p-play g-good, I may hire you n-next time instead of your d-d-daddy."

I said, "I want to thank you, Mel. This is genuinely lovely of you to do this."

Now, Englebert wouldn't do what Mel did for me. None of these big guys, but country people are wonderful, because they don't mind breaking their rhythm. Their fans are so loyal, Mel could have dropped his pants and said fart or something and they would say, yeah, do that again.

We had become great friends. The sad side of the Mel Tillis story is the way we parted. The day before the show closed, Bob Younts brought me a copy of the script of a movie called *Up Hill All the Way.* It was a movie project that Roy Clark and Mel were going to do together. It was about two Civil War returning veterans and their trials and tribulations. I read the script, and Mel gave me the part of the Garrison Commander. He announced it right in front of the whole band. I was thrilled.

Guess what happened next? The producer came in and said, "I'm sure this guy Cork is probably a good actor, but we're going to get Glen Campbell." They wanted a "star" name. The movie went in the toilet. Glen Campbell was as rigid as a piece of rebar. He's a wonderful entertainer, but not a great actor. I'm not saying I would have been better, but I think I might have been. The movie went right to video.

After that I could never get ahold of Mel. Isn't that sad? They took the authority and creative control away from him. I wrote him a postcard, "Mel, I understand." That's Hollywood. That's show business. It's all bullshit. I wrote that I wasn't angry about it and couldn't we still be friends? Nothing.

Years later my younger daughter Luann was singing in this shit-kicking bar at Singer Island when Mel came in with a bunch of his buddies. Luann said to him, "My dad worked with you."

"Who's y-your d-d-daddy?"

"Cork Proctor."

"I l-l-love C-cork!" he said.

But it's been twenty-some years, and I've never been able to reach him. I called and left messages at his room in Reno twice and then in Vegas once and finally gave up. I've been in the phone book for thirty-one years. I think you can find me. It was kind of too bad because I thought we had a nice friendship going.

While I was performing for Mel, Channel 2 came into the showroom and shot a video. Don't ask me how they did it, but they blocked out shots with a single camera so that it looked like they actually had two cameras. They shut down and moved the camera for a millisecond and then took another position. I got to the end of a bit and while I rambled—where are you from, what do you do—the guy repositioned the tripod. It looked like I had a three-camera shoot, which at that time would cost $5,000. I was wearing a double-breasted blazer, gray slacks, and $150 Italian shoes. The whole twenty-two minutes was on that cassette, and they handed it to me.

I must have made $150,000 off that video. I milked it for all it was worth; it got me club dates for the next ten years.

Enter the Cruise Ships

On my first cruise ship job in 1983 I worked with Carme and comedy/magician Jac Hayden on the Sea Escape, a little daily Scandinavian Line cruise that left Miami for a day. We sailed to Freeport and Nassau in the Bahamas, made a u-turn and came back. We were in Freeport for four or five hours and back in port by five or six at night. Carme got me that job by referring me to the guy who was doing the booking.

I was on many of their little cruises, and then the owners bought a big, flat bottom, ocean-going auto freighter and called it the Scandinavia. It took cars from New York to Miami to Freeport in the Bahamas and back to New York, 300 or 400 on the lower decks. Even though it was a big ferry, everything was enclosed like a cruise ship, and the top levels had all the luxury accommodations and amenities for cruise passengers. Later on, the cruise director was my friend Kenny Laursen.

It was a weird triangulation. We picked up people in Miami, went to New York, came back and dropped them off, picked up new people, went to the Bahamas, back to Miami, and back to New York.

There were a lot of serious Hassidic Jews on there from New York to Miami Beach and along the way they got sick. They were throwing up because this thing was so rough. The minute we got out by Cape Hatteras that ship pitched and yawed and bounced and rolled. We had to tie the piano down. We had to tie the piano player down. People were flying through the air. Later they discontinued the cruise part of the run because it was so rough for the passengers.

I worked that gig for the better part of a year and a half, until one day Jim Teter said, "Why don't you come to work for Royal Caribbean? They don't have anybody as crazy as you are." He said he'd fix it with Robin Netscher. Robin, an Englishman and former trumpet player, had hired the bands for RCCL before they moved him up to entertainment director.

Jim Teter told Robin Netscher, "I'm going to have this guy come and talk to you. His name if Cork Proctor, and he's the most unique comic I've ever seen."

When I went to Robin's office, armed with the videotape of the Mel Tillis show, I took Luann with me. Robin immediately thought she was my girl-friend. "I've heard that you are somewhat of a roué," he said.

"No, this is my daughter, Luann."

He laughed. "Yeah, likely story."

"Louie, show him your driver's license."

She pulled out Luann Proctor, and he said, "Oh, it is your daughter."

"Yes, this is my kid. She's my buddy."

Robin took the videotape into the conference room. He took his shoes off, put his head back, and watched. Then he stopped the tape and said, "What was that line you did there where you got the laugh?" It was something silly that I can't remember now, but he kicked the tape out of the machine, turned to me and he said, "What dates would you have available?"

YES!

That's how I got the Royal Caribbean gig. For years I've told guys, don't do this over the phone. Get on the plane. Fly to Miami and get in the guy's face. I stayed with RCCL nine years. My money went up and down from $1,200 to $2,500 a week. With Kathy in college at San Diego State getting a master's degree in health administration, I needed the money. I didn't have a choice. If the money went to $1,200 I kept working for them.

How do we know the ship will come?

If Robin called and asked me to jump on a plane and go to San Juan, Puerto the next morning, I did it. RCCL paid the transportation. There were many, many casualties where the ship got lost or the plane didn't land on time. I once sat in the airport in San Juan, Puerto Rico for nine hours. American Eagle

My Mind is an Open Mouth: A Life Behind the Mic

couldn't get a co-pilot. Then they'd get a pilot, and the plane wouldn't run. I was only trying to go seventy-five miles to St. Thomas. You could spit from there. I could have taken a power boat for $100. When I missed that, I had to fly to Antigua on Liat Air. LIAT—leavin any time. The plane was doing fifty-foot crow hops, up and down. I said to the guy next to me, who was going to put a desalination plant on Antigua, "We're going to die."

We were terrified. We were drunk, and we didn't care. Get another drink. The girl kept saying, "That will be $4 for the drink."

"The way we're getting treated by the plane and the weather you should be paying us to drink."

We were flying on a small jet, a British plane with tipped-up wings. One motor was acting up. I did think we were going to die. When we landed in Antigua at 10:30 p.m., the rain was hurricaning so hard water was bouncing eighteen inches high off the tarmac. We got drenched deplaning.

Inside the terminal I had a huge beef with the Antigua authorities. This guy began with, "Do you have a plane ticket to go back to Miami?"

I said, "No, I'm not going back to Miami. I am boarding the *Nordic Prince* tomorrow morning at this dock right here."

He said, "Well, how do we know the ship will come?"

I said, "Well, how do we know the sun will rise? We assume that there will be a twelve-hour period of dark and then we'll have light. The ship comes here every week. You understand?" I was in his face now. "The *Nordic Prince*. We bring a lot of tourists here. We spend a lot of money here. Am I getting through to you?" I was getting mad.

He got indignant. "I don't know if I like your attitude."

"Well, I sure as hell don't like yours, and I'm tired of talking to you."

I picked up the phone right there and called Vere Wynter, RCCL's representative in Antigua. An Antiguan by birth, he had a permanent office there and lived on the island. "Vere, this guy's giving me so much shit, I can't handle it. We're going to go out in the alley and one of us is going to die. Can you come down here and straighten him out?"

"Let me talk to him," he said.

The guy got on the phone, and still he declared, "No, we can't do that. He doesn't have a round trip ticket."

What the guy was trying to do was boost me, so I made noise in the airport. I said loudly, so everyone could hear, "Do you want me to give you money? Is that what this is all about? I can give you money. I just need a couple of witnesses over here. Would you folks come over here? I'm going to give this guy a bribe so we can stop this pointless discussion. How much money will it take for me to get you to stop busting my balls?"

"Oh, it's not about that," he exclaimed. "It's about the rules."

I leaned in close and hissed, "Let me go. The plane was late. I'm tired. I want to go have dinner. I've been in Puerto Rico nine hours. Have you ever been off this island? I fly all over the world and nobody bothers me. These are my papers. This is my passport. This is my ship ID card. I'm boarding the *Nordic Prince* tomorrow."

He finally let me go.

At that time I'd been with RCCL for four or five years and we weren't supposed to use more than $25 for dinner. I thought, bullshit, after that ride. I went in to the restaurant and asked the waiter, "Is the kitchen closed?"

"Oh, no, mon, you've got ten minutes."

"I want the biggest steak you have in the freezer," I said, "and I want it cooked raw, and I want onions on the side, and I want sliced tomatoes, and I want the biggest baked potato on this island, with sour cream, and I'm going to leave you the biggest tip you've ever seen in your life."

"Will there be something to drink?" he asked.

"There better be, my man. Start bringing that wine out." I had the best $100 dinner. I bloated myself.

Antigua is a beautiful island and Halcyon Cove was a great place. I loved the little violin frogs. There must have been eight million of them going *beep, beep, beep* all night long. Finally, I zoned out. I got up the next morning and felt like I'd slept thirty-five hours. I took a walk on the beach, zapped, and excited to finally board the *Nordic Prince* as scheduled.

Trouble in Paradise

Trouble in the Caribbean happened a lot. One time, Mexicana Airlines went down, and we had to travel from Playa Del Carmen, across from Cozumel, eight miles to Cancun in a van that I wouldn't put my dog in. I could look down and see the road through the floorboards. It wasn't all romance out there working the cruise ships. The risk was trying to get around from point A to point B and not missing the plane, and now it's a bitch because of customs and security. Entertaining was easy. The travel was hard work. I was exhausted when I got home.

Jackie Curtiss said, "They don't pay us to entertain; they pay us to travel."

But I had the best of both worlds. I could come back to Vegas and grab a month in a lounge or two weeks or sub for somebody. I was making good money, having fun. It was a whole new vehicle for me because I had not worked that level of cruise ship. Royal Caribbean was a great line. The ice carvings were gorgeous. The midnight buffet with the peanut sauce sautes and all the chefs dressed like Chinamen was world class.

One trip, I was sailing on the *Nordic Prince* out of Miami with a singer from Detroit, Bob Francis. He was six feet tall and huge, 325 pounds, so we nicknamed him, "Fluffy." We had worked together on different ships, and this time we were at the outdoor deck bar watching a lot of Canadians board, checking out the girls and waiting for the ship to sail. Also with us was impressionist Joey Van.

We had to be on board by 4:30 p.m. before the ship sailed at 5:00, but we'd been at the bar since 3 p.m. We were shit-faced drunk because none of us were scheduled to work that night.

"We should do something unusual today," I said.

"Now don't get us in trouble," Joey said. "I know you."

"We're not going to get in trouble. Let's go down and visit those Canadians."

We left the bar and went down to B deck, and in the hallways we could smell the cigarettes and Crown Royal. The Canadians were off to a good start, too. We heard screams and laughter and glasses clinking from two cabins across the hall from each other. Twenty Canadians partying their asses off, chain-smoking—a cloud of smoke.

We greeted them and heard, "Come on in. Have a drink? How ya doing? Where ya from?"

I said, "We've come to sing some Negro spirituals for you."

The guy turned to his wife and said, "Did you hear that, Mother? The boys are going to sing a Negro spiritual!" He turned back to me and said, "In Canada, we don't hear a lot of Negro spirituals."

Walking down the hall, we'd rehearsed this so we got close enough with the harmony. We sounded pretty professional. Bob did a "hmmmmmm" to get us tuned and we began, low and slow ...

"In the evenin' by the moonlight, you can hear those darkies singin'—mother fucker, mother fucker, mother fucker."

Those Canadians must have laughed for three minutes solid. One woman laughed so hard she literally fell off the bed, which generated a new round of drunken laughter.

Our new friend, when he stopped howling, asked, "Is that a real song?"

"If you want it to be," I said.

He nodded, "Well, that was really good."

When we left the cabin Bob Francis said, "It's over; we're going to get fired."

Joey looked at me and shook his head. "I might as well call my old lady and tell her I'll be off at the next port."

I said, "Naw, they're so drunk they don't know who we are, and they're not going to remember us. Watch, there won't be anything. First of all, they are so drunk when you come out on stage, they're just gonna think, have I seen that guy before?"

Not a word on the comment cards at the end of the week. God bless those Canadians.

Bermuda Run

For years I worked RCCL's *Song of Norway*, which went from New York to Bermuda. First day at sea and the second day we would tie up at St. George on the windward side of the island. We would be there overnight, and the next day dock right on Front Street in Hamilton, the capital city. Passengers and entertainers, if they weren't working that night, could depart the ship in

St. George and meet it the next day in Hamilton if they wanted. But not the crew; the crew didn't get to do shit.

Bermuda is 640 miles off the coast of New York and is not part of the Bahamas. People get them confused. Bermuda is all by itself and is still an English principality. The island is only seven miles long, and there are little jitneys, little water taxis, that take you around. There are great bars and places to hang out, pink sand beaches. I enjoyed walking the old Railway trail. There's not much crime because the criminals can't get off the island. The cops are all hired from Trinidad and Tobago, because the locals, who all know each other, don't want to be cops and have to arrest their own families. The government only allowed thirty-eight people to migrate a year and you could only have one car per house. You couldn't walk around with your shirt off, either. This was not your casual beach island.

I tried to do that run eight, ten, twelve weeks a year because it's such a great place. I would have one thirty-minute show going to Bermuda and one thirty-minute show for the same audience coming back. Wasn't that sweet?

Later when the *Nordic Prince* made the run from New York to Bermuda and back I worked on it, too. Sometimes I'd bounce around. I'd try to do the Bermuda run in the summer because it was such a beautiful island.

Hand Grenade Ad Lib

I was on the run to Bermuda, and all the guests were having a great time. I was making friends with a lot of people. I invited everybody to come see my show. One guy I chatted up had a visible zipper scar and wore a medic alert bracelet. His wife had a gravelly voice like Selma Diamond. She said, "He had open heart surgery."

That night, standing at the bar, getting ready to do the show, I saw them come in, wave hello, and sit ringside.

So in the show, microphone in hand, I walked over to them and said, "Well, sir, I can see you had open heart surgery."

"Yeah," he said, "but I'm doing okay."

I held the mic before his wife, who was chain-smoking, and said, "How's it going?"

Gravelly voice says, "He's doing fine."

"Looks he has a medic alert bracelet on." I swear to God, I don't know where this came from, but I raised his arm with the bracelet so 400 people could see it and said, "Look what his medic alert bracelet says." I peered closely at it. "Give. Me. Head. Until. I'm. Dead."

Hand grenade-scale laughter. When the show was over, the cruise director, Gene Cook, gave me a piercing look. "I didn't think you were going to work that strong."

I shrugged. "Did you hear that laugh?" Undoubtedly one of the best ad-libs I ever did in my life.

Cruising Women

Sometimes I was out in the western Caribbean for months at a time. On some of the better ships, even though it was down on B or C or D deck, there were still nice cabins. If I was making two grand a week, I could save a bunch. If you're cautious, don't gamble, drink or smoke, you don't spend much money. Many times somebody would buy the entertainers drinks. Sometimes I would be sitting drinking Stoli and some widow would introduce herself and say, "My husband died and I own Pete's Pawn Shop in Phoenix and can I buy you a drink?" Sure, whatever.

I met ladies who wanted to have an affair. But I wasn't that good with one-nighters on the ship. I worried because I saw a lot of women having sex with waiters who were bisexual. I thought, do I want to participate in that? I know guys who rolled that dice and have been lucky. But I saw how it worked. A widow with money, out on the romantic high seas with everybody fawning over her. The waiters would say, "Oh, you're the most beautiful thing in the world." She was an easy victim, and next she'd be coming out of some gay guy's cabin. I'm not saying that everybody does this—I'm not castigating passengers—but I saw a great deal of capricious activity. Once I told a married woman who'd been fucking a gay waiter that she might want to slip in to the doctor as soon as she got home, before she did her husband. I thought she should be prepared if she went home with a bug. What?! She went straight into shock.

But we'd have fun watching the women. It was common practice among the staff, many of whom were there to greet the passengers, but in reality to check out the women. Often Smitty, the bar manager, and I would stand, drinks in hand, at the rail with the executive chef and rate them—one to ten—as they boarded. "See the blond with the big red shoes," Smitty would say, "She'll be with me tonight." I never thought too seriously about it. I figured that, hey, if it happens, it happens.

And of course, it was risky. There was a rule that if you took a passenger down to your cabin, you were done.

The Ticket Game

When RCCL built *The Song of America*, I worked on it a week after the inaugural. I got asked to stay an extra week because the comic got sick. I was pretty flexible even though I lived 3,000 miles away from Miami. They would send me a ticket at the last minute. The FedEx guy would knock on the door at 8 p.m., and the red-eye would leave from Vegas six hours later, at two in the morning.

In the old airport where American Airlines was located, on the north side of McCarran, I had a friend named Rosemary who taught me how to work the tickets.

"Why don't you go ahead and book this fare two or three months out for $229 round trip," she'd say, "and then when they send you the last-minute $600 ticket, you bring it to me and I roll it over, and we give you more tickets."

"I like you, Rosemary." I would see her frequently, and we got a book exchange thing going.

What she was suggesting wasn't illegal. I would know in advance I was going, but the company would do the stupidest thing in the world—wait until the last minute to buy the ticket, then pay FedEx $20 to deliver it.

I probably got five, ten thousand dollars worth of free flights with American. I brought everybody out to the ship as my guest. I took twenty-one people as guests—Leo Lewis, piano player and conductor Andy Thomas, Tony Becker, John Meyer, a number of beautiful women, including Carolyn.

Both daughters got to go to Bermuda and the Caribbean several times. It was years before Royal Caribbean finally figured out the ticket deal.

What to do with a bad audience?

RCCL used to go to Montego Bay, Jamaica until the drugs got bad. The Jamaicans would hustle us getting off the ship so finally the company decided they didn't want to go there. They also stopped going to Santo Domingo in the Dominican Republic because people were given cavity searches at the airport. When they popped a cavity search on comedian J.C. Curtiss, he called Royal Caribbean, and they flew him immediately back to Miami and gave him a complete physical. About the next day, they stopped going to the Dominican Republic.

J. C. made it into a comedy bit: There are three silhouettes on the wall. The first picture is a guy standing with a briefcase and a hat and a suit. Second picture, the guy is naked. Third picture, the guy is bent over and there is an officer behind him with what looks like, well, we don't know what he's got. They say 'ding, ding, ding, which door do you want; one, two or three?'

With some of these island people, it's almost like the twelfth century, BC. We were bringing in a cruise ship with millions of dollars of potential sales, and they were giving our people rectal exams? I wanted to say, *What are you doing? You're stupid.*

Besides RCCL, I worked for NCL, Norwegian Cruise Lines. I did the Maya Magic run once, a jazz cruise with all black passengers. There was a lady sitting in the front row with bilious green hair. She'd been screwing with her hair and then jumped in the pool, and the chlorine turned it green. I leaned over and said, "Yo, mama, who be doin' your do-rag?" That didn't go over too well; boy, was she mad. That wasn't one of my good weeks, but quite honestly, they weren't a great audience.

When you bomb on a cruise, man, there is nowhere to go. You go to your cabin, and you open Jack Daniels. I would always try to analyze what I did wrong. Usually, it wasn't me.

One time on the *Song of America* I had a bunch of reborn Christians in the audience. I said, "What does Jimmy Swaggart know? A man trying to have

My Mind is an Open Mouth: A Life Behind the Mic

sex in a Corvette. He doesn't even know that it's not physically possible to do that in that car."

A guy came up and grabbed the mic out of my hand. "You will be taken to task," he announced. "God will punish you for this."

I didn't say anything. It was scary because he was a pretty big guy. I was afraid he was going to punch me with the mic. I raised my arm in a defensive block, prepared, ready with a four-knuckle punch. Then he handed me back the mic and walked away. I continued to do another fifteen or eighteen minutes. At the end of the show I apologized to the audience for "the gentleman." They booed him. He didn't realize that others on the ship didn't share his views.

Next day I was scheduled to get off the ship in San Juan, Puerto Rico. Before departing I was sitting in the office with the ship's manager, and we were having coffee with a little cognac in it.

"Don't worry about that guy," he said. "He came to my cabin and complained that you were blaspheming God. I said, 'No he wasn't. I was in the back of the bar drinking and smoking and having sex with a woman'." He faced him off.

Before I left, a woman said to me, "Mr. Proctor, I want to apologize for that man who was in the depths of Hell and worked his way back to Christian spirituality, and now God is everything to him. He didn't hear what you said. We heard what you said. We know you were setting it up about all these wretched TV evangelists, all of whom are in the American pocket. There are 200 of us on here, and the majority thought you were funny." It was gratifying to hear.

Hurricane Bob

RCCL had been warned that Hurricane Bob had come up the coast after hitting Florida and was now between New York and Bermuda, but the *Nordic Prince* sailed out of New York anyway so they wouldn't have to pay additional port rental fees.

We'd hardly passed the Verrazano-Narrows Bridge when the weather got rough. Soon we were sailing in twelve- to fifteen-foot swells. Billy Fellows and I stayed down in the crew quarters drinking while the ship rocked 'n rolled.

Passengers took their blankets and bedding up on deck because they all knew about the *Titanic*. It was a miserable goddamned night. We barely missed that hurricane. When we arrived in St. George, our first port in Bermuda, a bunch of people got off and made arrangements to fly home. The company gave all the passengers a free cruise.

Leaving New York in the first place after being warned about Hurricane Bob was a foolish move. If the ship lost power and went sideways in twenty-five-foot waves, we'd have gone down. They could have lost everybody.

Changes in the Cruise Biz

Toward the end of my years with RCCL, I got into an issue with the company over cabin status and passenger privileges that pissed me off. I did a good job for RCCL. I never let them down. In nine years, I never cancelled or was late or pulled a no-show. And now they wouldn't give me full passenger status where I could go on and off the passenger gangway with my guest. There I was with Carolyn, a beautiful woman all dressed to the nines going down the crew gangway, through the shit shoot, the garbage offramp below. It made me mad.

I said, "Wait a minute, you give other guys passenger status. Look how long I've been here. What's the problem?"

They said Carolyn could go off as a passenger, but I had to now go off as "crew." All the cruise staff deferred it; nobody could make a decision to change it. It was all about power. If I really kissed ass, the cruise director would say, "Oh, okay, you can go off the passenger gangway."

"What difference does it make?" I asked.

"You're crew."

"Okay, I'm crew, so what? Is the captain the crew?"

"Yes."

"Does he go off the gangway through the garbage shoot? I don't think so."

"Well, he's the captain."

"That has nothing to do with it. He's in the crew. Make sense for me here, wizard. Tell me what's going on."

They had the power, and logic didn't win the argument.

Sometimes they would change my schedule. Sometimes they would call it Adult Night Comedy, or Late Night Comedy. Then I could say this, but I couldn't say that. I understand that now there is a great deal of crudeness out there where entertainers can actually say hard core words. When I was out there, we couldn't do that. It was taboo. When I did it, it was infrequent and I got away with it, but it wasn't supposed to be. I got away with it because I was old, had some maturity and was long of tooth, but otherwise, the young guys couldn't do that because it was too flippy-dippy. People got offended when a young guy got crude. If it's in context and it's funny, nobody ever got mad.

I had nine great years. When I finally got into a beef, it was time to go anyway.

On the *Nordic Prince* to Bermuda I had a run-in with a twelve-year-old fat kid. On the formal night, this kid in the audience jumped into the middle of my bit about how lowly-paid teachers are for what they do. He yelled, "We don't need no stinkin' teachers!"

I trounced him. "You ain't got no stinkin' grammar, neither. Stand up and let's see you." He stood, everyone looked at him, and I said, "First thing we have to do is put you on a diet."

After the show his mother approached me at the bar. "You mortified my son," she said.

"He mortified himself when he heckled me," I told her. "Besides, he shouldn't have been in the room. Now go away before I say something I'll regret."

At the end of a cruise the company holds a drawing for every guest who fills out a comment card, with the winning name getting a logo ashtray or some silly thing. At the end of that week I got twenty-one bad comments for picking on that little boy.

The verbiage in the comment cards that week was so similar it was obvious the fat boy's mother told other people what to write. That boy's ass shouldn't have been in that showroom, anyway. It wasn't about vulgarity or adult material; it was a late night show that advertised no children. If there are children, they have to be eighteen and with a parent. The cruise director was there, and he should have said something. Eighty percent of that problem was his fault. And do you know what that fat kid's last name was? Rotunda.

That was my last cruise, in 1992. I didn't want to do it anymore. I lost the heart for it. It was time to go. It was a drag for Carolyn because I had taken her on her first-ever cruise, but I just couldn't do it anymore. It got too gay, with too many people in authority. I felt like I was doing the same thing over and over again and not getting any cooperation or support from the staff. I'll go to my grave saying if I had issues out there, part of it was because of the cruise staff not doing their job. If there is a sign over the door in the showroom that says "Formal Night," it means formal night. It doesn't mean come in Levis, cut-offs and a tee shirt that says "shit happens." I understand from friends who still work out there that the ships have cheapened the buffets, cheapened everything. They have whored out the standards on the ships so far that all they are interested in is how much are you going to drop in the casino? And how much is your bar bill? And how much can we automatically charge you for tips? The days of sophisticated cruising are now relegated to maybe the Crystal Harmony and the QE2. I never worked those.

Fun and Games at Lake Tahoe

For the month of March 1984 I was booked into the lounge at Del Webb's High Sierra in Stateline, Nevada. It had been open since 1965 as the Sahara Tahoe and the year before had been "westernized" and given the High Sierra name. Ed Nigro was the manager.

For the first two weeks the group appearing opposite me in the lounge was a progressive bluegrass band called New Grass Revival, featuring banjo player Béla Fleck. They had a million-selling record at the time, "Sinister Minister." Béla invited me to sit in and play brushes, which I enjoyed. After they left, Country Jazz Singer and songwriter Freddie Powers came in. He played guitar and sang on Willie Nelson's 1978 album "Stardust," and 1981 album "Somewhere Over the Rainbow." I'd known Freddie for years; we used to get high together.

Freddie and Willie and Merle Haggard were buddies. Once Freddie brought Merle to sit in. They were doing all those old Hank Williams and

Hank Penny songs and having a great time. Merle had on a white suit and a little hat like Charlie Chan. He came in for three nights till some idiot publicist wrote it up in the paper. Merle didn't want any recognition; he just wanted to have fun, so that was that.

But one of the nights we were all back in the dressing room, half-smashed on Heinekens. The door burst open and a guy came in, all excited. "Merle," he said, "there's a guy out there that was in the joint with you. He's got every album you ever made, you know; he just has to meet you."

Merle Haggard pushed back his little Charlie hat, looked at the guy and said, "I believe I've met all the people I care to." Guess Merle didn't have the energy to go out and shake the guy's hand and talk about shit they did in prison.

In the lounge a drummer and piano player were behind me, and I wasn't doing a lot of jokes. I was saying, "Come on in. Where are you from?" I had a few good nights, but not what I should have had. It never clicked. I scored pretty well because there were a lot of girls there, but I didn't do well professionally. I don't know why. I've never figured it out.

On one of my days off I was in the pit, playing 21, when this beautiful woman wearing a gorgeous beige pantsuit walked through the pit. I knew Joe, the pit boss, and asked him, "What's her name?"

"Carol. She's the shift supervisor."

"Well, you can tell her that from my perspective she's got the best-looking ass I've seen in years."

So he went over and whispered in her ear, and she smiled. Then she came over to say hello.

"Can we have drink when you get off?" I asked.

She smiled again. "Sure."

We went to the Blackout Bar and had a few hot buttered rums. She was wearing gold hoop earrings. I said to her, "Beautiful earrings." Then I looked her right in the eye and asked, "If my cock is as big as the circumference of your earrings, would you be interested in getting it on?"

I was staying there, courtesy of the hotel, and she came to my room. While I took a shower, she did a few lines of cocaine and took her clothes off. When

I came out of the bathroom with a huge woody, I had her earring on the end of my cock.

Opening for Eddie Raven

On New Year's Eve week I opened for Louisiana's Cajun country and blues singer Eddie Raven—Edward Garvin Futch—at the Reno Hilton. He was a big country star who had written hits for himself and other country artists.

That weekend Reno had the worst snowstorm and fog in history, and the airport was closed. I found myself working to forty people when there should have been 1,000. Henry Lewin's son, a nice young man, was running that Hilton. He said to me, "Don't feel bad."

I'd wanted to bring my current (very young) girlfriend up from Vegas because I had a suite as part of the deal. She couldn't even get out of Vegas. I asked her if she would take a bus. She said, "No, I'm not doing that." Okay.

Eddie Raven was a great guy. I had known him when he was on a rock 'n roll band in Elko in the sixties, and I mentioned it.

"You remember?"

I said, "God, Eddie, how long has it been?"

"Twenty years."

Roasting Chuck Yeager

In 1985 in Las Vegas there was a roast of Chuck Yeager to raise money for Angel Flight. There were 1000 people in the Judy Garland room at the MGM, all guys. Besides me, the roasters were Joey Villa, Pete Barbutti, Carl Waxman, and a comedian from the Pacific Northwest, Mike Nuen. We had all read the book, *Yeager*.

Chuck Yeager, the ultimate fighter pilot, flew everything. He flew a plane called the Dassault over the Orly French Air Force facility and commercial base at 700 miles per hour. He stood it on its nose and went up two, three miles, laid it over on its back and made a loop.

The French designer said, "That is impossible. That plane cannot do that."

Yeager had been raised on a farm where his father said, "Never run the engine wide open." So Yeager would come back with the plane all shot up, the motor with holes in it, and when they went out to fix them, they couldn't believe that the plane was still running. But see, he never stressed it, never tried to fly it as fast as he could.

The audience for the roast was all guys, with some pretty heavy hitters. Yeager's wing man, Bob Hoover, was there. Harry Wald from Caesars and Bill Creech, a guy who started out as a buck private and wound up a general.

Some great stories were told. When Yeager was on temporary duty, he was the first guy to break the speed of sound in a little X1 Rocket. It had a six-volt battery in it, and the engineer who was working with him said, "Chuck, we ought to put a discharge valve in here, because we have this special fluid in here for the little jet plane, and God forbid if anything happened to the little rocket"—it had wings like a bumble bee—"then you've got to get rid of all this fluid."

So right behind Chuck's head they put a garden hose valve and guess what? The next flight out in a B25 he hit the ignition switch and nothing. So, there he was with a full load of fuel in this little sled. He had to keep the nose up and circle long enough to dump it.

"I had some tense moments," he said.

But the guys in the audience apparently had not read *Yeager*. We're doing jokes about the first woman to break the speed of sound, Jacqueline Cochran, and we asked Chuck if he balled her.

"Were you up there getting head from Jacqueline while she was breaking the speed of sound?"

When he stood to rebut our roast remarks he said, "You guys did your homework."

After the roast he wrote me a nice thank-you note.

The Shrouded Lounge

In his Friday, March 1, 1985, *Las Vegas Review-Journal* column, Bill Willard called me, "The fastest mouth in the west" and wrote: "Practicing his diablerie nightly at the Mint. In the Merrimint Lounge. 'You're probably wondering what I'm going to do up here to try and entertain you. I'm wondering the same thing,' he says. 'If I do well here, I don't have to go back to the Union Plaza.'"

I had opened twice nightly in the Merrimint Theatre of Del Webb's Mint Casino & Hotel in downtown Las Vegas.

The *Vegas Visitor* also ran a blurb: "This comedic madman shows no mercy when it comes to his audiences, as they become very willing victims of his hilarious jabs."

The contract was through March 12, but the audience was almost nonexistent. It had nothing to do with me. Around the lounge was a curtain from the floor all the way to the ceiling and a little entry with a maitre'd but no signage. If you didn't know and you were timid and didn't ask, you'd never find it. The majority of people walking through the casino passed it. There were people who actually came down there, couldn't find the lounge, turned around, and went home.

Art Engler booked that disaster, but the money was great, three grand a week. The biggest crowd I ever had was a night when Sam Butera came in with his whole band. They were appearing across the street at the Four Queens, and I knew Sam from my 1950s lifeguard days at the Sahara. So we had fun that evening.

After I left, funny piano man Danny Marona came in and he didn't do well either. I knew one of the sound guys and he told me that nobody did well in that shrouded lounge. You can't do your act if nobody is there. You've got to have people, man; you can't rehearse comedy.

Garbage Dumping in the Cruise Ship Industry

For two weeks that summer I worked the *StarShip Royale*, which was the old Federico "C," out of Port Canaveral, Florida. This was Disney's first experiment in the cruise industry, and they called it *The Big Red Boat*.

As we were leaving Nassau on Sunday the air conditioning went out, and they couldn't get it to work. It was 100 degrees and 100 percent humidity. Off the Bahamas in broad daylight they were throwing big brown trash bags off the ass end of the ship. I was back there at the Sundae Bar with 500 passengers, watching this and trying to chill.

My Mind is an Open Mouth: A Life Behind the Mic

That night I went on stage and said, "Hey, did you see that today? They are making a movie, 'The Loch Ness Monster Comes to the Bahamas!'" All those bags together looked like Nessy.

After my show a cruise staff guy told me, "You shouldn't have said that."

"You shouldn't have been dumping that garbage in broad daylight."

Not long after that the cruise ships started to get fined if they were caught dumping garbage like that. RCCL got a $50,000 fine. They were supposed to take the garbage back to Miami or leave it at an island where it could be disposed of correctly. Those thousands of plastic wrappers are killing the fish. The undoing of garbage dumping in the cruise ship industry was the video camera. Passengers started videotaping the dumping of trash at three o'clock in the morning. They'd take it to the maritime authorities. Even though the ships are licensed out of the country, they are still subject to maritime laws.

That incident kept me from getting hired again on *The Big Red Boat*. I didn't want to go back there anyway.

The Writing on the Wall

I got an idea to run an ad in the Las Vegas newspaper to get myself a steady lounge job at home. I wrote, "COMEDIAN Big local following, tired of road, wants steady work at home. Will also promote & market, flexible. Reply Review-Journal Box X0053" and ran it July 30th in the *Las Vegas Review-Journal*.

Not one phone call.

Disappointed, I thought, something is going on in this town. The writing was on the wall, as we say. I'd had a good run in Vegas. Over fifteen years working up and down the Strip. Wait a minute, isn't my audience still alive? Don't they still go out? I guess a lot of them got older and weren't drinking anymore and didn't go out.

I thought somebody would call and say, hey, I'm looking for a guy.

The Landmark with the Unknown Comic

Then August 2nd, I went into the Empire Showroom at the Landmark for a month. Our show consisted of me, comedy/magician Fielding West and Murray Langston, the Unknown Comic who wore a paper bag over his head.

Kelly Stevens had the band. Mickey Finn had his show at the Landmark at the same time and produced ours to work back-to-back with him. He did two and we did two.

I was quoted in a newspaper column: "All three of us are getting along great, which is unusual when you put three guys who are half nuts together."

Of the three of us, Murray closed. He was funny, doing every traditional old joke in the world, but he's a pro. He easily got the audience on his side.

Closing night Murray got mad at me because I stayed on an extra ten or fifteen minutes. It's kind of traditional on the last night to screw off, and he knew how I worked. He was backstage screaming, "When is he going to get off?"

I said, "Okay, I'm leaving."

Next time I saw him I asked, "What were you mad about?"

"Well, I had to be somewhere."

"So what? It's not life or death," I said. "Where are you going at 11:30 at night? You got a club date?"

Of course he didn't. He wanted to get back to L.A. and get laid. That's the simple truth. Drive eighty miles an hour to get some of that good booty.

Lee Greenwood

In the 1970s Lee Greenwood appeared in Las Vegas at the Stardust. He was funny, part of the group Frankie Carr and the Novelites, doing comedic bits and doing them really well. After I saw the show he came out and I introduced myself and told him how funny he was. We had a drink together and mostly talked about divorce.

I followed his career. After he left the Novelites, he went into the Lord Byron Room at the Tropicana, where he worked for about a year as a single. During that time we spent a lot of time hanging out together. After that he moved to Nashville so he could have a career. He wanted to be a songwriter. When he left we shook hands, and said to each other, "If I can every help you I will."

Ten years later he called. I was surprised to hear from him, but it was like no time had passed.

My Mind is an Open Mouth: A Life Behind the Mic

"Do you want to go with me to Harrah's in Reno?" he asked.

Well, sure.

"Three thousand a week plus room food and beverage."

Yes!

We had a great week. But it almost didn't happen. Three days before the opening, on the way to Nevada, his two busses got into a terrible accident. He and his son, who was playing drums for him, got on a plane and flew into Reno. Lee was rattled when he got there. "We had a near-death experience," he said. Luckily nobody got killed, but his son had broken his foot. Still, he played those drums.

Lee Greenwood's "God Bless the USA" had just been out a few months and was already the biggest record in America. Every time he sang that song he got standing ovations. I bought him a beautiful pair of horsehide boots and a belt buckle as a thank you.

That week and the one with Mel Tillis were the two best jobs of my entire career.

Lee called me when I was in *Caribbean Carnival* in Valley Forge and asked me to go to Greenland with him for a Christmas show. I told him I couldn't get out of the contract. I wouldn't do that to Greg.

Lee Greenwood still always sends word through somebody that he says "hi."

The Meatball Festival

The Annual Meatball Festival in September was a fundraiser for Opportunity Village, a well-established Las Vegas charity that sells secondhand clothing and furniture and provides jobs for mentally-challenged people. Linda Smith, the foundation associate executive director, put it together with chef Jack Sheridan who managed the Vineyard Restaurant in the Boulevard Mall on Maryland Parkway. The Vineyard had a homey Italian atmosphere, and the soup was great. It was popular with Vegas locals.

For three or four years I emceed the Meatball Festival. The county would give us a trailer with a tilt-down stage for the parking lot. It went on all day, with thirty bands coming and going on that stage. When there was down time, I'd get up and do some time. I'd introduce people in the crowd. Jack

Sheridan, who has a good sense of humor, would dress up as a giant meatball and call himself, "Mr. Meatball."

But it was perceived value; the people in the crowd didn't pay anything, so they didn't care. They walked through with a baby, pushing a stroller, having a hot dog, eating an ice cream cone, not even going to applaud. But the idea was to make everybody aware of Opportunity Village and the good work they do, and the Meatball Festival did that. Opportunity Village is still my favorite charity.

"Giggles and Yocks" at the Marina

I wanted to do a late night comedy thing and Bill Willard came up with the name, "Giggles and Yocks." I brought Jeff Wayne and Kelly McDonald from L.A. to work with me.

Bob Brooker agreed to put us into the room at the Marina. At the end of the first week, when we didn't immediately draw, Brooker let us go. It was too premature. My God, it takes a while to generate a flow and a following. The Marina was a turkey. It never did great business, which is why it kept changing management from Brooker to this guy to that guy. I think there were two or three sets of owners, but Bob stayed there as manager for a long time.

The Toyota Cash Bash

From 1979 to 1986 I worked the annual Toyota Cash Bash at the Desert Inn Country Club for Floridian Jim Moran, one of the biggest car dealers in the world. He had Toyota stores everywhere. American Booking Corporation (ABC) entertainment agent Art Engler, who never even knew what I did, got me the job.

Moran had the idea to give the salesmen an incentive: if you sell four cars over our quota, you get to go to Vegas and participate in the "Cash Bash." Depending on how many cars over the quota he sold, the salesman got to pull a number of tabs off of a big tote board that lined the whole stage. They called them "pulls," and the salesman could pick his pulls from anywhere on the board. A man with a basket followed him to collect his pulls. Behind one pull might be as much as $15,000. The salesman and the basket man would then go to their own cashier, where the salesman would be paid the total of his pulls in cash. Brinks guys armed with shotguns stood everywhere.

The guys lined up, waiting to get up on stage. One guy would be so hot, he might have thirty pulls.

In between pulls I did joke, joke, joke, wait, joke, joke, joke, wait. It was like working a speed bag as a boxer. There was such a frenzy over the money that I had a little whistle I sometimes used to get their attention. I used every joke I'd ever heard, but there were women there so I worked pretty clean.

I started at one in the afternoon and didn't finish until 5:30 p.m. I was on that stage all that time by myself, no music. For this they paid me $3,000.

The Cash Bash was so successful that Toyota people came from Japan to watch, to see how it worked.

The last year I was to do the Cash Bash, Toyota changed the date at the last minute, and Art Engler neglected to tell me. I was out walking around with Murray, a banjo player from the ships, and decided to take him to meet Engler.

We walked into the agent's office. Engler said, "Where have you been?"

"What do you mean where have I been?" I said. "This guy came to town from Miami and we're out walking around."

"Today's the Cash Bash!"

"No," I said. "That's next week."

"No, they moved it."

They got magician Johnny Thompson—The Great Tomsoni—and his wife/assistant, Pam, to work the Cash Bash. He did every trick he had, cut the rope, comedy magic. John said he never worked that hard in his life.

But I had "burned" them, and it killed the job for me.

By the end of 1986, Art Engler had left American Booking Corporation and started his own independent booking office. In January, I received a 1099 from ABC. In all the years I did the Cash Bash I had never gotten one, and now I knew why.

The 1099 showed that I'd been paid $4,500 for the Cash Bash. Engler had been stealing money off the top. They'd probably given him the 1099s to pass on to me, and he threw them away.

I marched into his office in my cowboy boots, waving the 1099. "Mr. Engler, perhaps you'd care to explain this."

I towered over him, and he pushed himself back from the desk.

"Look, man, I don't mind that you took some extra, but you ruined our relationship. You cheapened it."

The look on his face told me he thought I was going to pull him over the desk and bitch slap him.

I'd assumed he'd been making a standard ten or fifteen percent commission. "Why would you do that, Art? You got a Cadillac, a pinky ring. I know you're cheap, but you didn't have to do that." I railed on. "All you had to do was say, Cork, I'm going to take a little more because I'm getting you more money."

I told him I was sorry I'd defended him so many times. People had told me he was a schmuck and a thief and I'd always said, "No, he isn't."

As I stomped out of his office I said, "Now I know they were right. I hope you feel good about it."

Sizzle at the Sands

Dick Francisco put a music/comedy mini-revue he called *Sizzle* into the Copa Room at the Sands. Besides me, he hired vocalist Phyllis Kelly, impressionists Babe Pier, and Kenny Cornell, who had been one of the original Jesters. Kenny, a funny guy visually, could make great faces and sort of swallow his jaw. Phyllis Kelly, a former Miss Louisiana with a beautiful smile, looked like "Wonder Woman" Lynda Carter.

Nine dancer/singers, choreography by Betsy Haug, $9.95 minimum. My money was $2,500 a week for three shows, six nights a week. That's eighteen times you're on stage in a week—a lot of time.

Tom Willer, the marketing director, hated me and tried to get me fired out of *Sizzle*.

Dick told him, "Tom, I call Cork my buffet comic. If you don't like the fruit bowl, he'll give you the dessert. If you don't like that, he'll give you the entrée, and if you don't like that, he'll give you soda. Go find me a guy who will work for this kind of money, is that good, shows up on time, knows his shit, knows how to talk to the audience, and I'll hire him. You bring me a guy like that and I'll put him in here for the night, and you come watch him. If we agree on that, I'll get rid of Cork."

Willer kept bringing Dick tapes of guys who swore in their acts. You couldn't do that in the show. I would insinuate a few things, but never that bad.

In order to get the job in *Sizzle*, I had to sign a waiver that said I would not, in any of my performances, mention Sands owner Howard Hughes, the Sands Corporation, Summa, any of its employees from the valet attendant to the gardener in the back, and if I did any of those things, I'd be fired immediately.

So each night on stage I would make jokes about it. "You know, I have a contract. I can't say anything bad about the joint. So, as far as I'm concerned, it's great." I'd leave it at that, and the audience would giggle. "You think I'm making it up. I'm not making it up. I have in my contract a rider that says if I step over the line, I'm out."

Wednesday, March 19, 1986, *Variety* said, "Proctor does twenty minutes … he has to avoid harpooning the tender execs, it's in his contract."

On press night, in the middle of my act the fire alarm went off. We already had the MGM Grand fire, and I can tell you when that alarm went off, all those press agents, notables, and other comped guys were scared to death. It didn't happen when the dancers were out there, it didn't happen when the juggler was out there. Nooo, when the comic came out, the fire alarm went off.

I had a glass of wine in my hand, and I wasn't even nervous. "You guys relax," I said. I figured everybody was overreacting. I didn't know til later that a guy with sociological problems named Thomas Little Owl lit a room on fire in the tower.

All these people in the audience knew each other, and the press was known for their proclivity for eating, drinking, and stiffing the waitresses. Sig Sakowicz, a heavy former *Chicago Sun-Times* columnist who was a huge eater and stiffed a lot of guys, was there that night. He had a local Las Vegas TV show and sometimes he wouldn't even go to the shows. Some guy would call him and say, "The girls are great and they had big costumes," and that would become his review.

I made a sort of sing-along sound with the fire alarm and said, "Folks, you know what that means—that means Sig Sakowicz just went through the buffet line for the third time."

At the end of the run, cast and crew were wringing their hands thinking, boy, he's going to crap on everybody tonight. I never said a word other than, "It's been great, thank you, Dick. I love you for giving me a chance to work and do what I do the best, which is be funny."

That night I called Remington Steele, my favorite Dobie puppy, on stage with me. He was gunmetal gray, so I'd named him "Steele" after the TV show. I'd been making jokes in the show about the puppies my Doberman had just given birth to. "Nine puppies," I said, "and after three weeks, the bitch, Raja, stopped feeding them, so I have to do it." I'd put a hand to my chest. "And boy, my nipples are sore."

Gray dobies are rare, and Steele was a bright little dog. The very young girlfriend was holding him in the wings, and I was talking into the mic when I called his name. He looked up because he could see the speakers and he thought I was in the ceiling. Then I put the mic down and called him. She set him down, he came running out, and I picked him up. Hugging him, I said, "I don't have a big finish, folks, but I have a great dog. Good night." I walked off and that was it.

The next morning Dick Francisco and I got on a plane for New York. I had a week on the ship to Bermuda, and I took him as my guest. Each time the ferry stopped we got off and rode mopeds to the next bar. We got shit-faced drunk, and when we were coming back in the rain from the Maritime Museum, which was also the old American submarine base, Dick fell down going down a corrugated grate onto the ferry. He slid down that ramp and his bike fell on him. I ran to the bar, and got as much ice as I could to put on his leg. I was afraid he had broken it, but by nighttime it was fine.

Sizzle had an eight-month run, but the tide had turned. There was no longer enough name value in a Cork Proctor or a Phyllis Kelly. The minute they added "topless" to the marquee, the crowd count went up 46 percent the next day. America still wants to see breasts. If you're from Podunk, Iowa and you've never seen great-looking breasts, it makes sense to me. Dick hired good dancers with great bodies; I don't think there were any synthetic breasts there.

Buying Haven

It was a cold day in March, and the very young girlfriend and I had been drinking plum wine all afternoon. *Sizzle* was going well, I was making good money, and I had a brand new 1986 Ford F250 Supercab, which I had purchased in St. George, Utah, because I couldn't get a deal in Vegas. My license plate read "Que Huevos"—Spanish slang for "What balls!" When I registered it with the state of Nevada, it passed because I told them it was Spanish for "What eggs" (the literal translation) and that I raised Cornish game hens.

We were riding in my new truck through a rural neighborhood south of McCarran Airport zoned RE—Ranch Estates—for horses, carrying a thermos full of Acadama. We were both trashed.

Out in front of a property on Haven Street a "for sale" sign intrigued me. We pulled into the driveway. A little acre and a quarter ranchita, the place had been built in 1970 and was beat up.

The realtor, Sandy Zimmerman, was showing it to another couple and asked if we wanted to see the house. The other couple had said, "Oh, no, this will take too much work."

The seller, Donna Sohn, had moved to Palm Desert, California. In a moment of drunken, cavalier flipancy, I said, "What's she asking?"

"She wants $82,500."

"Offer her $72,500."

I gave Sandy $1,000 earnest money, and an hour later she called and said, "Mrs. Sohn took it."

I signed an $18,000 second deed of trust, which I paid off ahead of time. Then the deed got lost and never re-conveyed. I had to go through a lot of work to get the deed back. I moved in a cowboy couple I met through some friends and got $500 a month rent, which covered the nut. I think the first deed of trust was $250 a month, so there was some positive cash flow. They lived there for ten months until I raised the rent to $600, and then they moved out in the middle of the night, stiffing me for a month's rent. Then I got lucky, renting it to a cowgirl cocktail waitress at the Sahara named Cheryl. She was a good tenant who stayed almost six years.

My impulse act to impress the very young girlfriend turned out to be one of my best real estate investments.

The Nightcap Lounge

After Dick and I returned from Bermuda I went to Bill "Wild Cat" Morris, who owned the Landmark Hotel. I knew him from Vegas High, and of course, I had lived in Reno with his wife, Vivian's family.

There was a little room in the Landmark that had been a poker lounge and was now called The Nightcap Lounge.

"Why don't you put me in this lounge?" I asked, and he agreed to a month's run. The schedule was Wednesday through Sunday at 10 p.m., midnight, and 2 a.m. The money was terrible, something like $1250 a week, but it was fun. It was starting to work, but at the end of the month I was depressed because not enough people were there. This is the same thing that happened at the Hacienda. I began to question how funny I was because there so few people were in the room. Freddy Powers, a guy who worked with Willie and Merle Haggard, came in and brought some people. Stars would come by and say hello. When I'd ask them, "Do you want to get up?" they'd say, "Oh, no, not in this room. I work at Caesars for big money. I'm not getting up here."

I'm Outta Here

By 1987, it was time to seriously break up with the very young—twenty-three-year-old—girlfriend. I was fifty-five-years-old, and I knew I had to get out of the relationship. It had started when I came back from Atlantic City. She was the daughter of a friend, and I had known her since she was fifteen. There was a party at Carme's house and, hey, magic, she was all grown up.

Built on passion, it was a strained relationship, and we had had some separations. She had been involved with some other guys, and I found out. Hey, she was young and experimenting. She wasn't evil. She was a pretty girl and guys hit on her. "No" can be a difficult commitment.

Her dad even told me it was doomed. He said, "She'll break your heart." But I thought, *You know what? I can fix her.* No, I couldn't. I couldn't do anything.

I just kept paying the bills and thinking, *God, I hope you like me.* What an idiot I was!

Those spring and fall relationships can work, but you have to be together. There can't be any infidelity. I traveled a lot and was suspicious of her behavior when I was gone.

From Catalina Island, I called my house. Our last conversation went like this:

Me: "Tell me you love me."

VYG: "Well, you know I do."

Me: "There is somebody in my bed, isn't there? Tell me you love me."

VYG: "I don't have to tell you that."

I could tell there was a guy lying there, and that's why she wouldn't say, "I love you." I got so mad I hung up.

She was too young, and it was an expensive learning process. That's when I went on blood pressure medication and when my hair started to turn white. It was karma, my payback from all the infidelity when I was with Louise. I was probably a bad dad and a bad husband and a bad everything. But, you learn, and you try not to do it again.

My M.O. when things get intolerable is to split. No confrontation, no paint throwing, no slashing of tires, no punching ice pick holes in a diaphragm. Just go away. Women can scream and yell and shake their fists and there's nobody to talk to. Where is he? He's done.

I knew I had to leave town. It's kind of like drug addiction and peer grouping. You get away from all the people who are shooting up and doing crack and crystal meth, and you get a new life.

So why not leave the country? My travel agent and friend, Ann Geno, and her travel agent friend, Nancy, were going to Australia, and I could tag along. We flew Quantas airlines in a jumbo 747. Being curious, I asked if I could visit the cockpit, and they said yes. I met the pilot and co-pilot and got to sit with them for a while. When that door behind them closes, they don't know anything that's going on in the cabin. It's all instruments and light as a feather, no vibrations.

Quantas also served free drinks, anything and all we wanted. Ann and Nancy and I drank Courvoisier for twelve hours, so I arrived in Australia shit-faced.

What a wonderful vacation: six weeks visiting Sydney, Melbourne, Brisbane, Alice Springs, Cairns, and then Auckland and Christ Church in New Zealand. We climbed Ayers Rock—which you can no longer do—and saw all kinds of sights. The Australians were courteous, extremely sensitive; they love to drink, and they're funny.

I went over there strictly to lose myself, forget the baby girlfriend, and maybe have an affair. I met a charming girl named Adrian from New Zealand and though we became traveling buddies, no we didn't. She came from a farm and was a great traveling companion. I did hear from her briefly but, you know, New Zealand is a long way away, and the chances of me seeing her again were remote.

I would have liked to spend more time in New Zealand. It's a gorgeous country full of friendly people. When I discovered the Milford Track on the south island I wanted to hike it, but it was already closed for the season.

Coming back I changed my ticket because I'd decided I wanted to see Fiji. Hey, I was already halfway around the Pacific. Fiji's capital is Suva. I stayed at the Castaways Hotel, not far from the airport. I invited the gorgeous concierge—part Samoan, Fijian and East Indian—to dinner and she accepted. In the Maharaja Room they cooked the East Indian cuisine tableside in woks, and we ate with our fingers out of stainless steel bowls.

Next morning I walked nine miles to another private hotel inland, a Hilton or Sheraton, I think. The air smelled so good. There were lots of palm trees and dense jungle, moist and damp. The road was good, though, paved all the way. People kept stopping to try to give me a ride.

"No, thank you" I said, "I'm just enjoying your country."

The hotel had a bar in the middle of the swimming pool. Boy, could they make martinis.

Bartender: "Would you like Bombay gin? How about our finest vodka from Russia?" After three of those, sitting under a palapa by the pool, I wasn't walking back to town. About that time a mid-afternoon monsoon hit, so I asked for a cab to take me back to the Castaways.

"How did you get here?" the driver asked.

"I walked."

There was a national labor strike going on, but luckily for me, the cab drivers were working.

Leaving Las Vegas, Maybe ...

By the time I returned from down under in 1987, I felt like I'd had it with Las Vegas. The lounges were disappearing to make room for more slot machines, I'd had a bunch of girlfriends who'd cheated on me, and I'd always wanted to just get in a trailer, go on the road, and see America. I'd even purchased a used 22-foot trailer with two doors and air on the roof, which now sat in the driveway of my house on Firethorn.

As I was sitting alone with a bottle of wine in my living room feeling sorry for myself, I began to reminisce about the girls in Vegas I'd met that I would never "get" if I left town.

Carolyn Hamilton's name popped into my head. I remembered her from the night ten years earlier when I'd met her at the Press Club. I looked in the phone book and lo and behold there were five C. Hamiltons and Carolyn Hamiltons. I called them all. I got recorders and left the following message on each: "If you are the Carolyn Hamilton who has the advertising agency, this is Cork Proctor and I want you to know that you've been my fantasy for the last ten years." Then I left my phone number.

Guess what? They all called back. One of them said, "I'm not the one you're looking for, but can we have lunch anyway?"

Carolyn told me later she only called back to tell me she no longer had the ad agency. She thought I was calling for a job. But she agreed to have breakfast with me at the Showboat golf course at Warm Springs and Green Valley Parkway.

So began a ninety-day courtship during which I never even kissed her. There she was with these 44DD daggers, but I said, "You know what? I just got out of a relationship. I don't want to do the what's-your-name-let's-get-a-bottle-of-champagne-and-jump-in-the-hot tub. Let's have a nice courtship and get to know each other." I was thinking, *let's find out what we like and what we have in common. Do we like to read? Do we like to travel? Do we like to take risks?* I think it is the ultimate way to have a relationship and make it stand on its own.

I sent her perfume and earrings from the Caribbean and took her out as soon as I got back to town. We took long walks together and talked. She said her friends asked her, "He hasn't made a move on you? Do you think he's gay?"

When she met my travel agent, Ann Geno, she told her she was kind of reluctant to start a relationship with a man who was going to leave town to "go see America."

Ann told her, "Ah, he's been saying that for years. He's not going anywhere."

Rodeo Week

Traditionally in Las Vegas, the first two weeks in December are dead. Because most people are home getting ready for the holidays, all the showrooms go dark and the singers and dancers and showgirls and crew all get their vacations. So some years ago the Chamber of Commerce decided that would be a good time to host the National Finals Rodeo. And it worked. Now the first week in December the town is full of cowboys and cowboy wannabes.

Cowboy-at-heart Michael Gaughan hosted most of them at the Gold Coast. All the rodeo events were held at the Thomas and Mack. Michael called me and asked, "Do you want to work the week with Johnny Tillotson?"

"Sure."

"Well, the rodeo people won't like you," he said. "You're gonna die, but I'm gonna put you in there anyway."

Despite Michael's dire prediction, John and I worked well together and were well received by the audience. I was on at 9:45 p.m., 11:30 p.m., and 1 a.m. John performed at 10:30 p.m. and midnight. On Friday and Saturday nights, I did a show at 1 a.m. and he finished with one at 1:30 a.m.

I had met John before when he was married to a dancer, but we'd never worked together. I had a great time teasing him from the stage: "Now, John, all those albums you're selling, those jams and jellies—you are gonna declare those to the IRS, right?"

My Mind is an Open Mouth: A Life Behind the Mic

His wife, Nancy, who had an infectious laugh, stood at the side of the stage each night, shaking her head and laughing.

Ex-lovers Passing in the Night

Very Young Girlfriend and Carolyn's Ex-Boyfriend, the one she didn't marry, came to the Gold Coast on the same night, while I was there in the lounge with Johnny Tillotson.

VYG was leaving the Gold Coast, alone, at the same time the Ex-BF was coming in, accompanied by his family and some friends. Carolyn and I were standing just outside the lounge, a few feet apart, talking to some people.

"What are you doing here?" he asked Carolyn.

"I'm here to see Cork."

The ex-boyfriend's friend blurted, "Oh, he's very funny," and his wife gave him the kill look.

At the same time VYG asked me, "Is that your new girlfriend?"

"Yeah."

"Oh."

Oh, those ex-loves, both of whom lasted four years.

The Milford Track

I planned to take three weeks' vacation in March 1988 to go to New Zealand to walk the Milford Track. I thought it would be a wonderful adventure and a great way to start a serious relationship with Carolyn. I always remembered that I'd gotten there at the end of the season, too late to walk the track, and I knew I wanted to return.

The Milford Track, in the wettest, isolated part of southwest New Zealand, is the 53.5 kilometer (thirty-five-mile) switchback in the Fiordland National Park. This famous walk goes from Te Anau up over McKinnon Pass and down the other side to the fiord that is Milford Sound, passing through scenic Alpine vistas and temperate rain forest. Everything we wouldn't need on the track was stored at a hotel office in Te Anau, and after three nights in huts along the trail, we arrived at Sandfly Point (aptly named) from where we were bussed back to Te Anau.

Carolyn could only be away from her business for two weeks, so after we walked the track and she left, I remained in Auckland. I visited the Kauri Tree Museum, where these fossilized red trees, almost as hard as ebony from Jamaica, had been made into beautiful furniture.

From there I went on to Tasmania, which has a wealth of history. Hobart, the capital, even has a casino. I stayed two nights in a nice little hotel in downtown Hobart, half a mile from the casino, for $25 a night. I visited a Tasmanian Devil farm, and even got to pet one. There are always nine in the litter, and only the four strongest survive because the mother only has four nipples. I also had a date with a blond 21 dealer with a great ass from the casino. We went to dinner at an old family restaurant. Afterward she drove me to the highest point in the country, from where we could look down on the town of Hobart and the ocean beyond. But I didn't make a move on her. No, I got in trouble doing this before.

Comedy Under the Balls

Michael Gaughan, who owned the Gold Coast, was adding a west end to the hotel that included a lounge. He offered it to me to run as a comedy room, and I accepted. Upstairs was a bowling alley, so I started referring to what we were doing as, "Comedy under the balls."

From the day it opened on July 25, 1988, the room was a challenge because of its no-cover, no-minimum policy. I've always found that the price of admission affects the response.

Seven nights a week, from 7 to 11 p.m., with new comics each week. I emceed and featured two comics. I hired everybody funny I knew plus comics who were recommended to me by comics whose judgment I trusted. Kelly McDonald and Larry Omaha and Gene Michener, America's first wheelchair comic. I hired *Star Search* winner Earl Burks and his Wonder Dog Winston, this huge sheepdog that he would bring out on stage. A good friend who appeared on and off at the Mitzi Shore's Comedy Store at the Dunes had a clause in his contract that said he couldn't work any other room in Vegas, so he worked for me under a phony name. Jeff Wayne became Wayne Jeffries for the duration of the gig. I always had a woman on the bill, too. I hired Glitter and Kim Richards and Pam Worthington. I gave Carla Rae her first job. She had these little toilet earrings, and one of her lines was, "If you can't hide it, decorate it."

Even though some comics normally got paid more than others, I wanted to be equitable, so everybody got the same money, $1200 a week.

Most of these comics were coming from L.A. "You're going to have to give a room," I told Michael.

Michael's response? "No, we can't afford it."

So I found a cheap, clean motel, the El Mirador, owned by Tom Frias, who owned all the cab companies. For $106 a week, my comics stayed on the south end of the Strip kitty-corner from Holy Cow. A Chinese restaurant was in front and the El Mirador was in the back. Frias owned that building, too, but leased out the restaurant.

I didn't hire Sandy Hackett because he told me he was going into the Tropicana as the star. I figured, why would he want to come and work this toilet lounge with twenty-five bucket seats with their asses toward the stage?

There's a piece of research and design. Instead of setting it up so that customers sat down at school desks with video poker machines and the bartender could walk up from behind and take your order, there were a few cocktail tables and stuffed chairs with a bar of video poker machines between the back of the room and the casino. A little creativity could have made a perfect room out of it. So that's where my humor started.

"How can you win when you have twenty-five people's backs staring at you when you walk out on stage? Mr. Gaughn has infinite wisdom, but he doesn't get everything right. He has fifty-two partners here. With fifty-two partners, I don't know whose ass to kiss."

In his *Las Vegas Sun* column, Joe Delaney beat Michael to death for the bad sound system we suffered through. Finally, in frustration I put my own sound system in. My friend, comedy magician Jac Hayden—"Mundane the Grate"—helped me wire it.

But it was still a rough room. One night, it wasn't even 7 o'clock yet and I was onstage doing a mic check when a guy threw a rolled newspaper at me all the way across the room from the bar. He sailed it underhand like a Frisbee. It missed my crotch by an inch and a half and knocked a water glass out of my hand. I leaped from the stage and chased him, but he ran, disappearing in the casino crowd. I was pissed. Who knows why a guy would do something like that? The show hadn't even started.

I was conscientious about managing the room. I had the latitude to leave occasionally for a week or two here and there to work out-of-town gigs or travel, and when I left, I let Fats Johnson or Bernie Allen or Peter Anthony take over the room.

Old Girlfriends

In the Gold Coast lounge I was in the middle of a comedy bit when my ear caught a side conversation at a front table. Two pretty young girls were talking to each other.

"He used to date my mom," one of them whispered.

"Really? He's got gray hair!"

"Well, whadda you want? He's old!"

What Kind of an Entertainer?

The trailer I'd bought before I started dating Carolyn, when I wanted to go on the road and see America, was now parked next to the place on Helm Drive, two blocks south of Sunset, that I rented after I sold the house on Firethorn. John Meyer, a retired sea captain, owned the property. He had a row of original El Rancho Vegas duplex bungalows he'd bought and moved onto his land, and I rented one for $300/month.

After a year and a half, I quit the Gold Coast West Lounge to take a job for producer Greg Thompson in a show called *Caribbean Carnival* that he had at the Sheraton in Valley Forge, Pennsylvania. I still had my trailer, but I didn't take it with me.

I said goodbye to Carolyn. "I'll call you when I get to Valley Forge."

I got in my '86 El Camino and drove out of Vegas, elated to get away from that lounge. I've always loved El Caminos. This one only had 39,000 miles on it when I bought it two grand below wholesale out of a bankruptcy handled by Nevada Bank of Commerce. The car had been sitting for a long time when I bought it, and I fixed it up.

My Mind is an Open Mouth: A Life Behind the Mic

I drove out Route 60 heading east. I left Kingman and turned north. I had my bike in the back, a thermos full of coffee, and the tunes playing. I was so jazzed, so thrilled because I didn't have to babysit those pain-in-the-ass comics anymore.

In the middle of the night I was out in New Mexico doing sixty-six miles an hour when the speed limit was seventy-five. Out of nowhere came a state highway cruiser, black and white. I'd just bought this car, so it had no license plate, just a bank report of sale taped in the lower right hand corner of the windshield. But I had it insured, everything right in my name, and all the paperwork sitting on the seat next to me.

When the patrolman pulled me over, I didn't know what he was going to do. I hadn't seen a car in forty miles. Just the two of us in the middle of nowhere. I turned the inside light on, rolled down the window, and put both hands on the steering wheel. I looked in the rearview mirror and saw him unsnap his pistol. I was sure he figured maybe he'd gotten somebody. No plates. What did he know? He had a dangerous job.

He walked to the window, and I said, "Good evening, officer."

A big guy, 6 foot 3 inches, maybe 250 pounds, he bent a little and looked in the car. "Do you have a weapon in the vehicle?" he asked.

"No sir, I do not. The back is open and you're welcome to look." Before he could even ask, I added, "You'd probably like some paperwork," and handed him the stack from the seat, my driver's license, proof of insurance, and registration right on top.

He took it back to his car, and I could hear him talking. "Yes, it's an '86 El Camino." Da, da, da, "No plates; run it." So they ran me down, and I was clean as a whistle. He came back, handed me my papers, and said, "Mr. Proctor, I'm going to give you a warning citation." Thank God he didn't call me Alfred because I would have wanted to punch him. "You have a taillight out. I'd like you to get the light fixed as soon as you can."

Since I'd only had the car three days, this was the first time I'd driven it at night. "Officer, I'll go to the next truck stop."

The guy was all right, he was courteous. I didn't blame him for stopping me. I was out there all alone with no plates and a taillight out.

As he put his book away he asked, "What do you do in Las Vegas?"

"I'm an entertainer." I started the engine and put the El Camino in gear.

"What kind of an entertainer?"

The comedy brain is capable of doing one of these things every once in a while, where it's right on the money.

"A good one." And I drove away.

We be Dancin'

Caribbean Carnival was in the Lily Langtry Theatre-Restaurant at the Sheraton Valley Forge. Taped music and a drummer, with Argentinian performers Los Huincas Gauchos, singer Kathi Collins, and magician Phelston Jones.

The owner of the hotel, Leon Altamose, was a cool guy who had stood up to the union when they gave him a horrible time. He liked me, and somewhere I have a letter from him saying I was the best comic he ever booked. With the gig I had a room in the hotel, where I added a little microwave and some plastic dishes so I could cook some simple things.

The hotel was across the street from Valley Forge National Historical Park, where park rangers in American revolutionary uniform manned the original little cabins built by the soldiers of the Continental Army the winter George Washington was there. Every day I rode my bike. The parka I wore read "The Survivor" and attracted some attention when I was out biking and the temperature was nine below. I'm sure they were thinking, *That son-of-a-bitch is insane.* At the end of the nine-mile run around the park was a Methodist Church where I would treat myself to the hot cider and cookies they sold.

On our day off, I'd go with two or three of the cast into Philly on the speed train. One of the dancers wanted to go see Chick Corea. She paid her own way, and I said, "Sure, I'll take you." I think it was the old Orpheum Theatre.

After the show got out, about midnight, we had to cross a well-lit parking lot to where my El Camino was parked. About thirty black guys were together in the parking lot. I think they'd been to see the concert. One of them hailed me with, "Hey, what you be doin' with that young sister?"

I grabbed her and did a little whirl. "We be dancin'."

They laughed, we got hastily into the car and left. I wanted to get out of there while I was lucid and alive.

Valley Forge Potluck Thanksgiving

Carolyn came for Thanksgiving. It snowed for the first time in twenty-five years and she was thrilled to see the park cabins in the snow and imagine how those soldiers survived that revolutionary winter. She had also discovered that she had gone for a year to the same Seattle high school with Greg Thompson. She brought an enlargement of his high school photo with her, a young kid in a white suit with a little black bow tie, quite different from his high-heeled boots, eighties rock star persona. She gave it to the delighted cast, who had copies made at Kinko's and mailed them to their friends in Greg's other shows in Japan, Bermuda, and the Caribbean. For the next six months, when he went to visit one of his shows, he ran into his high school photo pinned up backstage.

Carolyn and I had the best dinners. We were young and in love—well, we weren't that young. We found a beautiful restaurant called The Kennedy-Supplee Mansion. Built in 1852 by granite stone mason John Kennedy, who called it "Kenhurst," the hipped-roof mansion design is Italianate, with a central four-story tower. The rubble stone foundation is almost two feet thick, and there's lots of cast iron filigree work on its balconies. The inside was green and gold with eleven-foot ceilings and flocked wall paper and all button-tufted couches, fancy plaster cornices and bands of decoration called Egyptian Revival style. In 1911, the mansion was sold to J. Henderson Supplee, one of the last Civil War veterans in Montgomery County. The Kennedy-Supplee mansion is listed on the National Register of Historic Places. Since it was right next door in the Valley Forge National Historical Park, we went for dinner between the matinee show at three o'clock and the evening show at eight.

We went over to Buck's County on the Delaware River where the play-house is and stayed at the Wedgwood Inn, the Bed & Breakfast of the year.

At a restaurant called David's we saw a young boy in his military uniform dining with his father. Neither one of them was saying much. The boy sat very straight. I couldn't help but remember my own military school experience, and

I still say it's a terrible place to send children. They come out twisted. 'Screw the discipline and you'll be a good soldier stuff.' I didn't want to be a good soldier. It's just not wholesome when the dad leaves and the kid goes back to the hall alone.

The manager of the Sheraton Valley Forge was this strange chick named Mary. On holidays, Mary would take the cast and crew into the restaurant and give us some shit food. I suggested that for Thanksgiving we get her to give us the room; we'd buy some beer and wine and make a pot luck. The cast and crew loved the idea.

When I told Mary she didn't have to feed us, she copped an attitude.

"Come on, Mary. What difference does it make?"

So she gave us the room, but she wasn't happy about it. A strange woman. I'll leave it at that.

Tuco, the father in the Los Huincas Gauchos act, had his wife Nellie with him. She was a great cook and made some wonderful dishes. Everybody brought good stuff. It was a memorable holiday dinner.

Look Out, Friar's Club

While I was appearing in *Caribbean Carnival* my old friend, Catskills comedian Dick Capri called and asked if I'd like to come have dinner with him and do a few minutes at the Friar's Club in New York City. The Friar's—my God—Lucille Ball's picture is there! Pictures of comedy giants who'd performed there. Going in, I was intimidated.

I told Dick, "We'll talk about the few minutes when I get there."

I took the speed train from Philly, met Dick, and we had dinner. While we were there, Vic Arnell and Stewie Stone got up and did some time. I was looking around at all the pictures on the walls. I'd never been in that kind of company, and I was terrified.

But I did it. I got up and told the truth. "I'm wetting my pants here. I'm a west coast guy. We're not used to this. We don't have a Friar's Club in Vegas."

I felt that I did well. Dick said, "You were funny. They loved you, man. I want you to come back."

"Sure, why not?"

David Jonas, who had been Freddie Prinze's manager, introduced himself. "Where have you been?" he asked.

"Working every toilet in Vegas, up and down the Strip."

"Would you like to come to New York?" he asked.

"I don't know, Dave … I met this lady and we're kind of having a courtship. I think this is a keeper. She's not just somebody I'm going to jump on in a hot tub. I think this is a long-term relationship."

"I'd like you to come here," he said. "I can get you some gigs in the Catskills."

Now my idea of a career move at this point in my life was not working to old people in the Catskills. I'm not even sure those joints are open any more. I'd already worked to the old people in rest homes, the shut-ins, and the angry people playing bingo at the Aladdin:

"JUST CALL THE NUMBERS!"

I was doing a couple of jokes. "I can see why you're all alone and how is that laxative working? Hey, I'm not even getting paid for this, don't you want a few laughs?"

"WE WANT TO PLAY BINGO."

Snotty old bitch, I wanted to go down there and punch her lights out. Boy, if I ever get that old, I want somebody to come up behind me with a machete and say, "Say hi to Jesus." Get it over with.

"I don't want to do that," I told David. "If you've got something that makes sense, great, but I've already done that."

I didn't go back because I'd started with Carolyn and I didn't want to move to New York. I thought that maybe I'd had my turn at bat, and I didn't want to put a relationship on hold for show business. Fuck show business—I just met somebody decent.

The 1990s

High Voltage

By 1990 I was back in Vegas doing another Greg Thompson show, *High Voltage*. This was in the showroom at the Dunes, newly owned by the Asian guy, Nangaku. I was working with the Gotham City Daredevils, a cycling act, and again with Tuco's family, Los Huincas Gauchos.

High Voltage had a media theme, and I was doing a take-off live newscast. "All the news today," doing a funny thing and still doing my stand-up in another segment of the show. In the "news" segment I created a piece called, "The Top Ten Shows on the Strip." All the show people came in to see it because I lambasted everybody. I called *Siegfried and Roy* the number one show and described it as, "Two ex-cruise ship waiters who make giant white pussies come and go."

In his *Las Vegas Sun* column, Joe Delaney wrote about me, "the caustic one was razor-sharp in all three appearances; the first at a TV news desk; the second in that setting but dealing with Las Vegas entertainment, a neo-classic piece, plus a without-a-net audience encounter…no one does this better."

The funniest thing that happened in that show happened backstage. I like espresso, and I brought in a Krups espresso machine. I shared the "star" dressing room with the lead male singer, Jon Halbur, and rather than keep the espresso machine to ourselves, I thought to share it with the rest of the cast. I went to them and said, "I'll keep it in the main dressing room, and you guys can all make espresso at night before you go to work. That'll get you pumped up."

They liked the idea. Sure thing.

I was going into the main dressing room each night to get my espresso before the show. A few weeks later one of the dancers, who virtually had no breasts, complained to the company manager, and ultimately to Greg Thompson, that I was back there ogling the girls' breasts. Pretty funny when you consider that they're onstage showing their tits to 800 people. The last thing I was interested in were her inverted nipples.

I told her, "Honey, I've got a woman with 44DD boobs. If I want to see tits, all I have to do is go home and see the best pair on the Strip."

Nobody else in the show cared. But she made such a big stink, it pissed me off. I yanked my espresso machine right out of there. I'd worked with strippers for years as a drummer and worked with them as a comedian. Breasts, everybody's got them. What's the big deal? I never could fathom that.

I saw that dancer later after she married one of the guys in Greg Thompson's production company. "What was that all about, anyway?" I asked.

"My dignity," she said.

Pulleez.

Nangaku, the Dunes owner, was surrounded by thieves, kind of like Howard Hughes and the Mormon mafia. Nangaku was surrounded by guys who knew nothing about the casino business, show business, or anything else. They were constantly chipping away at the show. Change this, change that, get rid of stage hands—they drove Greg crazy. Every week it was something, but he didn't make the changes. He'd sit with them and say, "We can't do that." Then they wanted to cut the money. Contracts are always subject to being broken.

Nangaku was a disaster for the Dunes, and they lost millions. The show was doing well, and we were full every night, but it didn't last long. We might have been there four months before he closed it.

Let me say this: Greg was paying $600 a week to his dancers. That was phenomenal money. No other dancers on the Strip made that kind of money. He paid well, and we were all sorry to see *High Voltage* close.

The Charity Wedding

By 1991, four years into our relationship, I started introducing Carolyn with, "This could be my next ex-wife." It was a joke.

She finally said, "You have to quit doing that. People are beginning to ask me, when's the wedding date?"

I think a lot of her friends said, "What about this guy? Is he going to get serious?" She already had a couple of failed marriages, quite honestly, and a bunch of failed relationships, as I did. I think we are about fifty-fifty, though I may have had the edge, being eleven years older.

"We could have a conversation about it," I said, and that's how we got engaged. "Let's go on a dive trip to Belize and get married there. Then we'll have a big party for everybody when we get back."

"No," she said, "That'll piss off our friends. It'll be the same amount of work and cost the same amount of money to have a wedding here, and our friends want to come."

So we decided to get married in a gay-nineties theme wedding downtown at Main Street Station, ask our friends for a $25 donation per person in lieu of a wedding present, and donate the money to our favorite Las Vegas charity, Opportunity Village. Between us we had two TVs, two microwaves, two toasters, two vacuum cleaners, and five toilet brushes, so we didn't need anything.

Friday night, November 1, 1991, of the weekend we got married we treated all our out-of-town guests to dinner at the Bootlegger Italian restaurant on Tropicana and Eastern. From there we all went over to Catch A Rising Star at Bally's, where I was appearing that weekend in the midnight show. At eleven the next morning we were at Main Street Station for the wedding rehearsal.

My friend Mickey Finn, a fantastic ragtime piano player, was appearing on the circular stage at Main Street Station and was also their marketing guy, so he helped us put the wedding together. Carolyn and the wedding party came down a descending staircase in the back of the room and walked to the round center stage. Then I came down the fire pole in the middle of the stage. At the rehearsal they kept telling everyone, "Don't look up, don't look up. If you look up, you'll give it away."

Saturday night we treated the wedding party to dinner at our favorite Mexican restaurant, El Sombrero, down on Main. Jose and Theresa were kind enough to close the restaurant that evening for us and our guests. Afterward, off to *Catch* again for the midnight show.

We were married at noon on Sunday, November 3, by Dr. Toni Hart, who has the Hart Family Mansion at 6th and Charleston and is also the mother of the former Landmark girlfriend, Linda. Afterward the Mickey Finn people did their lively, energetic show for our guests. Another former girlfriend and excellent vocalist, Loretta St. John, sang. We had 250 people in Victorian and early American costumes. My friend Gene Paulson even wore a gun. Leo Lewis was the first guy there and the last guy to leave. Dr. Lonnie Hammargren, the neurosurgeon, came in playing a violin. We heard later that Steve Wynn even crashed the wedding. We raised $6,000 for Opportunity Village.

Some of our friends responded surprisingly to the charity part of the wedding. One called and said, "We heard you're charging for your wedding."

I told him, "Were you planning to buy us a wedding present?"

"Well, sure."

"What kind of a wedding present can you buy for $25? You're getting off cheap."

A comic friend of mine from L.A. called to say he and his wife couldn't afford to come to the wedding. Carolyn told him, "Quit smoking for two months and you'll be able to afford it."

He called me to complain. "When I told Carolyn we couldn't afford to come to the wedding, she copped an attitude," and told me what she'd said.

"Well, she's right!"

Kelly McDonald, who had a legitimate reason not to come because his wife, Ann, would deliver their first baby any minute, got in the car with Jeff Wayne and drove five hours in the morning from L.A. to Vegas to attend our wedding, then drove five hours straight back to L.A.

Go figure.

Carolyn had one friend who couldn't come because she had to hold her dead aunt's garage sale, and another who said she couldn't afford it, when she'd just ordered new dining room drapes. I had a guy in another state who was building a house and the cabinets were supposed to be delivered that day—in the end, of course the cabinets didn't come on that day. I had another "friend" who didn't want to miss a golf tournament and another who forgot the date! I couldn't help wondering what these guys were thinking. It's not like we get married every day of the week, so if Sunday doesn't work for you, you can come on Tuesday.

I saw this as a rare, rare occasion—a charity wedding—but we got terrible local press coverage, terrible pictures, the worst. The *Las Vegas Sun* sent an Asian kid photographer who hardly spoke English and didn't know it was a wedding till he got there. Then they printed a picture of the only three people NOT in costume, with one-third of the shot the brim of another woman's hat. The *Review-Journal* printed a picture of the entire wedding party, with Carolyn looking on as I kissed Dr. Hart. I honestly wondered if there was a local media conspiracy against me.

Several months later, the event was featured with our picture in a column in *Brides* magazine.

The Funny Farm

Monday morning after the wedding we drove to Temecula, inland from San Diego, California, where I had a week scheduled at Fats Johnson's comedy club, The Funny Farm. Fats, a singer comedian who had been with the New Christy Minstrels, had rented a bay in a shopping center for the club. Each week he featured another comic besides himself. One show a night.

He put us up for the week in a nice little condo, and during the day we explored the Temecula Valley, Southern California's Wine Country. One day we went to a vineyard on the side of the hill for lunch. We had a lovely table outside on a patio. The food was exquisite and we ordered mimosas.

Then I looked over at another table.

"You're not going to believe what's going on behind you," I said.

Carolyn followed my gaze toward a group of seven people, including a little baby. The mother, in broad daylight, surrounded by diners, had the baby positioned on its back on the table and was changing its diaper. Apparently, they had finished their lunch, because when she'd finished, they all got up and left in a Rolls Royce.

That was our honeymoon.

Mr. Bull Horn

On the show with me that week at the Funny Farm, Fats had booked Glen Super. He used a bull horn, so his entire act was "Mr. Bull Horn here. Some coffee would be nice." He milked that for years.

He had been opening for the Beach Boys in the big room when I was working Caesars at Lake Tahoe in 1980. Actually at the time Bruce Johnson offered me the job, but I told him, "I'm not really an opening act for a multithousand stadium. I've only worked lounges and a lot of my act is one-on-one." It wasn't about being funny—I guess I could alter everything I do, but I was in love with Very Young Girlfriend at the time and didn't want to go on the road that much. Too many women—probably killed my career.

When I met Glen Super at Caesars he'd pulled a kind of "I'm a comic in real show biz," snotty attitude. I thought that kind of rudeness was a cheap shot.

Four years later he worked at Mike Kaley's Laugh Stop in Palm Springs the same time I was there. Once again, he and his little group of friends were standoffish. Those L.A. guys all thought they were hotter than a pistol. I was angry at them anyway because when I'd arrived at the condo reserved for the Laugh Stop comics, I'd gotten a bad reception.

When I asked "Could you tell me which condo belongs to the Laugh Stop?" I got a wave of hostility from the manager. Seems one of those guys had taken a girl into the jacuzzi and not only made love to her, but had a bowel movement in there. He left this chicken shark floating around, and the next morning all the retirees came out to see that brown residue, whipping from side to side in the bubbles.

Now Glen Super and I were together again at Fats' Funny Farm. Opening night, the press was there and also Bob Fisher, who owned the Ice House in Pasadena. I was scheduled to perform before Glen, and I ripped the place apart. I trashed him, I trashed Bob Fisher, I trashed everybody in the room. It was a hot audience, and I was at my peak. As I left the stage to thunderous applause, I walked by Glen Super, who now had to get up and follow this wrath of World War II. I just smiled and said, "Top that, Mother F—!"

Fired Up

When Carolyn and I first got together, I had her go talk to a guy I was seeing, a psychologist named Tad, so she'd have an idea what she was getting into with me. In his southern Texan drawl, Tad told her, "Well, ah cain't talk about Cork, but we kin talk about yee-ou, and why y'all are attracted to Cork."

Anyway, she felt insecure, I guess with reason. One day I made a flippy, off-the-cuff remark: "Hey, I didn't take you to raise. Do I look like the welfare, charity group? You're a grown woman. You have a degree." Even after we got married, I was reticent to pool our resources because she didn't have much. Like many professional women, she'd just been working.

One day, I found out that she had signed up with Amway. On the edge of tears, she said, "I need something to give me some security for my future, my retirement."

Okay, so I began to participate with her. Many people view Amway as a scheme. I didn't particularly look at it that way—as a pyramid scheme. It does work if you are willing to participate seventy-five hours a week. Give up everything else because all you're doing is selling soap. We went through motivational trips to Salt Lake City to see Amway rallies at the Salt Dome, thousands of people screaming, "Fired Up." I was thinking, *these people are on some mood-altering drug.*

But we grabbed the enthusiasm and solicited all of our friends. Tony and Maggie, and Fats Johnson and his wife, Beverly joined us. The legs are the people under you, kind of like worker bees. They do what you are doing, and if you get enough of them, you have this financial support group.

Carolyn was driven. She thought that otherwise she was going to be left along the road. She had no trust in the future of our marriage. I didn't particularly see her insecurity. However, knowing that she'd already been married to two guys who unloaded her, I guess there was reason for doubt.

We did that for the better part of a year, and we were doing pretty well. We had solicited some friends and showed them the plan. It was a hell of a learning experience. We rented a little motor home and took our Border Collie/Akita mix, Puck the Wonder Dog, and went to Salt Lake City. We went to a lot of rallies. We heard a lot of good speakers. We also heard a lot of terrible speakers.

One day I said to Carolyn, "What are we doing?"

We didn't have enough of an edge to see a future in the Amway business. You've got to sell a lot of products and the people under you have to do it, too. I think it's a young people's business, people between the ages of twenty-one and forty. We were way over that. Our Amway experience ended without bitterness or malice. When people ask me about it, I say, "Yes, it does work. You can make money, but it's a commitment." It's worse than a marriage. In a marriage, you don't go out five nights a week, wear a suit, and "show the plan." And in your plebian state, open the door for the guy above you at a rally and park his car. There was too much ass-kissing in it for me.

There is a lot of stress. I was in my sixties and Carolyn was in her fifties and we were mature enough, at that point, to see it for what it was. We said, yes, we can do this thing, but do we really want to? Carolyn is as tenacious as a junkyard dog, but we both decided at the same time to give it up. We recognized the fact that it can get too slick. And I value my time. My life has been focused around having a good time, dating, sleeping around, whatever, accompanied by dining and drinking.

We met some nice people, though. Luckily, a lot of the guys had built enough of a platform—legs—that they could make it. We have friends who were in the program who went to Emerald Level, then woke one day and realized they had no life. They had their day job and they had Amway. They realized that they were virtually strangers with their kids. It was a Herculean task to do it well and keep everybody happy. We invested a lot of money, not in products but in motivational tapes, all of which we summarily gave away.

Forbidden Vegas

My next local Vegas job was in a show for producer Dick Feeney, *Forbidden Vegas*, September and October, 1991, at the Sands. Actually, I think it only lasted a few weeks. Dick Feeney kept his word and paid me the money. We had a guy in the cast who was a Wayne Newton lookalike. We had a guy imitating Kenny Rogers. We had sketches about Siegfried and Roy, etc.—kind of a left-handed look at the town.

I don't think Sheldon Adelson liked it. He's a tough guy. I don't think he likes anything, but that's my opinion. I thought *Forbidden Vegas* was going to sustain because we got a lot of laughs. It was well received. Who knows? It's one of those things where the timing is wrong. You are close, but not close enough. I thought it was good, I enjoyed it, but of course, I'm flexible. Where do I enter the stage and where do I exit? If I'm working, that's enough.

Comic Relief for Burned Sign

The week in 1992 that I was scheduled to open at Catch a Rising Star with Bernie Allen and Fielding West, the Bally's sign caught fire. A guy dropped a wrench on the sign and when it went down, it apparently bounced into a transformer and knocked out the sign. One whole side burned. They didn't fix it right away because of some insurance issue. There would be no marquee on the Strip advertising our appearances.

I said, "Let's have some fun. Let's march on the Strip and advertise ourselves." Bernie and Fielding were all for it.

Carolyn made some big signs that said, "Will work for laffs - Cork Proctor, Bernie Allen, and Fielding West, live at Catch a Rising Star" and "See the Vegas Veterans of Comedy." Tuesday, January 7, the day we were to open, there the three of us were marching up and down the Strip in front of Bally's, looking like picketers, shamefully marketing ourselves.

When the suits at Bally's saw us out in the street, they went ballistic. Tom Bruny, their director of advertising, came out and demanded, "What's going on? Has this been cleared through legal?"

By now, two or three TV camera crews were there. Legally the hotel had no power to stop us, because we weren't on Bally's property. We were on the sidewalk of the Strip.

"Hey, Tom," I said, "We're having some fun. It'll be great film at eleven."

The woman who was the pseudo-entertainment director for Catch a Rising Star also came out onto the street and screamed at us.

"What is all the bull about?" I asked. "They're going to do a nice piece on us at eleven o'clock tonight. It's funny, and it won't hurt anything. The sign is burned down in case you haven't noticed, and it's been burned for six weeks. Why are you screaming at me?"

Later that night Catch a Rising Star manager Don Lake got in my face, saying, "You shouldn't have done that." He was being an ass about it, too.

"Don, what do you care?" I said. "It's no skin off your nose. You couldn't buy that kind of great pr." I couldn't believe how uptight they were about what we did.

I made some enemies over that, but it didn't matter. I didn't want to go back there anyway. I didn't want to go back to Bally's, and I didn't want to work for that bitch pseudo-entertainment director again.

Fielding West had this wonderful little white dove in his act named Bob the Bird. In his pocket he also had a rubber bird that looked like Bob. Bob the Bird did tricks; he went up the ladder, he went down the ladder, and then he pooped on Fielding, who looked at him and said, "I said SIT!" Then in a sleight of hand, Fielding appeared to pull Bob's head off, but it was the rubber Bob.

This woman, using her pseudo-executive authority, told Fielding, "You can't do that in my room."

It made me mad that she didn't get that this was comedy. This was why we were there, to get laughs. From then on, she was persona non gratis with me. Later I ran into her at a friend's birthday party. As soon as I walked in the front door and saw her I said, "Hey, f— you, strong letter to follow."

Carolyn said, "Boy, you really like to burn those bridges."

I said, "You know what? If I have to spend the rest of my life catering to people like that who have the IQ of a mint, I'm not going to do it. I know my job. She didn't know her job. She took way too much latitude with the program."

The problem is, when you get 400 comics working for you over two or three years, they start kissing your ass so they can get more weeks, and she actually started to believe her own importance. She was just a woman who got lucky.

At eleven opening night Channel 8's Dave Courvoisier gave us a beautiful piece. He even laughed at the end of it and said, "It goes to show you what happens when there is an electricity failure." He made a nice light issue out of it.

Fielding and Bernie and I worked out the week, but those Bally people were all so tense. I thought, *you poor bastards*. No testicles at all in that group.

The Three Stooges Construction Company

Before we got married, Carolyn sold her house and moved into a warehouse on Eastern Avenue, where she ran her graphic design business out of the office in front and lived illegally in the back. After a year living at John Meyer's property on Helm, I sold my trailer and moved into the warehouse with Carolyn.

After we got married, we decided to look around the southern end of the valley for a little ranch property to buy. I had $20,000 to put down. We were looking at $150,000 to $200,000 homes and they all needed another $20,000 to make them livable. Cheryl, my Sahara cocktail waitress tenant on Haven, was talking about buying her own house, and Carolyn said, "Why don't we move in there and use your twenty thousand to remodel a little. Then we'll have a low mortgage payment."

We agreed and then decided to gut the place because there were a lot of things that had never been permitted and weren't correct. I fixed them. We retrofitted the windows, added skylights, took out a wall, and totally rearranged and rebuilt the kitchen. We were excited about moving in.

I hired two Italian brothers and another guy to do the construction work. I called them the Three Stooges Construction Company because the brothers turned out to be wired all the time on cocaine and the other guy was loaded on pot. They did a few things right and a lot of things wrong. It took longer than we expected, but it finally turned out okay.

One Sunday afternoon when Carolyn and I drove over from the warehouse, we came up the driveway and saw a guy trying to break in the front door. He ran when he heard the truck. Right then we decided we needed to start sleeping there. The new berber carpet was down in the bedrooms, so we moved in, even though the kitchen wasn't completed.

The Return of the April Fool

Michael Gaughan hired me for two weeks in April of 1993 to work again in the West Lounge of the Gold Coast. I wanted to do a postcard mailing to everyone I knew, so Carolyn and her junior graphic designer Theresa helped me design and print a clever direct mail piece in orange and dark blue. I called it the 'Return of the April Fool' because I was opening on April 1st.

We addressed and mailed 500 funny fold-over cards with a tear-off that people would send back. The tear-off was addressed to Michael and "demanded" that "Cork Proctor be held over."

Those return postcards came back to Michael in volumes. Dave Barry, the syndicated columnist from the *Miami Herald*, sent back one on which he wrote, "I think you should hold Cork over, and I promise not to bring any guns to the West Lounge."

We got an unbelievable 37 percent response to the mailing.

Michael kind of blew it off, but he told his secretary, "Sheri, you've never seen anything like this, have you?"

She said, "No, I certainly haven't."

By the time they'd collected a boxful, he gave them to me. He said he didn't want them.

I said, "You don't have to keep them. It was just to show due diligence on my part."

Michael is a strange dude. He wouldn't admit it to me, but he understood the impact. He knows what advertising does, and he knows what direct mail does. He's a genius. He's not always on the money, but he's real close.

Early Show for Families—Late Show for Adults

Greg Thompson never got big bucks for his shows. He would go to a hotel and say, "What do you want to spend?" and they would say, "$29,000 a week" and he would make it work. He was so creative with what they gave him to work with. He should have been on Broadway.

I've worked for a lot of guys and seen a lot of shows, and you've got to have that preproduction money. Greg never had outside money. David Merrick said in order to have a production show you have to have sets and screens and scrims and all. You can't do that on a limited budget, but Greg's creativity always made the production look huge.

His 1995 show at Harrah's in Reno, *The Great Wild, Wild West Show*, won Reno's Show of the Year. I was the "cowboy" comic. I provided my own costume: cowboy hat, striped gambler's pants, cowboy boots, white shirt, and eight or ten different western vests I had made by a Reno seamstress.

It was an 8 p.m. show in a tiered, 400-seat showroom, and the girls were covered—that is, not topless—so it could be marketed to families. I was pretty much on good behavior.

Greg put in a different show for Harrah's at 11 p.m., targeted to an adult audience, *Playboy's Ecstasy*. Rock 'n roll music and topless dancers. For that show I wore a white suit, and could say more bizarre things.

One night I approached a bunch of people directly in the front row. "Where are you from?"

I put the mic in one guy's face and he said, "Taiwan."

I opened my coat to display the label and said, "Look, I'm wearing your shit."

The people laughed, but Greg got a complaint letter from the Harrah's suits who were afraid they were going to "lose our Asian database."

You reach a point where you want to go to these people and say, "It's comedy, for God's sake. Don't you have anything better to do with your time?"

By the nineties I was making good money for the shows, almost $1,500 a week. People think I made a lot of money, but I never had a $100,000 year. When you amortize it out, I probably earned $50 a week over the last forty years. I don't even want to think about it.

Phyllis Diller

Between Greg's 7:30 p.m. and 11:30 p.m. *The Great Wild, Wild West Show* at 9 p.m, Harrah's would bring in a headliner. One week it was Phyllis Diller. Her week started on Monday night, when we were off, so Carolyn and I went to see her show. Afterward we went backstage, and I introduced myself.

Pretty soon everyone had left her dressing room except Carolyn and me and the tenor saxophonist in the house band, Gordon Anderson. Phyllis, in her mink coat, blue knit cap, and bunny slippers, opened a bottle of Chivas and we proceeded to talk about the business, laugh and trade jokes while we drank. She told some incredible stories about her early years at the Purple Onion in San Francisco, when women just didn't become comedians, and she was a minority.

We laughed, and I threw a line, and she cackled and said, "Oh, that's sooooo funny. Do you do that in your act?"

"No. It just comes out."

After she did that a few times, and I answered, no, she asked, "Well, what the hell DO you do in your act?"

Three and a half hours later, the Chivas bottle was empty. Gordon was drinking O'Doul's, so it must have been just the three of us who drank all that scotch … and we were trashed and still laughing. We helped Phyllis find a security guard who escorted her to her room.

The funny thing was that after drinking and laughing till four in the morning, the next day I didn't have a hangover. I think all that laughter released some endorphins that must have counteracted the effects of the alcohol—or something.

The Day Job

When he was building the Orleans Hotel/Casino on West Tropicana, Michael Gaughan asked me if I wanted to be the hotel's entertainment director. He offered me a salary of $50,000 a year.

I'd worked for Michael on and off for decades. I was flattered in one respect, and I also saw the job as something that would enable me to stay home. I didn't want to be gone all the time, going somewhere, getting on and off boats and planes. I'd had enough of both—the rush from the airport at San Juan to get to the ship in a gypsy cab with bald tires and a statue of Jesus a foot high on the dash. After a while the novelty wears off. I'd been on the road for years, and I was married now. I wanted to hang out at home and enjoy my life with my wife.

After I said yes, Michael reneged on the money.

"I'm going to pay you $48,000."

I should have said, "Michael, you know what? If $2,000 makes that much difference, forget it." I'd already be taking a $30,000 a year pay cut to take this job, since I had been making $80,000. That was probably a harbinger of things to come, had I been paying attention. But as I said, I wanted to get off the road.

Carolyn always thought the job was worth a lot more, and Michael may have offered it to me because he felt sorry for me. Maybe he felt I didn't have anywhere to go or anywhere to work. He may have. I don't know; I never asked him.

Even before the hotel opened, I walked onto the site and saw them pouring a concrete stage in the lounge. That's unheard of in show business. Stages are made of wood so they resonate, so they are warm, so contact is easier on the legs of the dancers. Theater stages are always made of wood, like musical instruments. Here was a concrete stage in the dark, 2½ feet too high, with foreboding-looking chairs, ugly carpet, and no sound mixing booth. It was the worst lounge I ever saw in my life, and there was nothing I could do about it.

The Branson Theater

Michael planned to name the showroom "The Branson Theater" and open with Rex Allen, Jr.

"Why?" I asked him. "What does Branson have to do with a New Orleans theme? Why don't you call it The Louis Armstrong Performing Arts Center, get a plaque for the wall with a special declaration?"

"Who ever heard of Louis Armstrong?" Michael said.

"Well, who ever heard of Rex Allen, Jr.?"

"Have you ever been to Branson?"

"No."

"Then you're going."

He paid for me to take Carolyn and go to Branson for a week and see all the shows. When we came back I said, "Okay, now I've been to Branson, and I still think you should call it the Louis Armstrong Theater."

But it was going to be the Branson Theater, and that was that.

Coast Resorts

Michael's other hotels had all been limited partnerships. With the opening of the Orleans, he wanted to create Coast Resorts—Barbary Coast, Gold Coast, and the Orleans—and take the corporation public. To go for a public stock offering he had to meet lots of SEC regulations. That meant all the key people had to be squeaky clean. He hired Harlan D. Braaten, property controller from Harrah's in Reno, to manage the Orleans. He replaced Jim Abrams, the manager of the Gold Coast with ex-FBI agent named Michael Growney.

They brought Rick White down from Harrah's in Reno as marketing director. He didn't get along well with Michael, because Michael micro-manages stuff. If you're going to sit on everything and watch everything and make the decisions, then the guy loses the empowerment to do his job because he can't. He knows no matter what it is—marketing, advertising, whatever—somebody's going to come in and say, don't do that or take that out. When it comes to managing underlings, there was no difference between Michael and Howard Hughes.

The Orleans Hotel/Casino opened the 13th of December, 1996, the same week the movie *Titanic* debuted in the Orleans movie theaters (days ahead of the rest of the country). I had a sign made for the band that played that night that said, "This is the original band from the Titanic."

Chuck Norris was a VIP guest, mainly because he was a partner with points in the joint. There was no advance publicity. Chuck slipped in and slipped out. He was one of the fifty-two partners. I enjoyed meeting him.

The casino was full for the opening, but I felt it was all thrown together at the last minute. Very stressful—lots of stuff went wrong—yet everyone seemed to have a good time.

New Year's Eve; Where's the Sound?

As with any new hotel opening, a lot of things were unfinished. As an example, we were a few days away from a New Year's Eve show in the ballroom. I'd booked a rock 'n roll band referred by Johnny Tillotson.

Because of piss-poor planning design, there were no provisions for microphone hook-ups. They planned to use the ballroom for everything from fights to weddings, and they had no facilities for sound. No speakers, no cables to which you could attach speakers.

I went in there with Michael and Fred McClure, director of construction operations and chief of maintenance. I looked around and asked, "Where are all the wires?"

Michael said, "Well, aren't they there?"

Fred looked and me and shrugged his shoulders.

"We need a snake," I said. This is a wrapped tube three and a half inches in diameter with twenty-four outlets inside that are called sends. You plug them into the mic and into the amp on the other side. They were in a hurry and didn't build it into the wall. It should all have been wired before the sheetrock went up.

As you approach the ballroom, you open the doors and a sound booth is there because it is always at the rear of the theater with the stage on the other side. The wires for sound had to go up through a column in the ballroom and into the ceiling, drag across seventy-five feet and down to where the stage was.

The kind of snake we needed came from a New York company that provides sound equipment, Excelsior, where we could have it custom-made with an extra fifty feet. The snake would be sent out to Las Vegas by air freight. It arrived three hours before the New Year's Eve event was scheduled to begin.

I must have had a premonition. I said to Carolyn, "Let's just go by and see if they're fuckin' this up."

Sure enough, we walked into the ballroom where Fred's maintenance guys were installing it, and I saw the wrong ends hanging down from the ceiling—the female ends to the stage instead of the male ends, which go into the microphones.

They were good maintenance guys, but they didn't know anything about mics.

The guy pointed to the instructions. "That's what it says."

"I don't care what it says. It's in backwards. Pull that out of there."

They must have trusted me because they didn't call Fred. One of them said, "Well, Cork, you're an entertainer, I guess you should know."

"You can call Fred if you want," I said.

They shook their heads. "No, we'll do it your way."

So I was able to straighten that out, just in time.

Michael was fortunate that he had people like me and Rick and some other guys who sidestepped some real nightmares in there after the opening.

Deja Blues

I missed playing drums and was thrilled when Michael didn't object to me having my own band in the lounge in the afternoons. We opened the hotel with my band, Cork Proctor's Deja Blues, noon to five, five days a week. I bought two Hammond B-3 organs out of Circus Circus and a Leslie speaker. I hired some of the best players in the world: Charlie McClain, who had been on Kenton's and Woody Herman's bands, Tommy Rich, a wonderful guitar player, and my dear friend Dick Green, who I've known for forty years.

I also hired Kenny Harkins, who had been one of Sinatra's piano players, to come in and play organ. He was a wonderful player, but Kenny still had a lot of snootiness in him, and I ended up having to fire him. I called the guys to the bar one day to have a drink and said, "We're losing our hearing, Kenny. You cannot put that Shur S 58 microphone inside the cabinet of the Leslie speaker for the Hammond organ."

It was chaos, and some of the guys in the band had given their notice. Kenny was obstinate, and I knew I had to fix this. I said, "Kenny, this is hard to do, man. I like you. We've been friends for forty years, but you have to go."

I split the money right down the middle with the band. I had my accountant, Susan Lambros, withhold the taxes so nobody wound up upside down, as musicians are prone to do.

I think Deja Blues performed in the lounge for three months before it became too much responsibility. When I dissolved the band, it was a mutual decision. I kept Charlie McClain and Tommy Rich on banjo, added trombonist Jimmy Dell, who had previously been with the Goofers, and turned them into a strolling house band. It was classy. They walked around the casino playing old Louis Armstrong tunes.

Cajun Music and Cooking

The lounge music was frenzied, but it was exciting.

I worked with an agent called Louisiana Sue, and brought in zydeco bands like violinist Tom Rigny, and Al Rapone's band. Al was Queen Ida's brother, and he and his wife gifted me regularly with homemade boudin from New Orleans. Al had a happy, gravelly voice, and when he called he'd always say, "Hello, this is Al Rapone on the telephone."

Al offered to cook a traditional Cajun dinner at my house. I invited in a few friends, and Al and his wife cooked jambalaya, gumbo, crawfish, and a bunch of other stuff from scratch. The kitchen smelled wonderful; we ate and drank and laughed like fools, and Al wouldn't take any money for the supplies. After they left, our kitchen was a disaster; the weight of the gumbo pot had broken one of the electrical elements on the stove. But it was all well worth it.

After awhile everybody in the casino hated the Cajun music, though, because it gets repetitive. The pit complained about the washboards, and I couldn't get the guys to stop micing the washboard. After six months, Frank Toti said, "That's enough of that shit," and we went to cover bands.

Rex Allen, Jr. and "Gone Country"

Most of the time, when Michael makes a decision, he is 100 percent accurate, but when he makes a mistake, it's a big one—like The Rex Allen Show. There has never been a show that bad in the history of Las Vegas. I don't know how Michael found it. I think his wife and Rex Allen went to high school together. There was some weird, convoluted connection that I never could figure out.

That piece-of-crap show with Rex Allen, Jr., *Gone Country*, was so bad, the biggest night he ever had was 140 people in an 850-seat showroom. And ninety-six of them were comped.

A theme place, The Orleans, with a country show; it doesn't work to put rednecks and Cajun people back-to-back. They're not each other's biggest fans.

Rex Allen, Jr. was an arrogant guy. Within thirty days he had alienated everyone of any importance in management, me included. In fact, he alienated me the first time I met him, when I was still in *The Great Wild, Wild West Show* in Reno.

Michael showed up in the audience unannounced one night, and he had Rex Allen, Jr. with him. I'm sure they came to see the show because it was so successful. In the show Greg Thompson had a piece at the end where the lead male singer came out and sang, "I'm Proud to be an American," backed by the entire cast waving little American flags. After the show I took Michael and Rex Allen, Jr. to dinner. I said, "Did you see anything in the show you liked?"

Jr. said, "Well, not really."

That piece of business with the flags showed up in his show, which showed how full of shit he was.

Even the media hated *Gone Country*. The hotel had trouble getting press coverage. Joe Delaney told me, "If I review it, Michael will never talk to me again."

Michael closed *Gone Country*, released Rex from fulfilling the contract, and paid him off on the whole thing. One afternoon soon after, I was walking through the showroom when I realized from the light source that the back doors were open. Wait a minute, I thought, we weren't moving a band in or out. I walked backstage and found some guys loading sound equipment and computers onto a big yellow Ryder U-haul truck backed up to the door.

"What's going on?" I asked one of the guys. He told me they were moving Rex Allen's stuff for him. Rex Allen never had any "stuff"—that shit all belonged to Michael. Rex had conveniently absented himself from the scene, so I called the head of security, Skip Wilkes.

"It looks like Rex Allen is stealing shit," I told him.

Skip arrived immediately, looked at the computer stuff, and questioned the workers.

"Mr. Allen is taking this to his house to do some work at home," one of them said. What b.s.! While the guys stood there, bewildered, Skip called Michael.

"I don't care what it takes," Michael said. "Let him have it, just get him out of here."

Thirty years ago he could have had him killed for doing inappropriate things with the company's equipment.

After the Rex Allen, Jr. disaster, Michael hired Roy Jurnegan, an old biker guy with pink glasses and a Mercedes Benz who used to be a gopher for Don Laughlin down at the river, to manage the room and hire safe B and C acts like the Smothers Brothers, the Righteous Brothers, Roger Whittaker, Tony Danza, Frankie Valle. People who were not exactly stars anymore, but still drew well.

It hurt me that Michael took away my authority to book those acts. I knew a lot of them, and I could get their current going rates out of Pollstar. He didn't need to spend another salary in the form of Roy Jurnigan when he'd already hired me for the job, but that was Michael's call. He liked Roy. Maybe he was the kid that Michael never had.

Demoted to Lounge Manager

The crowning blow came when I opened the new 1999 Directory for the Coast Resorts Corporation and it said Cork Proctor – Lounge Manager. They had actually demoted me without my knowledge. I fault myself now for not leaving that day. I should have written him a post-it that said, "F— you, strong letter to follow," and walked.

Maybe Michael was toying with me to see how far I'd go. Maybe he was waiting for me to leave. He doesn't negotiate well with guys. If Rick White had said he wanted another $20,000 a year, Michael would have said, "Well, you can't get it from me." Guys were quitting and he would never say, "Why don't you stay? What if I give you some more perks?" Michael never offered anything.

I was in a top corporate job, and I was never given a level one comp stamp. I still had to go to somebody else to get food or drinks comped. I could get a room taken care of, but I never had the ability to walk in and get a show comped or anything. The whole thing was embarrassing. I knew how to hire and contract talent. I knew how to do good things, and I knew what to do to fix things like the snake for the ballroom on New Year's Eve.

It got worse by the month. Another wearisome thing was the realization that I did have great ideas, but I was hampered by budget. Here was a 250-million-dollar hotel and I couldn't keep Michelle Renee, a classically trained harpist, playing in the Canal Street Grill. After a month, Michael blew her out, saying, "We can't afford a musician for the Canal Street Grill." What can one harpist cost when they're making money hand over fist from the gaming tables?

Another example was the sound mixing booth for the Orleans Theater. They did finally stop calling it The Branson Theater after Rex Allen, Jr. left. The sound mixing booth was in the wall above the showroom, two stories up and enclosed in a little cubicle. So, the sound technician could never get an accurate feel of what was coming into the showroom because he was isolated.

I said, "Michael, you need to move that sound booth down to the back of the main floor."

"It would take up nine seats," he said. "I don't want to give up nine seats."

Seven years later, he moved it. Rumor has it that Bill Medley told Michael, "We've suffered through this for years. Come on, fix it."

Now when you walk into the showroom, off to the right from the center doors is a roughly six-foot by seven-foot booth with a sound engineer with cans on—a headset—who gets what we call a line patch or direct feed right into his ears. So if the guitar is too loud, he fixes it right there. If the bass player is not loud enough, he can bring it up. That's his job, to make everything come out in a nice uniform sound so that the music is not oppressive. People don't go in to have their ears hurt. They go in to see the show.

If the sound isn't right, it's the fault of the guy sitting at the sound board. It's not the act's fault because their main speakers—the mains—are up front like in a movie theater. On stage are monitors in little boxes two feet high and four feet wide. Those are the stage monitors. They tell the performer what he sounds like, but they don't tell him what he sounds like coming through the main speakers. As a net result, a translation is always there, and it's usually not for the benefit of the audience. Sound engineering is a delicate job, and unfortunately sometimes they put kids in there who don't know what they're doing.

I felt like the Orleans came across as cheap. The difference between Michael and the Fertittas, for example, is that the Fertitta joints—the Station casinos—look like they spent the extra millions. Michael's places look the way the budget works. So many times I heard, "We don't need this. We can't afford that." Finally I said to myself, *They're never going to change. What am I doing here?*

In all fairness, I think Michael had too much on his plate. I think he realized that I was more than competent, but he didn't want to give me the credibility or authority I deserved in case I asked for more money.

Yes, Michael gave me the job, but I earned my money. I had to put up with crap from his buddy, the FBI guy who ran the Gold coast, and a bunch of other guys who treated me like, well, aren't you supposed to be working now? I said, "I am working now. I'm going to be able to fix anything that goes wrong in this lounge."

The Guy from Pima College

Carolyn and I took a week's vacation and flew to Tahiti. We spent most of the time on the island of Moorea. A few days before we left, we were having a beer in a little café in Papeete because it was pouring rain outside. A guy walked in by himself, and I recognized him as a tourist we had seen in the pineapple fields. I called to him to join us. Over more beers he told us he was a professor at Pima College in Arizona. He'd been working as a trainer for the Peace Corps and was on a three-month sabbatical, traveling around the South Pacific.

"Is the Peace Corps still around?" Carolyn asked. She was interested because she'd done some graphic design work for them when she worked at an L.A. ad agency in the sixties.

When he heard about our backgrounds he said, "Oh, you'd make perfect Peace Corps volunteers."

"Aren't we too old?" I asked.

He explained that there is no age limit for Peace Corps volunteers. When I jokingly said we'd like to go to Dominica because we heard the diving is great there, he said his good friend was Dominica's Peace Corps country director. We were surprised to hear that there were Peace Corps volunteers in the Caribbean, which is normally thought of as a vacation paradise. But of course, there's a lot of poverty in the Caribbean.

He gave us his card, which we subsequently lost after we got home. But the seed had been planted. Eight months later, I came home from the hotel one day so disgusted I said to Carolyn, "You wouldn't believe what's going on now. It makes the Peace Corps look good."

We talked about it a little, and she said, "Well, if you're going to make jokes about it, do you want me to call and get more information?"

Yeah, sure.

Next thing, the regional recruiter from San Francisco, May Ng, came to Vegas and interviewed us. In the first application, you could cross off parts of the world you weren't interested in, and we crossed off Africa and the Middle East. Carolyn told the recruiter I had a little arthritis, and we didn't want to go anywhere cold. She said no problem. "There are still a lot of warm places in the world."

Then we had to get medical check-ups. We were taking it one step at a time, to see what would happen next. We wanted to go to South America and learn Spanish, so when they called from D.C. and offered us a choice of "Eastern Europe or Inter-America" we chose Inter-America. That encompasses the Caribbean, Central, and South America. When they next called and offered us Suriname, which we had never heard of, we thought, why not? We figured we'd go down there, and if we didn't like it, we'd come home. I built a guest house in the back yard just in case.

We made arrangements for some friends to stay in the house with the dogs for two years, and began packing our personal belongings. Carolyn closed her graphic design business and sold her computer equipment.

Thirty-three months after the Orleans opened, I gave Michael my notice. "I'm going to go and join the Peace Corps." I wanted to rub his nose in it. Like, *Michael, I don't need this shit.*

My Mind is an Open Mouth: A Life Behind the Mic

He said, "Should we give you a party?"

"No, thanks."

I left the Orleans the last Friday in August 1999 to go with Carolyn to do "Rural Community Development" in the Peace Corps in Suriname, South America.

No more show business.

Epilogue

July 2012

After a year in the Peace Corps in Suriname, South America, the governmental powers that be decided they really didn't have job for Cork, and he returned home to Las Vegas with what Peace Corps calls "Interrupted Service."

Cork entered semi-retirement, performing gigs between travels to countries like France, Holland, Thailand, Taiwan, China, Spain, Portugal, Germany, and the Czeck Republic.

He continues to make his home in Las Vegas and indulge his interests in reading biographies, travel, and hanging out with friends.

It is with ironic appreciation that Cork notes his eightieth birthday Comedy Roast has taken place at Michael Gaughan's Las Vegas' South Point Hotel & Casino, and proceeds have been donated to Cork's favorite Las Vegas charity, Opportunity Village.

—Carolyn V. Hamilton